GREAT SECRET
OF
BOBBY FISCHER

Nenad [signature]

The Greatest Secret of Bobby Fischer

NENAD NESH STANKOVIC

THE GREATEST SECRET OF
BOBBY FISCHER

THE FINAL TRUTH ABOUT THE GREATEST CHESS PLAYER OF ALL TIME

ILLUSTRATION BY NENAD NESH STANKOVIĆ

The Greatest Secret of Bobby Fischer

THE GREATEST SECRET OF BOBBY FISCHER

⌘

Nenad Nesh Stanković

Translated by
Randall A. Major

EVERLY BOOKS
PUBLISHING CO.

New York   Boston   London   Paris   Toronto

THE GREATEST SECRET OF BOBBY FISCHER

First Edition
Printed In the United States of America

The Greatest Secret of Bobby Fischer

54 24 66 74 12 98 15 01 14 20

by

EVERLY BOOKS
PUBLISHING CO.

Everly Books Publishing Co., 375 Hudson Street, New York, NY 10014
United States of America
www.EverlyBooksPublishing.com

Copyright © 2010 by Nenad Nesh Stanković. All right reserved by author. Except where permitted under the United States copyright Act of 1976, no part of this publication may be reproduced or distributed in any form or by any means, or stored on a database or retrieval system, without the prior written permission from the publisher.

LIBRARY OF CONGRESS CATALOGING-IN-PUBLICATION DATA

ISBN-13: 978-1481922340
ISBN-10: 1481922343

PUBLISHER'S NOTE

Without limiting the rights under copyright reserved above, no part of this publication may be reproduced, stored in or introduced into a retrieval system, or transmitted, in any form or by any means (electronic, mechanical, photocopying, recording or otherwise) without the prior written permission of both the copyright owner and the above publisher of this book.

The scanning, uploading and distribution of this book via the internet or via any other means without the permission of the publisher is illegal and punishable by law. Please purchase only authorized electronic editions and not participate in or encourage electronic piracy or copyrighted materials. Your support of the author's rights is very much appreciated.

The Greatest Secret of Bobby Fischer

to my Mother and Father

The Greatest Secret of Bobby Fischer

The Greatest Secret of Bobby Fischer

Table of Contents

Acknowledgements	xi
CHAPTER 1. A WORD AT THE BEGINNING	1
CHAPTER 2. AT THE DOOR OF A MYSTERY	5
CHAPTER 3. THE SUSPICIOUS TRAVELER	11
CHAPTER 4. ABOVE THE DANUBE AND SAVA	22
CHAPTER 5. THE BOY BEHIND THE MASK	65
CHAPTER 6. WAVES AND STONES	81
CHAPTER 7. SEPTEMBER FIRST	106
CHAPTER 8. THINKING ABOUT THE UNTHINKABLE	119
CHAPTER 9. LIKE IT ONCE WAS, LIKE IT NEVER WAS	132
CHAPTER 10. RIGGED GAMES	166
CHAPTER 11. AVALA-AVALON	181
CHAPTER 12. THE HUMAN TOUCH	219
CHAPTER 13. THE END OF A NEW BEGINNING	227
CHAPTER 14. NISTAR	259
CHAPTER 15. AGAINST THE WIND	264
CHAPTER 16. THE MAN IN THE MIRROR	279
ABOUT THE AUTHOR	285

The Greatest Secret of Bobby Fischer

ACKNOWLEDGMENTS

Working on the English translation and American edition of the book before you confirmed once again my deepest spiritual belief that nothing happens by accident and that a "secret connection" links all places and times, bringing people, events and happenings into relationships that would be otherwise unbelievable or impossible if a powerful, edifying desire did not make them real and necessary.

Hence, I direct my gratitude to the CREATOR of those circumstances and opportunities, no matter what name we call Him in the language we speak or what form He is given in the system of thinking available to us.

My memories, full of love and respect, take me back to thoughts of Mr. Svetozar Gligorić who recently passed away, the greatest Yugoslav and Serbian chess player of all times and an exceptional man in a myriad of ways. I am grateful to him for the attention he gave me over the past decades and for the opportunity to inspire my soul with his memories of days gone by and the events he witnessed.

I am certain that one other person from the chapters ahead of us deserves a literary description in an all encompassing biography. Mr. Janos Kubat is a journalist, publicist, sport and chess activist, but above all he is an inspiring person. He offered great support while I worked on the book, and has honored the author and the book with his presence at the promotional events for it.

I extend special gratitude to an exceptional person, a respectable businessman and true gentleman, editor Christopher Douglas, who, with his devotion and remarkable support, made it possible for the American edition of *The Greatest Secret of Bobby Fischer* to appear so quickly.

I agree with the opinion in literature that "translation is as demanding as writing, and with absolute right and great pride I can say that Mr. Randall A. Major is as responsible for the final form and appearance of this work as the author. While congratulating and slightly envying the students of the University of Novi Sad for the opportunity they have to be led through the wealth of the English language and its literature by this reputable teacher, I must say that it is difficult for me to find the words to thank Mr. Major for his dedication and effort, and for the kindness I have felt and received from him in our working together.

Almost every day for more than two years, I have had the privilege of exchanging ideas in long conversations with American philosopher, thinker and writer, Mark Thomas Wayne. This man of exceptional intellectual dimensions had and has the spiritual courage to set the questions of Heaven and Earth before himself, searching for answers to them, which either lead his soul to the dangers of the abyss or edify him to unfathomable heights. The stimulus he has given me in this way has been exceptionally important.

I offer my gratitude to all who have supported me in the translation of my book into English, above all to Mr. Nebojša Nenezić, whom I consider to be my closest collaborator on the road to success of *The Greatest Secret of Bobby Fischer*.

—Nenad Nesh Stanković

The Greatest Secret of Bobby Fischer

CHAPTER 1.

A WORD AT THE BEGINNING

Many years have passed since the events occurred which are described in the book before you. Perhaps someone will ask why it is only now that my memories are being dedicated to paper. Is it really necessary in these times to open this chapter again, now closed so long ago?

For me and my understanding of the world and life, there is only one explanation. It cannot be found in the sphere of rationality. If it were, this book would have appeared long before in the times when there were a multitude of concrete, monetarily attractive offers from all over the world for it to come out. Such flattering temptations were accompanied by status worthy of the challenge. In addition, from the point of view of business, it would have been much more profitable if this manuscript had appeared while Fischer was still alive, or perhaps in the days immediately after his death. As someone who does marketing, I am quite sure that these words would have been seen more clearly, that they would have certainly taken flight in the media spotlight from the perspective of everyday reality.

Today, when writing has been democratized to the absurd and when overproduction "devours" specialness in all segments of our lives, does this manuscript stand a chance to be noticed? Thankfully, my heart mystically guides my mind, forbidding it to make such calculations and speculations.

Nothing can happen before its time. Rewarded by the freedom of will, by its inviolability, we continue to head down the paths laid out for us and indicated to us by immeasurable love, at times gently, at others cruelly, not to punish us or cause us pain but to teach us.

The Greatest Secret of Bobby Fischer

Walking down the road through various scenes, tranquil plains, inaccessible heights, menacing forests, unstable weather conditions, scorching days, thrashing rain, snow flurries and blizzards, I arrived at the moment which was waiting for me. That is why I am here just now, with this story I am offering you.

The thing that you must take my word for, because disputes are already calculated into the result, is that everything between the covers of this book is described exactly the way it happened. In order to support the facts, in the end when the final calculation is made, there will be no damage done or favor won by anyone. Because the truth is sufficient in itself.

I did not wish for the privilege of citing certain sources, references, or newspaper articles, because I fought for authenticity by observing firsthand the protagonist of this book and the historical framework of these events. Thus, though as powerful as tornado, the only motive I have carried in my heart is actually to share with everyone the knowledge and cognition I obtained, no matter how vainglorious or prosaic that may sound, with all those who truly want to know more about the greatest chess player of all time and about his most carefully guarded secret.

This book is thus not about chess theory and practice, but a text about a man who was inspirationally and brilliantly creative in his own time, and for all times hence. Naturally, I acknowledge the possibility that others might have different understandings, points of view or descriptions of Fischer's personality. However, we are confronted here with Bobby Fischer in his fifties, a full twenty years after Reykjavik, and almost twenty years before he departed for the north, where the sun sets for the greatest.

I would like to emphasize that Fischer's opinions, thoughts and qualifications which I am presenting here, those related to individuals, phenomena and events, are exclusively the product of his perception, that is, they are the expressions of such an incredibly complex soul. They are clearly delineated from my observations which attempt to describe and explain, with no intention of supporting or negating in any way. I must say that the description of Fischer's overwhelming anti-Semitism was a particular challenge to me. To write about him as a person and not grapple with this most delicate and painful subject would be to flee from the truth. In his later years, those which I do not testify to in this book, Bobby's rhetoric which he used to express this dark part of his mind, was to become even stronger and more aggressive, and it went far beyond the descriptions I offer here.

Likewise, the terms "champion", "undefeated world champion", and so on, in relation to the protagonist of this story, are used more for stylistic and synonymic variety than as value judgments. I apologize to all those who are not mentioned in the chapters ahead, but who certainly deserved to be part of the events described because of their role and significance in them. I hope that this will be justified by the fact that this book, will be dedicated to them, to the temporal framework of the nineties and the turbulent events outside of chess.

If there are mistakes of fact related to chess in the text, or contradicting details, that is only because I did not wish to change them after the fact, so that the authenticity of what I heard directly in Bobby's voice, and also that which I sensed directly and thus experientially retained in my memory, would not be desecrated by *ex post facto* observations.

Because this is what happened.

Then let it be so.

And let it remain so.

The Greatest Secret of Bobby Fischer

CHAPTER 2.

AT THE DOOR OF A MYSTERY

I believe that this story begins long before July 29, 1992, when I met Robert James Fischer, "the uncrowned king of chess", "the genius from Brooklyn", among all the other names in the fourth estate for the owner of one of the most intriguing biographies of the twentieth century. Perhaps the roots of all these events lay back in those days when, as a boy, I used to fervently search for articles about the legendary world champion in Yugoslav[1] dailies and weeklies. I must admit that I was never terribly interested in chess but I certainly was fascinated by anything that had the undertone of a secret or a mystery. The rare headlines in the press were exactly like that:

"Where is Robert Fischer? Has he really been spotted in Argentina?"

Others claimed:

"Fischer is in the Philippines. He is negotiating a comeback with Campomanes." Or:

"Bobby Fischer, captive of a bizarre religious sect holding him hostage in Mexico. Would he ever play again, was he following the events of the chess world, and ultimately, or perhaps firstly, why had he withdrawn from public life?"

Questions, questions. All of that aroused my childhood imagination which placed him in my fantasies somewhere at the end of the world, and unraveling his enigma managed to bring

---

[1] This text includes four geographical and historical concepts: The SFR Yugoslavia, the SR Yugoslavia, the Federation of Serbia and Montenegro, and finally Serbia. In ten stormy years, as a result of well-known circumstances, the territory where these events happened changed its name in accord with the new borders being drawn on the map.

him back to the game on 64 squares. Certainly there was no way I could have guessed that my dreams would come true and that I would, through the quirks of destiny, be privileged to get to know the personality of Robert Fischer, perhaps more so than any other person.

Why would such a carefully guarded door open up to someone like me? I am sure that there are many reasons.

This text is related to the period of July, 1992 through September, 1993, when I was with him all the time. The idea of the people who stood behind the entire project of Fischer's return to public life, which was only partly a chess event and much more a complex political-financial story in the middle of the conflict of the Balkan "tribes", was that I was to be introduced to him as the person who would take care of his most immediate security. Of course, that was one of the most important segments of my activities which I was completely prepared for due to my earlier work. However, the focus was supposed to be for me to use my abilities to get as close to him as possible in order to dampen the danger of his untamed character, his whimsical nature and his destructive foul moods, so that the entire upcoming spectacle would have a happy end.

The reputation which preceded me, fortunately, was confirmed after two weeks by the fact that Bobby expressly demanded that I be constantly at hand. As our friendship developed, I quickly took care of all the secretarial responsibilities and solved all the technical-organizational problems that arose for us before, during and after the "the Rematch of the Twentieth Century."

For me it was especially significant, as a sign of his enormous trust, that Bobby also entrusted me with all contact with the journalists. This development also pleased Mr. Jezdimir Vasiljević, the owner of Jugoskandic Bank, who was the organizer and sponsor of the match, because it relieved him of all his worries about the whimsical world champion. Thus, my working hours extended to all twenty-four, because I had to be available at all times of night and day. Much later, a few days before we parted ways, over dinner in one of the many restaurants in Budapest,

Bobby said to me, "You know, Nesh," that's what he called me, "you're the only person to spend so much time with me." Then he looked over at Philippine Grandmaster Eugene Torre and Hungarian-American player of the old school Pal Benk who were keeping us company that evening, and he burst into laughter and added, "I mean, the only one who lasted that long." He continued by adding the story of his "strange" friend Sam Sloan with whom he cruised Manhattan for six months, covering every inch of the heart of New York. They spent time together every day during that period, but then "poor Sam" disappeared without a trace. I liked the story, but I did not feel like laughing, because I myself was fairly worn out and exhausted after something more than a year with him. Even Bobby's old friends, Argentine Grandmaster Miguel Quinteros and the above-mentioned Eugenio Torre, who kept company with him in alteration during his stay in Yugoslavia, later in Hungary, had difficulty staying with him more than a couple of months in continuity. The reasons for that should be sought for, above all, in Fischer's fierce individuality, his self-sufficiency which often demeaned all those around him, and which had destructive influence on the people around him.

The mitigating circumstance for me should have been the fact that it was my job, and that I attempted to respond to all his challenges like a professional. However, Bobby and I quickly became friends, and so from the very beginning I had a feeling of enormous responsibility, along with a desire to precisely and accurately carry out each of his plans.

With equal seriousness and care, I chose the materials for his shirts and suits since he always had them tailor made, organized dinners on his sudden whim to visit a typical Serbian restaurant at three o'clock in the morning, or took up the task of finding the address and telephone number somewhere in Europe for the man who Bobby suspected was the new friend of his ex-girlfriend, Miss Zita Rajcsányi. To aid me in my orientation, he gave me the man's nickname and height. No matter what happened, whatever the chess genius wanted was satisfied in a way that met his very best interest. I know that Bobby appreciated the sacrifice, the understanding and loyalty, and he returned it with a trust that surprised many.

There was one other factor which, at the very beginning, positively or perhaps decisively helped to establish such a relationship. It happened as early as the first couple of days of Fischer's stay in Yugoslavia, before we were to depart for Sveti Stefan for the great spectacle for which the million-strong chess public all over the world had been yearning for twenty-odd years.

At that time, Bobby was still quite withdrawn and distrustful of everyone around him. Our conversations until then had been brief and conventional, dealing mostly with his daily plans and desires. During one such discussion in the sitting room of the house which was our first home in Belgrade, he suddenly changed the subject to a new topic. He was most interested in the war which was already raging in the territories of the former Yugoslavia and the stance of the international community toward the conflict.

I saw this motif many times later as well. By asking a question to which he already had certain and uncompromising answers, Bobby was testing his partners in conversation. If he did not like what you said, your short-lived "acquaintance" with the chess legend would abruptly end.

Over the next ten minutes, I expounded my opinion on the subject. I entered into the genesis of the conflict of the "brotherly" nations and into the historical aspects of the war. Desiring to be as detailed as possible, I touched upon the stance of the international community along with some of the conspiracy theories that were widely circulating at the time. By the expression on Bobby's face, I saw that my effort was not in vain.

There was no way I could have known at the time that the bastion of Robert Fischer was based on a belief in one such conspiracy which was directed at all of humankind, but which especially focused on his life and career. This belief was not just a strong belief, but also the universal principle by which Bobby functioned, on which he based absolutely all of his decisions from the most important – like his withdrawal from public life – down to the most common ones every day.

That was our first conversation on the subject which was to dominate the next fifteen months. We often spent hours on the beach on Sveti Stefan while many curious onlookers wondered what Bobby was talking about with his bodyguard.

Here it should be added that, over this entire period, many important and exceptionally significant personal events were happening to him. After more than twenty years of absence from public life, this was a fast return for him to be under the lights of the chess arena and in the center of the media hype. During the match he had significant ups and downs in form, to which he reacted emotionally, and the whole event was under direct threats from the US government. Then, there was the departure of Mr. Vasiljević from the country, their unresolved personal and financial relations, and also his wrenching emotional decline after his break up with the young Hungarian chess player, Zita Rajcsányi. I lived through all of that, and so much more, with him, and I had the opportunity to see him in moments of joy and great excitement, but unfortunately also when he was assailed by crises and when he suffered deeply. It is known that in such situations a man will also manifest that part of himself which is otherwise in everyday circumstances hidden and inaccessible to other people. It was actually that depth in the personality of Robert Fischer which was most interesting to me. It was there that lay hidden the answers to the questions I had always had about the mysterious chess champion.

And so, I found myself at the door of a mystery.
Yet, to enter that door, first I had to knock.
So, I did.

CHAPTER 3.

THE SUSPICIOUS TRAVELER

Today, when I turn my thoughts back to the time I spent with Robert James Fischer, it is no coincidence that one particular scene most often comes back out of the multitude of those experiences. I see him in the balmy July early evening, walking across the endless plain of Vojvodina, down a wide dusty road leading through green fields and pastures outside of town, while the sky above Kanjiža[2] is burning with the color of the setting sun. With his characteristic plodding stride, this ever wandering Ahasverus[3] and chess-playing Don Quixote bore within himself some kind of terrible loneliness as he passed through the melancholy of the twilight on the plains; I managed to capture the chill of that solitude and retain it in my memory. The small number of friends and occasional, temporary fellow travelers could only be witnesses to his seething internal conflicts, the constant friction he had with the external world, but above all the personal tragedy which actually lies a the root of the fate of all genius.

The great Serbian writer, Ivo Andrić,[4] wrote long ago: THE ARTIST (in the case of chess, Bobby was truly that), THAT IS A SUSPICIOUS PERSON, A MASKED MAN IN THE DUSK, A TRAVELER WITH A FORGED PASSPORT. THE FACE BENEATH THE MASK IS MARVELOUS, HIS STATUS IS MUCH HIGHER THAN WHAT IT SAYS IN HIS PASSPORT, BUT WHAT DIFFERENCE DOES IT MAKE? PEOPLE LIKE THAT

---

[2] A spa in northern Vojvodina near the Hungarian border where we spent time in June and July, 1993.
[3] From Old Testament mythology, the man God cursed so that he could not die or find peace, but rather had to roam the earth forever.
[4] Ivo Andrić, winner of the Nobel Prize in Literature in 1961.

The Greatest Secret of Bobby Fischer

UNCERTAINTY, THAT SHROUD OF SECRECY, AND THAT IS WHY THEY SAY HE IS SUSPICIOUS AND HYPOCRITICAL."[5]

This ever dubious traveler left Los Angeles on a July day in 1992, traveling via Amsterdam and Budapest to cross the border at Horgoš into the land that was to be his host for slightly more than a year, and which was already under a tight blockade by the international community. In the early afternoon of the third day after Fischer's arrival in Yugoslavia, I was finally and certainly able to accept the role offered to me for the years to come. Although I had followed all of the events related to this truly significant mission from the very beginning, it was inevitable that I would join it later, because in the Serbia of that time there was someone whose importance surpassed that of the arriving chess master. However, that confluence of circumstances was to have a positive effect on my position in the further preparations for "the chess match of the century".

Namely, Bobby was exceptionally unhappy with the fact that a photographer at the Budapest airport managed to capture his disembarkation from the airplane and thus, before the time was right, revealed to the world his intention to return to chess. One other incident those days seriously brought the decision Fischer had made into question. Accompanying Mr. Jezdimir Vasiljević, Bobby visited the TV studio owned by this man, who was a significant Serbian business man at the time. This visit was recorded by a "hidden camera" so that an audience of millions was informed of Fischer's arrival that same evening on the main channel of the state-owned television company. The champion was furious. It took a lot of time and words for Mr. Vasiljević to convince him to unpack his bags again, because Bobby had prepared them to leave. The banker swore a hundred times that he had no idea about the secretly operating cameras. As proof, he offered the sacrifice of the station chief who was fired on the spot (at least that is what he promised Bobby). For his part, Fischer showed his good will by agreeing to answer a couple of questions

---
[5] Ivo Andrić, *Conversation with Goya*

which Mr. Vasiljević asked him directly, in front of the cameras of TV Serbia. Thus, it was officially confirmed that the legendary chess grandmaster was in Belgrade and that, as he said, "the match will take place unless Spassky doesn't show up."
The direct consequence of these mistakes was to be a change in the organizational team. Most of those who had worked on it till then were reassigned so that their places could be taken by real professionals with years of experience in their specific fields. My place was to be in close proximity to Bobby. Whatever the case, the primary disagreements were left behind, but much later Fischer would be bitterly sorry for forgiving Mr. Vasiljević so easily.

Bobby Fischer's first residence in Belgrade was in the exclusive residential area of Dedinje, at 38 Užička Street. This well-maintained villa, old in years and style, used to belong to the Republic of Macedonia, more precisely to its representatives in the federal government, all the way up to the disintegration of the Yugoslav federation. The high fence and thick walls offered a proper amount of security and privacy, and the gardens around the house and the fresh air of "Belgrade's Beverly Hills" provided the possibility for walks and relaxation. Bobby was satisfied with the arrangements, but he would later confide to me that the house of his dreams would be different. That ideal home would have to have a modern architectural design, with lots of space and large rooms, built of massive concrete blocks, but with only a few windows. This "modern day fortress" would be situated in some quiet and ecologically healthy place, and it would be surrounded by high walls. Bobby actually longed for a large marble snail shell where he could find sanctuary and reclusion from all the troubles of this world, and where he could enjoy the things that satisfied him to his heart's desire. By the dictates of destiny, he spent most of his life in hotels of various categories all over the planet.

In the years preceding these events, he lived in difficult conditions, practically on the edge of poverty, in a part of Pasadena which was primarily inhabited by retirees. The "Macedonian villa" was a significant step toward a better and more comfortable life. Bobby moved into his rooms on the second floor. The spacious ante-room was turned into his chess office, containing: a table with 64 black-and-white squares, a chess set, two chess clocks (one classic model and one prototype of Fischer's new patented one), a lot of books, journals and magazines scattered about, and the ever-present radio.

When I entered the room the first day, and it was always the same afterwards, when the champion was not playing or analyzing them, the pieces were always in the same position. They were gathered and mixed in the center of the board. They were never set up in the opening position, never stored away from the table, they were always in the described position. In the following months, I had the opportunity to watch Bobby training almost every day. At the end, regardless of who his partner was, he would return them to their resting position with a swift motion of his hand. This constant ritual was much more than a habit. On one hand, it was a magical rite for luck in chess, and on the other it was a practical security measure so that someone he did not trust would not be able to see the final position on the board after he had played the game out and analyzed it.

In this improvised working area, there was also some of his luggage which could not fit in the room where Bobby slept. From Los Angeles, Fischer had brought a lot of things in ten old suitcases of varying sizes and shapes. They were all made of genuine leather. High quality accessories made of this material – jackets, shoes, bags, wallets – were a great passion for the champion. The objects of his passion were mostly from Argentina, a land famous for such goods.

That first day around noon (I was supposed to wake Bobby up at that time according to the agreed schedule) when I went upstairs, the bed in his room was already empty. Then I heard whistling coming from our guest in the bathroom, obviously in a good mood, as he performed his morning ritual, so I hurried downstairs to order the attendants to make breakfast. Some ten minutes later, the squeak of the wooden stairs announced that Fischer was on his way down. I waited for him in the sitting room and wished him a good morning. He lightly nodded his head, returned my greeting and went on into the dining room.

If I had not watched some "secretly" recorded films, I probably would have been quite taken aback by the physical appearance of the legendary chess player. This was no longer that young man from the old photographs which I remembered. Before me was a fifty year-old man with thinning hair, a thick red moustache and beard streaked with gray.

His face showed traces of the years rushing past, but the quick glance which penetrated me from his piercing eyes hinted at an enormous energy. What did surprise me was his build. When he walked past me, I realized that he was just under my own six-foot-four. His shoulders and arms were, in their width and strength, more like those of logger from the American north, or a discus thrower, than those of a man who was superior in the most intellectual game in the world.

His broad hips and powerful legs gave his appearance an impression of stability. Although he was a good swimmer, a walker of stamina and a bad tennis player with an intense desire to improve, his build was surprising and it was explainable only by his exceptional genetic predisposition. When he saw Bobby on the beach at Sveti Stefan, one of my friends said, "If this guy, by some accident, had chosen body-building over chess, Schwarzenegger never would have won so many titles." When you add his size 13 feet, which carried his 240 pounds, then it is no wonder that it seemed to me that the earth trembled when he walked past me.

Then he sat down at the long dining table and began eating the breakfast which had been laid out for him. From the corner of my eye I watched him as he hungrily downed eight scrambled eggs with lots of ham and a large salad of mixed vegetables, and washed it all down with orange juice and milk. During the match, the daily papers would often mention his marvelous appetite. Certain reporters, in search of sensational stories and bizarre stuff, claimed that they had seen him eating apricots and peaches including their pits, or that a breakfast of a dozen hamburgers was the usual start of his day.

Peaches and apricots were not his favorite fruit and he ate them more rarely than others, and when he did the pits remained intact, of course. The fact that he had not tasted a hamburger in the preceding twenty years was of no consequence for the representatives of the Fourth Estate.[6] It was true that Bobby had an exceptionally big appetite, but that was quite normal for a man of his size who was also psychologically and physically exhausted every day. In a very short time, he could mix all sorts of food and drink without upsetting his stomach.

The thing that immediately caught my attention was the way Bobby sat at the table. He dipped his right shoulder so that he was practically hugging the plate. For a moment it seemed to me that he was trying to protect his food from someone.[7] While eating he mostly used just his fork, tearing pieces of food from its tines. He would pick up his knife only when there was a tougher piece of meat.

During breakfast he listened to the music coming from his transistor, carefully placed on the edge of the table. On this morning, he chose a station with typical Serbian folk melodies. Bobby would later often remind me, "I am the greatest expert about radio media in the world."

From his boyhood days he had been fascinated with that small, magical box which gave him the power to travel the world by twisting a knob. Ever afterward, no matter where he was, no matter what he did, that small apparatus accompanied him. If he was out walking, he would carry one in his hand (Bobby had one special model, light and small, perfect for that occasion), when he was swimming, a transistor would be on the edge of the pool (a

---

[6] Bobby, namely, despised all kinds of fast food mostly because of, to his mind, its low quality and because of the fact that he thought all chains of such food were an expression of raw capitalism and imperialism.
[7] Such a posture when eating is characteristic of people who lived for a long time in insecurity (for example, individuals who have done prison time), because protecting one's food is one of the basic conditions and instincts for survival. As time went by and Fischer relaxed, this habit soon disappeared.

special yellow waterproof model), while he was in bed he listened to a slightly larger one with a map of the world in the background of the dial.

During our long walks I was to hear many lectures on the history of various radio programs, with a special accent on the American talk shows of the fifties and sixties. Bobby actually knew everything about them. I am certain that there was not a single song from that period, which we consider nowadays to be *evergreen*, to which he had not memorized all the words. He would often recite them or sing them to the rhythms coming from his radio. It was interesting that he did not isolate himself from his old "friend" even when he played training games or analyzed them. Once I asked him if it ever disturbed his concentration. He answered with a simple, "No."

Carried away by my careful observation of details, I almost failed to notice when Fischer finished his meal. He got up from the table, passed silently past me and went up to his rooms. I immediately telephoned Mr. Vasiljević to tell him that Bobby had finished his meal and that it would be a good time for him to come to the house on Dedinje.

That day the phones were ringing off the hook at the villa. Even though Fischer's arrival in Belgrade was no longer a secret, his place of residence was not known to the wider public. The people I talked to were mostly interested in Mr. Vasiljević and Mr. Kubat, the match organizer and the man who played an enormous role in the champion's return, and they were trying to find out something more from the answers I gave.

Only Mr. Pashayan, a former American congressman, asked for a direct connection to Bobby. Because of the sensitivity of the moment, I told him that Fischer was asleep, which was true, and that I did not dare to wake him up. This made the still powerful ex-congressman very angry, but there was nothing that could be done. In the forthcoming days, he was to call often and try with requests, but even more often with threats, to forestall the beginning of the match.

After an hour, Mr. Vasiljević, appeared in the company of Mr. Kubat. At the time, the summer of 1992, Jezdimir Vasiljević, popularly called "Big Daddy Jezda", was considered to be an exceptionally successful business man, one of the most powerful Serbs. It was said that his empire was growing at a fantastic rate and that the wealth of this "Serbian Onassis" was already so vast that he was numbered among the more famous world financial moguls. His ownership of the Sveti Stefan resort and of a part of the coast in Budva, his purchase of the Belgrade racing track and many other spectacular investments that were mentioned in the press gave all of these stories an air of reality. The fact that this business man had invested five million dollars in the award funds of the upcoming match contributed to the fact that his name appeared all over the world with the news of Fischer's return.

He and Janos Kubat trotted up the stairs and came down with Bobby a half an hour later. It was time to move out. The agenda for the day was the purchase of materials for the suits our guest wanted to have tailored. The clothes he had brought from Los Angeles were in really bad condition. The t-shirts, shirts and pants he wore those days were full of stains and patches, so the purchase of new clothing was necessary.

Shopping in the very center of town caused quite a stir among the passersby. The security around the honored guest to the capital of Serbia and Yugoslavia managed to keep the curious onlookers at a proper distance, and the citizens applauded and shouted greetings to the famous chess master. Fischer obviously enjoyed all of that and, somewhat awkwardly, smiling, waved back at them.

When the purchases had been made, the happy group went out to eat at a well-known Chinese restaurant. In the forthcoming days, oriental cuisine was to be our main gastronomical focus. That evening, Bobby chose sweet and spicy pork, chicken in curry sauce, squid Sechuan style, duck with walnuts and cantaloupe for dessert. He ate slowly, conversing about his present and future plans, and the meal lasted till after midnight.

Outside, a peaceful and balmy Belgrade evening was waiting for us. A gentle breeze carried the scent of earlier times, the expensive parked cars spoke of the present, while the sky above us was secretively silent about the future. Perhaps the stars saw better and further, but at that special moment it seemed, without

exaggeration, that the asphalt beneath our feet was the center of the world.
　The morning and the evening of the first day.
　And everything was looking good.

CHAPTER 4.

ABOVE THE DANUBE AND SAVA

Though filled with high tension and tempestuous events, Robert Fischer's first days in his return to public life and his arrival in Yugoslavia passed in an almost identical rhythm. Bobby did not come out of his rooms before noon, and most often he appeared somewhere between one and two. He would come down to the dining room with its long hardwood table and have an enormous meal. During that late breakfast, if there was anything else he wanted he would simply raise his hand and gently wave me over. From the small office where I usually was at that time, which was practically an extension of the dining room, I could easily see his signal. Most often he would ask for another carton of orange juice or milk, and sometimes for a few more fried eggs. I would immediately go to the kitchen, repeat the champion's wish, and then wait for the elderly attendant so that I could follow him to the table. I noticed that Bobby liked this customary procedure because, from what he admitted to me later, it showed that he was being taken care of down to the minutest of details. That belief was altogether true.

    The house where we were staying was located in Dedinje, a part of Belgrade that was covered by a special security protocol because of its residential character. Nearby, there was the "Bosnian villa", which belonged to the Republic of Bosnia and Herzegovina until the disintegration of Yugoslavia. In those days it was being used by the official representatives of the Bosnian Serbs. The leader of the SDS and the first president of the Republika Srpska,

The Greatest Secret of Bobby Fischer

Radovan Karadžić, often stayed there.[8] Not much further away lived the president of Serbia at the time, Slobodan Milošević. Even though we were in a maximum security zone, Bobby's temporary home had special protection. In spite of the fact that the large yard of the former Macedonian villa had a driveway that exited on two separate streets, only one of the gates was open, the one that led to Užička Street. The other, leading to Tolstojeva, was carefully locked and watched by a guard. At the main entrance there were always two armed guards, while five other people were always in position around the house itself. During the day, I would be on the ground floor of the building, and while I was off duty at night that space was occupied by two special forces agents from the state security agency of Serbia. Perhaps it will seem to some that such stringent measures were overdoing it, but the media significance of the event, its multitude of domestic and foreign political connotations, accompanied by a whole series of events related to Jezdimir Vasiljević and his *Jugoskandic Bank* and also to the match itself—all of this attracted a wide scope of interests and individuals from practically the whole world, and such guardedness made absolute sense.

According to an unwritten rule, Bobby would go back upstairs after breakfast and there he would prepare to work as he waited for Grandmaster Svetozar Gligorić. Gliga (his nickname) would arrive usually around three in the afternoon, always accompanied by the sounds of the motor in his old Volkswagen Beatle. Giving a warm greeting, he would quickly climb the stairs and knock on Bobby's door.

A famous player, journalist, and chess theoretician, Mr. Svetozar Gligorić was born in 1923; during his lifetime his name became synonymous with Yugoslav chess and he was one of the few people who managed to gain and keep Fischer's confidence over the years. Their friendship dated from way back in 1958 when Bobby spent a few days enjoying the hospitality of Grandmaster

---

[8] Due to a confluence of circumstances, Radovan Karadžić would often be our neighbor at the Interkontinental Hotel in Belgrade were he often later stayed with his entourage, up until the SR Yugoslavia imposed sanctions on the Bosnian Serbs.

Gligorić in Belgrade before the tournament in Portorož. From that period, the young American chess player remembered the good food, the long talks about everything related to chess, the excursions along the clear and clean Sava River in which he swam and along the banks of which he rode a bicycle. The fifteen year-old wunderkind player fascinated his host with his knowledge of the history and development of this ancient game, with his talent and prospects, but also with his chess curiosity, which he sometimes took so far that it was trying to one's patience. This was understandable when one realizes that, on Bobby's mental lists, Mr. Gligorić occupied a high ranking, especially in the field of theory and tactics, and in the journalism on this field, where the Yugoslav grandmaster was among the best in the world in the young man's opinion. The young Fischer wanted to use that profound source of knowledge to its maximum.

On the other hand, since he was delighted with the giftedness of his friend over the decades, Gliga was always happy to help, using his vast experience in sports and life. He thus enjoyed quite a special, privileged status in Bobby's world, and he had lived through all those years and all the champion's phases, without significant disturbance in their relationship. However, in order not to produce the wrong impression that Mr. Gligorić was constantly applauding Bobby, cow-towing to the ideas and approaches of his younger colleague, it should be emphasized that he was and remained actually the ONLY ONE who "dared" to oppose Fischer in terms of his most intimate chess beliefs, and yet Bobby never got angry with him. Bobby attributed that opposition and those differences of opinion to Gliga's advancing years and his decision to be a part of the establishment, and his desire not to risk his comfortable position, his chess and personal reputation, because of some foolish decisions at the end of his career.

Perhaps one of the sentimental and analytical biographers of Fischer would try to describe their relationship as father-son, because of the champion's life story and the difference in years, but several significant elements were missing from such a relationship from the events that I witnessed between them. On one hand, Bobby was always unusually kind and considerate to his old friend and showed him unreserved sympathy; Mr. Gligorić was always very rational and observed more carefully everything that happened between them and around them. Seen from the outside, it was as if Mr. Gligorić had a clear and defined limitation in his friendship with Bobby that he did not want to exceed, and that their relationship could be observed only through that prism.

To be fair, mention should also be made of those who claimed that the famed Yugoslav grandmaster did indeed pay the price for his closeness with Fischer by the fact that he was never elected to the top positions in FIDE, as well as in the publicly expressed antipathy toward him by some players from the former USSR, Kasparov in the first place and Karpov to a lesser extent. I once asked Bobby what he thought about this problem and I got a fairly indefinite answer; he thought that the factor of their friendship certainly had an influence on the fact that Mr. Gligorić was never chosen to the position of FIDE president, but the extent to which that was decisive, even he could not be sure.

Here mention should also be made of the late Mrs. Dana Gligorić, the wife of the grandmaster, a person of marvelous gentility and spiritual edification; often for hours she would gently hold Bobby's hand, as if he were a child, telling him about the old days and counseling him about how to make his life happier. Disarmed by her warmth and love, he would smile and promise her that he would take seriously her reflections on his marriage and establishment of a family. When he came to their home, Mrs. Gligorić always waited for Bobby with a table covered in his favorite foods, and she was such caring hostess that she never left anyone unimpressed. On several occasions when I was searching for Mr. Gligorić on the phone because of various agreements, in his absence I had the opportunity become convinced of the special, almost maternal love that this exceptional lady nurtured for Bobby. Speaking in her gentle voice, she would ask in detail about all of his everyday life, adding a myriad of her own observations, thoughts and advice about the best way to help him find and maintain balance in the real world.

The Greatest Secret of Bobby Fischer

The undefeated world champion and his friend from Belgrade would work hard until nine in the evening when they would take a break for supper. The first few days they did not want to interrupt the good tempo they had achieved by indulging in gastronomic pleasure in one of the restaurants from Belgrade, but rather decided to eat in the office upstairs. Usually they would order roasted pork or lamb, a lot of mixed salads and mineral water.

After supper they would continue with their preparations for the upcoming match and tried to get into proper competitive form, although Bobby persistently claimed "I don't need any sort of special training because my whole life is constant preparation for chess and it makes me ready all the time to answer any challenge." Grandmaster Gligorić insisted that they keep working, though he admitted that he was pleasantly surprised both by the high level of Fischer's game and by the fact that Bobby was apprised of everything related to modern chess, of the new trends, and in the significant specificities of the styles of all the modern players. In the long years of his self-isolation, Bobby had not been wasting time, so it seemed.

In parallel with this most important segment related to chess, because of the brevity of time before the beginning of the match, it was necessary to work on other necessary elements so that an entire mosaic of preparatory work had to be carried out by the given date. On Fischer's insistence, his overall appearance was the first thing in order. The clothes he had brought from America were practically useless and clearly reflected his financial situation in the previous decades. Everyone knew of his legendary affinity for the elegant suits that he bought in his youth so that he would dominate among the grandmasters both in style and in the quality of his dress as a whole. Thus, before us was the long and tortuous task of bringing Bobby's image into accord with his express wish to return to the chess arena in the best possible condition. And just how difficult that task was to be is best illustrated by the case of Fischer's infamous shirts.

Since Bobby was disgusted by anything off the rack, which was perhaps understandable because of his hefty and rather awkward build, we put in the effort to bring in a master tailor from a famed shop with a long tradition, someone who could meet his needs. Having obtained many recommendations from people who had proved that they know what top quality really is, we brought in a lady, as the best of the best, who by her very appearance, style and elegance exuded confidence. In addition, her obvious work experience suited Fischer and he, without hiding his happiness, congratulated me, already pleased in advanced that he would have first-rate shirts.

It all began in the best possible way, because he immediately agreed to and praised the materials she offered him, and then after an hour of thinking and a little help from me with the choice of colors, he ordered four shirts each in white, blue, ocher, green and pink. The seamstress took his measurements and carefully listened to his specifications down to the last detail. Bobby especially emphasized that the collars had to be stiff and high, so that his ties would sit nicely against his neck.

Everything was absolutely clearly and precisely agreed, without any lack of clarity, and the two of them parted smiling, satisfied that such fine cooperation had been established. The next fitting was set to be in a couple of days.

The poor seamstress could not have guessed that this was only the beginning of her Golgotha which she would certainly remember to the end of her life. Already at the first fitting, Bobby wiped the smile off her face with his complaints that the model she offered him was tight in the waist. Even though everything was done according to the agreed measurements and despite the fact that everyone present said that it looked excellent, his subjective opinion was the last word. Naturally things like this occur in the process of tailoring and sewing, and there was no problem to have another fitting in two days so that everything could be fixed according to Bobby's wishes, but not even then, in spite of the fact that every one of the picky client's demands had been met, he was not satisfied because he now said that the shirts were too loose. The kind woman, helplessly spreading out her hands, made an appointment for the next day, promising that she would make the new alterations by then. By now you can guess, on that day the cut was not the one that Bobby had imagined. Now the tense situation was made worse by his angry mumbling, by the tears of the frustrated designer and my verbal efforts to settle things down. In any case, the fittings from that day forward occurred daily, lasting for hours, and they went on for more than a month, right up to the beginning of the match on Sveti Stefan. Just as the crisis about the fit at the waist was overcome, troubles started with the stiffness of the collar and then with its height which was lengthened and shortened day after day, first by a centimeter, then by a half, and in the end there was a nasty trench war for every millimeter between picky and indecisive Bobby and the seamstress whose hair had suddenly begun to go grey. When Fischer finally gave his fated "thank you, now it's fine", we all sighed in relief, especially the tortured designer who cried for a long time after her client spoke these words, and she caught the first plane for Belgrade as fast as she could, declining Mr. Vasiljević's offer to remain on Sveti Stefan as long as she wanted for a nice and well-deserved vacation.

The efforts around Bobby Fischer's new suits and leather jackets were neither easier nor faster. The procedure was similar because he demanded the near impossible, a perfection understandable only to him. The problem was that the meaning of that concept changed quite often, so that a finished jacket which he was quite pleased with one day had to be taken apart at the seams the next day because of a sudden redefinition of the category "lovely" that had come about overnight. He almost ruined an ideally cut leather jacket once so that he could check to see if the inner lining was of all natural materials. Tailored suits to measure were Bobby's ideal of dressing. In order to reach that almost unattainable goal, a master tailor was needed, and he had always chosen them by the rule "the older the better". In Bobby's vocabulary, the term "old-fashioned" was synonymous with high quality. In his memories of past times, he was full of praise for tailors from Zagreb and Varaždin who long before, during his visits to Yugoslavia, had made suits for him that really pleased him. The extent to which his passion was well-known and constant is confirmed by an anecdote that occurred later in Hungary, where the protagonist was the sly and humorous Mr. László Polgár.

After we had been in Budapest for several weeks, Bobby decided to update his wardrobe once again, and thereby to try out the school of tailoring and sewing in the capital city of Hungary. So, he asked Mr. Polgár to help him in that effort. One day we went to a lot of stores and salons which Mr. Polgár had recommended to Bobby, full of enthusiasm and with an honest desire to make him happy. However, the picky guest found some problem or fault in every one of the tailors, ranging from their age, their general appearance, all the way down to the vague feeling that the tailor in question would not be skillful enough to meet his demands.

After this unsuccessful odyssey and Fischer's disappointment, we traveled to Nagymaros, a prestigious weekend getaway spot on the banks of the Danube, at the invitation of the kind Polgár family because they had a summer home there. After several days, during the morning break, while the famous sisters together with Bobby and Eugene Torre were relaxing over tea and cookies, the *pater familias* entered the room out of breath and ceremoniously announced, "Mr. Fischer, all of your troubles have come to an end." After several moments in which, in the manner of an experienced psychologist, he let the tension rise among those present, he continued with an explanation that there was someone in town who could surely fulfill all Bobby's conditions and that he would come to visit us during lunch.

A celebratory atmosphere, ripe with expectations, filled the entire house and everyone in it already at noon, so that no one was even thinking of food when we sat down at the table two hours later. Then Mr. Polgár peeked into the room, with a mocking smile on his face he looked everyone over and gave me a secretive wink. In a pompous voice that sounded like a game show announcer, he cried, "And now…!" closing the door for a second and then throwing it open wide, as if he were raising the curtain on a stage, he presented his discovery to the awestruck audience.

Before us was a man who László took by the arm, or rather supported by the arm, which was more than needed because of the man's age. While some in the room giggled and discretely cast glances at Bobby, the master of ceremonies went on, "No one can doubt the experience of this man before you, because he has spent seventy of his ninety years working as a master tailor, working for the aristocracy, and then for the Party leaders in the time of communism, which is certainly a guarantee of quality. I believe he is ready for one final effort, for one more suit. So, Mr. Fischer…?"

Everyone in the room was laughing out loud while Zsuzsa, herself shaking with laughter, hardly managed to translate Mr. Polgár's words, because he spoke English very poorly. After a couple of minutes, the visibly disappointed Bobby joined in the fun without anger, because he saw no ill will in this little joke. The old tailor, quite merry himself, somehow touched, took his place at the table where he answered many questions through an interpreter, as his would-be customers took an interest in his craft.

This odyssey around Bobby's clothing and the updating of his wardrobe which took place almost at the very beginning of our work together, besides being interesting as an anecdote, made me powerfully aware that there was undoubtedly only one way one must go in order to work with him over a longer period of time. On the basis of these episodes it was immediately clear to me that there was no such thing as an insignificant detail for Fischer, no small or less important things, no mistakes that could be corrected, but that he raised everything from the very start to the level of being crucial and vital. In later reflection and re-living, which for him usually meant re-interpreting and re-thinking already made decisions and opinions, which he usually did a few hours after an event, everything always took on a new form and meaning. Thus, every day spent near him and with him, naturally under the condition that you were motivated to be there, was a real 24 hour dance on the razor's edge where the outcome was never certain. It was enough if a single detail, a carelessly spoken word, or a movement made at the wrong moment, to bring down an entire avalanche of doubt in him which, regardless of your status up until that time in Bobby's world, certainly resulted in the erasure of your name from Fischer's list of the living.

Noting these facts further convinced me that the most functional model of my behavior was to be that I support Bobby absolutely both in word and action in all measures and directions, and that later, once I had his confidence, to try to make his life simpler and easier at least on the practical level.

This effort on my part was inspired by my desire to get to know my charge as profoundly and clearly as possible, but also by the powerful empathy I felt for him beyond our professional duties and relationship. Because the more I got to know about Fischer's personality, as I understood it better, in many segments, naturally though I did not necessarily agree, the more I wanted to help him and protect him from the numerous, mostly negative, influences from outside of chess, especially since the tragedy of his conflict with the world touched me deeply.

Therefore, it is no wonder that I analyzed, with great care and detail, all of Bobby's demands (even the smallest ones), regardless of what they were related to, and then met them with precision. In those early days, if he wanted to get a haircut and beard-trim, I would take him around all those barbershops that corresponded to his description of the ideal one. Although it was hard to find such shops in Belgrade, because Bobby wanted an old-fashioned barber who used only scissors and comb (he was disgusted by electric apparatuses in this craft), after a discussion with the barber he was offered and at least one hour of watching how each of them worked, he would choose one. When he wanted to have his shoes fixed (they were of an odd shape and design, bought during his last visit to Germany, and he was particularly sensitive about them) he chose the cobbler with equal care, one who was capable of such an undertaking according to his criteria.

I did not change these established rules the whole time I worked with Fischer. Later, he would allow me to take care of such important "small things" for him, with the comment that I would surely do it his way. Naturally, I had to make a lot of decisions by myself, especially the bigger ones, particularly after Mr. Vasiljević departed, and I undertook that privilege and responsibility with an eye to doing so in accord with Bobby's principles and wishes.

*

The house in Dedinje was *terra incognita* for everyone except a small group of people who was directly involved in the preparations for Fischer's return and the upcoming match. It was understood that no one uninvited was allowed to encroach on the privacy that was so important to Bobby, or allowed to disturb him, but there were also certain individuals who were singled out.

In order to highlight his favorite on the list of animosities, Fischer told me that he absolutely refused to have Mr. Dimitrije Bjelica disturb him.[9] When he spoke of this journalist and former friend, Bobby always used a bunch of negative epithets, attempting in anger to describe the man's character and work.[10] Generally speaking, Fischer counted Mr. Bjelica in the ranks of his greatest enemies and accused him that he had used their former friendship to write falsehoods and lies about Bobby, of having material gain from doing so, and above all he considered Bjelica to be a hypocrite for coddling and ingratiating himself to the Soviet chess players.

The price for Bobby's opinion was paid by practically all Yugoslav chess players who were not allowed to come anywhere near him as he prepared for the match. Grandmaster Gligorić and Mr. Kubat, the organizer of the upcoming match, asked him several times to receive Ms. Milunka Lazarević, a chess player and chess world personality, but Fischer did not want to hear of it. Yet, this did not keep him from hungrily eating the cake she sent him as a welcome present.

The regulars at "our" villa were, in addition to the above-mentioned security team, Mr. Jezdimir Vasiljević and Mr. Janos Kubat, and an engineer named Aleksandar Mihajlović, who was

---

[9] Dimitrije Bjelica, a well-known activist in chess, writer, publicist and journalist.
[10] As stated in the introduction, Bobby Fischer's opinions about individuals, situations and events are being presented in the form which I literally heard from him. At no single moment, unless I explicitly indicate it, do they contain my opinions or judgments.

working on the construction of a new kind of chess clock according to Bobby's ideas. From time to time, Mr. Vasiljević would be accompanied by his best man and lawyer, Mr. Protić, and another lawyer, Mr. Miljević, whose role in the legal procedures of Fischer's return were of exceptional significance. That was where the list of the privileged ended.

However, sometimes it would happen that someone, carried away by their own wishes and ideas, would try to put themselves on the list of the privileged. All over Yugoslavia of the day there was a lot of joy and excitement because of the fact that the grimness of everyday life was to be painted with the colors of something special by the event, the prologue of which was occurring in the capital of the "ostracized" country. In the squares, streets, restaurants and cafes, every detail was excitedly repeated as it reached the wider public through the media or newspaper commentaries. While the citizens of the capital, whose hospitality was and still is a matter of fame, manifested their satisfaction at every turn because of the presence of the grandmaster in their midst, there were also those who in some special, different way wished to show that and prove it. One quiet morning, while Bobby was still asleep, I was having coffee with one of my confederates on the veranda of the Dedinje villa. Then I noticed something strange happening at the front gate. The guard was arguing fiercely with someone through the half opened entrance. Using hand gestures and body language, he beckoned me over and we headed toward the front gate. When we got to him, we clearly recognized the tone and type of the conversation. Namely, our colleague was trying to explain to an over-exuberant citizen of the capital that it was not possible to enter the grounds. Wanting to hear and find out what was really going on, I entered the conversation with our unexpected guest. It was a certain gentleman, at the end of his working day (the empty parked taxi before us told us what his job was), and he wanted to show his indescribable joy at Fischer's arrival in Belgrade and, as he said "to play a couple of quick chess games" with him. In a blue t-shirt and faded jeans, he was exceptionally likeable because of the volcanic energy he was investing to carry out his plans. While I tried once again in a polite way to explain that this was absolutely impossible to this typical representative of the straightforwardness, stubbornness and hospitality of my people, he took off running toward the house with a quick movement and "superhuman" decisiveness. Naturally it was not difficult for us to stop him after just a couple of seconds, to firmly but carefully (because he did not have bad intentions) convince him that his attempt was senseless. As we put into his taxi, he was waving his arms and legs, constantly repeating at the top of his voice, "I just want to play, I want to play…!" When he calmed down after a few minutes, I sent one of my cohorts up to the house to bring him a small chess set which we gave him as a souvenir of this day, and then he went back satisfied to his everyday life. I am certain that, to this day at a taxi stand somewhere in my big and beautiful Belgrade, he is retelling the story about how "he was close to defeating the greatest player of all time."

The controversial, for some Serbs fatal, person of Mr. Jezdimir Vasiljević, the owner of *Jugoskandic Bank*, a financial mogul who had invested enormous funds in this sports spectacle and grandiose media event, gave the whole atmosphere a special aura. This quite capable businessman, who had returned to Yugoslavia after several decades of absence at the end of the 1980s, made several small business investments, trading in automobiles, televisions, video-recorders and so on, attracted quite a lot of media attention at the time with his unusual television appearances, and this caused a lot of commentary but also aroused a lot of curiosity. His commercials went on during primetime, promising the masses, potential bank customers, fantastic interest rates of 14% per month on foreign currency savings at his savings banks. This man, not very tall and a bit plump, with a strange haircut and long sideburns, seemed to have arrived by time machine from the seventies, dressed in a white tuxedo with fat pipe in his hand, was offering people quick and easy earnings at a time when war and poverty was the cruel reality for most families in this region.

He was born in 1948 in the village of Topolovnik, in the municipality of Veliko Gradište, and he finished elementary school there. Once he told me that his great love for music and the clarinet was motivated primarily by the desire, with one of the cultural and artistic folklore groups, to cross the border and head into the wide world. At the age of twenty he was already trotting the globe working at a variety of jobs as a tire repairman, sugar cane cutter, movie operator, stockbroker, diamond trader, pilot and Interpol inspector. He often showed us his small but powerful palms, proud of his hand covered with scars and knots that testified to a lot of hard work. He subsumed all of his other business activities to the pyramid scheme *Jugoskandic* savings banks. Even though the president of the Serbian government at the time, Radoman Božović, clearly announced in the media that the government did not stand behind *Jugoskandic* and *Dafiment* banks,[11] the number of clients rose every day at an unbelievable speed, which again allowed the "nimble" creator of the whole story to accumulate a financial base for a variety of profitable deals available at the time.

It was thus not strange that many, repressing the memory of the bitter experience they had had only a few years before with the state-owned banks confiscating their savings, rushed to entrust to Big Daddy Jezda with their cash reserves, hard earned and saved for "a rainy day." Certainly there were many who, in those muddled times, made a lot of money in many, often illegal ways, and there were quite a few individuals who made dozens of thousands of dollars every day with millions in investment. Almost no one asked how the whole thing functioned, or how it was possible, in a country where the economic crisis had already reached a dramatic level, that the monthly interest was twice as large as the normal annual rate in the renowned European banks.

Jezda himself was an exceptionally cordial and straightforward man so that everyone around him admired him and liked his treatment of his workers and the mutual respect which was dominant. That feeling was not the result of material status, their

---

[11] "Dafiment" Bank, a copy of the *Jugoskandic* savings bank, though founded later, was owned by Dafina Milanović, now deceased, who was also legally processed before she died.

salaries were certainly larger than the average in Yugoslavia, but not higher than those in the better-standing private companies.

The Bobby Fischer headquarters, as they called us from the outset, had quite a special and separate place because of the specificity of our tasks, completely independent of the *Jugoskandik* empire. That position was conditioned on the demanding nature of our ward and resulted in a privileged status within the framework of the organization of the match itself.

Therefore, I had two relevant coordination points from the very beginning – Jezda and Bobby. As time went by, Mr. Vasiljević would come by ever more often and stay longer with us, even when he had no particular reason.

Desiring to maintain my loyalty to both of them, I often balanced between Fischer's principles and Jezda's necessary practicality, which was quite difficult at times. The successfulness of my efforts was confirmed by the very flow and finish of the match, but the balance was lost forever with the departure, the flight, of Mr. Vasiljvić from the country. Their relationship passed through several phases, but the very beginning was surprisingly harmonious and tolerant.

The Serbian businessman was quite happy and satisfied that he was actually the man whose name was to be connected to Bobby's return to the world chess scene. This was an ego stroke for him because, in the chess following public, it was well-known who and in how many ways people had tried to convince the undefeated champion of the world to play again. Besides that, he understood very well that the exclusivity of the event would ensure another sure component in the life of any world-renowned millionaire, one that would bring him international credibility. On the domestic scene, the fact that he had invested five million dollars in the prize fund, in buying the resort of Sveti Stefan even more so, and that the entire match organization was to cost several million more, all created an impression of certainty and stability in his empire, as if it were built to last forever, among the citizens who were simply bombarded with these figures through the media. Much was said and written those days about the patriotic motifs for the organization of the upcoming spectacle, because the international community's embargo was already biting deep, and the presence of the American sixth fleet in the Adriatic created a sense of general insecurity.

Although Mr. Vasiljević himself gave a series of "patriotic" statements in which he connected the upcoming events with "the strength of the Serbian people which no one can do anything to harm", the later development of events was to show that it was a set up, both because of his attempt to penetrate to some extent the media blockade which was part of the general sanctions toward Yugoslavia, and also for domestic political reasons. From all the above mentioned it was clear that Big Daddy Jezda had plenty of motives to satisfy the demands of our guest from America.

On the other hand, after Bobby Fisher had made his final decision to make a comeback and to come to Yugoslavia, he had already completed the hardest part of the battle with his own dilemmas and fears, so he did not want to gamble easily with the capital he had earned with great effort. Receiving such a warm and heartfelt reception, maximum attention and the wish to meet his every need, along with all the other comforts and the ideal overlap of his personal efforts and the circumstances, he was more than happy to forgive and forget some things.

Here I mean above all the above-mentioned secret recording of his visit to Mr. Vasiljvic's TV studio. Conciliatory statements after that incident, guided precisely by the reasons just mentioned, were the key elements of this first phase of their mutual tolerance.

It should also be emphasized that from those early days all the way until they parted, Bobby did not hide his fascination with his host. He was not impressed only by the money, luxury and luster, but rather a specific kind of feeling which he experienced thanks to Big Daddy Jezda which emanated from everything Mr. Vasiljević represented at the time, and especially his position in society. Fischer had been received by important political figures in many countries where he visited (he often talked enthusiastically about Philippine former president Markos) but, by his own admission, he had never gotten so close to the sources of true power as he did then in Yugoslavia.

The Greatest Secret of Bobby Fischer

His feeling was intensified by Jezda's stories in which there were occasional exaggerations, and which contained at times a bit of well-intentioned falsehood. However, no kind of overstatement was even necessary because that summer the whole country seemed to be Jezda's backyard in which everything was possible, and in which Bobby would make all of his dreams come true.

*

The beginning of August was marked by exceptionally high temperatures, and Belgrade was the hottest city in Europe for a few days at 97 degrees Fahrenheit. The house in Dedinje offered a lot of shade and protection from the high temperatures, but the intensity of the events and the dynamics of the goings on threatened to bring on a different kind of heat.

Apart from his daily routine, Bobby was waking up quite early and as early as seven he would ask me to bring him copies of all the more important Yugoslav newspapers. He would appear at the top of the steps in his favorite ocher bathrobe, which barely reached his knees; he would call out to me and give me the sign that he was ready for his morning dose of news.

He would rush back to bed and begin paging through the papers, trying to understand as much as he could by himself. Now and then he would ask me about a word, about how it was read and pronounced in Serbian, and then ask for its transcription into English.

I was quite surprised by Bobby's ability to read and understand the language of the land of his hosts. The explanation could be found in his relatively frequent and long stays in Yugoslavia, even though they had taken place long before, in his association with Yugoslavs, especially Mr. Gligorić and Mr. Bjelica, but also in his fantastic ability to remember words quickly and easily, to understand their meaning and connect them into a logical whole. In addition, he also had a powerful desire to learn and to perfect his linguistic abilities, not hesitating to freely check his newest acquisitions with everyone, regardless of whether it was in conversation with a famous person, or if he was just ordering food in a restaurant. It is certain that, thanks to these character traits, he had managed to learn Spanish perfectly, and he understood German and Russian well. However, my surprise was no less when he once told me privately that his fundamental motive for learning Spanish was his desire to easily follow a kind of Mexican sexy comic strip, a couple of copies of which he had bought in Los Angeles in his younger years. I was therefore not surprised when, during the match, a packet arrived from the USA containing a pile of this "literature", which had obviously remained a passion of his over the years.

After about ten minutes of leafing through the papers by himself, Bobby would ask me to translate in detail all of the things that were related to him and the upcoming match. The texts and commentaries from the pens of Yugoslav journalists were, without exception, emotionally charged and full of enthusiasm because of the champion's return, and because of the fact that he chosen precisely our country for his new beginning. Carefully chosen words glorified his life and his chess career, and his triumphs and successes were hailed in retrospective accounts. Only in places, as a side note, some would ask about his current shape and competitive ability, but this would immediately be followed by the certainty that there would no problems with that either, no disappointments. Of course, Bobby was exceptionally satisfied by the kind disposition of the printed media. On the other hand, just so things would not be completely idyllic, there were those papers and magazines who published the thoughts and opinions of those who were not exactly enthused by Fisher's return. He was especially irritated and angered by the statements of certain chess players whom he *a priori* considered not only potential competitors in the sport, but even more so he thought of them as personal enemies.

For example, in those days the Belgrade daily *Politika* printed the statement by Garry Kasparov that "the match in Yugoslavia would be the clash of two retired champions for the highest purse in the history of chess." A few days before that, the same paper had published the claim of his wife Maria that "that will not be a big event." Kasparov had somewhat earlier already attacked indirectly, saying that "Mr. Gligorić questions his development" (?!).

As time went by, Garry was to radicalize the verbal aggression through the media more and more. The extent to which the hatred and obvious jealousy obsessed the current world champion's entire being actually even became irrational, and this would be reaffirmed by the fact that he awaited in Croatia, on Brioni, for the beginning of the duel on Sveti Stefan, thus turning that country into his observation tower for this event, which was of course a political and sport statement in opposition to Fischer, in opposition to the country where the American grandmaster was residing had chosen for his comeback. In this way, unfortunately, all of Garry Kasparov's statements would fall into oblivion in which he spoke with respect of his famous forerunner on the throne of chess, including the one in 1991 where he made the claim that "modern chess actually begins with Fischer."

As opposed to Kasparov, Anatoly Karpov, who had received the title as the champion of chess without a battle from FIDE, taking it over from undefeated Fischer on April 3, 1975, saw the new situation as a possibility for potential huge earnings in the events which would follow the "revenge match of the 20th century." His statements were thus fairly measured and well-balanced, with the ever-present note that he "would love to play against Fischer."

As I read and translated such texts from the papers, Bobby would comment on them loudly, if by comments we mean he would use the most varied and nasty of rebukes and curses. Naturally he had formed his opinions on these grandmasters long before, and their newest statements, even those which were positive about him, certainly did not budge him an inch from his beliefs. Bobby Fischer did not say, either collectively or individually, the names of Garry Kasparov or Anatoly Karpov without the qualification "CRIMINAL!"

The attention of chess followers was also attracted by an interview with one other great of the game on 64 black and white squares, with the "patriarch of Soviet chess", Mikhail Botvinnik, who tried to make a comparison of Fischer and Kasparov through time and space. He claimed that the two of them where similar in terms of assertiveness and calculation, and that Kasparov was better at combinations while Fischer was better in the endgame. He highlighted Bobby's contributions to chess theory with his new ideas in the French and Spanish defense, and two unique openings in the match for the world title with Spassky.

As the texts, commentaries and interviews grew in number, we spent longer and longer on these morning briefings. Since Bobby would go back to sleep after that, we decided to take up a new practice in which every day, after I had carefully and in detail looked through all the available domestic and foreign press, I would present him with a summary of the most important things. Among other things, the time till the match was growing ever shorter, and our obligations were multiplying in a geometrical progression.

An exceptionally important element of the preparations was also the work on a new model of the game clock. Everyone was expecting a lot from the results of that project: for creative Bobby the affirmation of his idea about the modernization of chess, but above all, together with Mr. Vasiljević, enormous financial gain from its exploitation.

The essence of Fischer's idea about this new way of measuring time in chess was born from his belief in the injustice of running out of time, because of which it often happens that "higher quality and more talented players in much better positions lose because of the flag falling on the clock." Bobby would add, "Of course the time of a game should be limited, but chess must be returned to its basics, and those are talent and mental strength, while seconds should be given to the track runners."

That change in quality would be ensured by an agreed fixed starting time. For the upcoming match it was to be 1 hour and 51 minutes, to which one bonus minute would be given to each competitor after each piece movement. After playing a certain number of moves the players would be rewarded with new time for thinking. Fischer and Spassky would receive an additional 40 minutes after the fortieth move, after 60 moves another 30 minutes, and after the eightieth move another 100 minutes. An alarm would sound as a warning automatically the first time at 55 seconds, then at 16 seconds and finally at 8 seconds before time ran out. This concept would be true for fast games and blitz games, with the proviso that the game length and all the bonuses would be adapted to those shortened forms of chess.

In spite of its technical complexity and the perfectionism of its designer, the prototype of Fischer's new clock was satisfactorily produced to Bobby's great delight. Perfecting it and putting the finishing touches on it, both essential and visual, was a daily chore, but the basic esthetic form was achieved due to the abilities and efforts of the engineer, Mihajlović. Partial to adding his own specific tone and elements of exaggeration to everything, Jezdimir Vasiljević spoke enthusiastically about this project and proudly announced that this game clock would also have high technology and micro parts from *AIRBUS* airplanes.

The extent to which work on this project was complex and expensive is indicated also by the fact that couriers traveled to Budapest almost every other day (because the Socialist Republic of Yugoslavia was already feeling the consequences of the international embargo) in order to obtain the necessary parts for construction and production. Once when one of them had set off to purchase a miniature part, on the Hungarian border the customs officers took forty thousand German marks from him which he was carrying to buy the part. All desperate and dejected, he returned to Belgrade where he was supposed to tell Mr. Vasiljević that the money was gone forever. However, Big Daddy Jezda immediately cheered him up, right in front of Bobby, with the words "such trivial stuff won't interrupt our work." Already the next day, the courier left for Budapest, this time with security measures in place and with a safe passage through the border formalities.

Before the beginning of the match, two such clocks were ready. Fischer kept the first one with himself all the time, and the second was used for the games, under the watchful eye of Mr. Mihajlović the engineer.

*

The Greatest Secret of Bobby Fischer

The fact that Robert James Fischer was in Belgrade left no one riding the fence in those days. While this interest was reflected in the media by the number of journalistic texts and TV and radio reports, in the wider public this event pushed into the background all the burning themes that burdened reality in this part of the world at that time.

Many respected people from the popular and cultural scene showed an interest in getting into contact with Bobby Fischer in a variety of ways. Equally varied were their motives for doing so, but surely for most of them the media boom around the match itself was the most important, along with all the events preceding it. It had a magnetic effect on many.

Bobby himself, of course, was not prepared to respond to all those invitations and offers. He personally would not have answered a single one of them positively, but because of the overall atmosphere and his primary "tolerance" as described above, he did make a few exceptions. Namely, on the first of August Jezdimir Vasiljević told me that the Yugoslav premier at that time, Milan Panic, would like to meet with Bobby Fischer as soon as possible.

After the first conversation on the topic, we got a rather indefinite answer from Bobby which aroused hope after all that such a meeting would take place. In the light of the urgency of the matter, the incredibly busy schedule of both participants, the political and personal opinions of my protégé, it was necessary that we go over this topic once again.

I must say that, from the very beginning, Bobby's familiarity with the everyday political situation in Yugoslavia was quite surprising. As I spent more time with him, I came to recognize that observing and analyzing global events, especially those in the fields of politics and economy, were the most important activities outside of chess to him. In order to obtain information, he regularly read dozens of leading world daily papers, all the relevant magazines in English, as well as those in languages he understood; he followed the daily news on a large number of TV and radio stations, and he sought as many facts, opinions and impressions as possible from those people he talked to. All of the things he learned as such were carefully and thoughtfully analyzed, systematically fed into the consequences of his firm convictions about the "real meaning of world history and politics, usually hidden from mere mortals." Of the thousands of bits of information that reached Bobby Fischer, he was actually searching for support for his vision of reality. If something did not fit into those principles at first, or if it seemed to contradict them, in his mind that was just because the real meaning of the observed phenomenon was still fuzzy and foggy. Bobby's studiousness went into unfathomable detail. If he wanted to pass judgment on a given political personality, he would persistently gather all possible facts about them for a long time and carefully stack them in his memory. Through contact with the people around him he tested various possibilities and solutions, but the final stamp was given by that Bobby Fischer who would often analyze a photograph with the observed person for hours, searching their face, the sharpness of their gaze, the setting of their jaw or the way they combed their hair, and then offer a final answer to the questions of their capability, decisiveness and honor. His opinion formed in this way was an axiom, and it was not something to be further checked into or even discussed. From the very first day I met him, Bobby often bragged that thinking through things in that way he had never been mistaken about a person, event or thing.

When I reminded him about his claim to his errorless analysis, as we left Yugoslavia, he intentionally answered me with a cliché and an ironic smile, "There's a first time for everything." Then he sighed, and with a wave of his hand and an icy tone in his voice he added, "But it happened too late in life for me, and it was very painful."

However, in August of 1992, Bobby Fischer had clear opinions on the Serbian and Yugoslav political scene and about the general situation in this area torn by war, because from the first moment when the match with Spassky was already a real possibility, he had directed his attention to this part of the world. When he arrived in Belgrade, he constantly kept up his practice of following all the events in the society of his host country. I was thus not terribly surprised by Fischer's rather cool reaction to the proposal of the federal premier, because I already knew quite well that Milan Panic was certainly not one of Bobby's favorites in the region. Furthermore, Bobby thought that the choice of this American businessman of Serbian background as the premier of the Yugoslav government was a catastrophe, the event having taken place on July 14 of that same year.

Driven by the desire to confirm his opinion of Mr. Panic by meeting him, but also to make another gesture of good will toward Mr. Vasiljević above all, Fischer agreed to the premier's wish. The meeting was set for Tuesday, August 4, in the building of the Federal Executive Council in Novi Beograd.[12]

That beautiful sunny day was no different from any other, because Bobby did not change the slightest thing in his morning routine. Indeed there was no need for that because he showed no visible signs of nervousness or excitement.

Around noon I helped him choose the best of the clothes he had and to get ready, because his wardrobe was rather meager since his new clothes still were not finished. We were quickly ready to leave, and we headed for Novi Beograd with Mr. Vasiljević and Mr. Kubat.

The Yugoslav premier, Mr. Milan Panic, received us in his already well-known hyper-happy style, which was launched as an essential element of his "optimistic" personality from the first moment he appeared on the political scene. After a long and energetic handshake which was accompanied by his usual smiles and loud, repeated words of welcome, the so-called conventional part of that conversation typical for such situations. Mr. Panic was interested in Bobby's stay in Belgrade, from his place of residence and food, all the way down to the champion's health. The premier mainly addressed only Fischer, obviously referring to the fact "that they were both, you know, Americans", desiring by that to establish a high degree of closeness and friendliness. But Bobby's rather cool and forced answers immediately indicated that it was

---

[12] Federal Executive Council, an institution of the once large and now non-existent Yugoslavia. Its building in Novi Beograd was at that time the seat of the Federal government, thus the common government of the two remaining members of the new Yugoslavia (Serbia and Montenegro).

going to be very difficult. Mr. Panic tried to capture the heart of is his guest with charm and humor, especially emphasizing all those elements of life that might ultimately connect them. Here he used a wide range of arguments: the already mentioned fact that they were countrymen, the fact that he was once a representative of bicycling for Yugoslavia, he was a successful athlete, and even an anecdote in which his chauffeur, sometime and somewhere in Los Angeles, had played a game of chess with Fischer. However, Bobby remained unimpressed by all that. As his ace in the hole in trying to establish a more intimate relationship, Mr. Panic offered maximum support and aid to his "compatriot" during his stay in Yugoslavia, concluding that "such a great in chess and sports must have special treatment, and that he and his place in government were a guarantee for Fischer's comfortable and safe stay in our country."

However, it was completely clear that none of what was said left any kind of impression on Bobby whatsoever, and once the premier saw this he changed the subject and made a long and heartfelt introduction to it, as it was actually the main reason for their meeting. In a much calmer voice, carefully choosing his words, after a couple of comments on the complexity of the foreign and domestic political situation of the country where he was residing, Mr. Panic looked Fischer right in the eye and announced that he "had been asked by certain circles in the USA to communicate their concern over the situation that had arisen by his coming to Yugoslavia and his readiness to participate in the announced chess spectacle." This "concern", according to the premier's words, was primarily related to Bobby himself because it was "certain that such a flagrant breaking of the UN sanctions would surely cause a reaction from the American government, which again might have a negative effect on his life and career." "So," he went on, "in terms of the responsibility I have taken on, it is my duty to ask you to think through the whole thing once more time."[13]

---

[13] The UN sanctions against Yugoslavia included sports (!), and Bobby Fischer actually violated them by appearing; likewise he violated that part of them related to

The Greatest Secret of Bobby Fischer

While Mr. Panic was saying this, a discrete, ironic smile could be seen on Fischer's face, which seemed to express his expectation of such an intervention, and he thus quickly and gruffly answered that "all concern for him which came from the USA, and especially from the institutions of the government, was completely void of meaning, because no one ever worried about him there and his decision to make a comeback and play the match in Yugoslavia was final, and he no longer wished to talk about the matter." Bobby did not respond to several other objections by the premier, so that an uncomfortable silence filled the room. Mr. Vasiljević tried to overcome this tortuous situation by assuring everyone present that there was no need to worry and that everyone would benefit from the upcoming event. He laid special emphasis on the media potential of the match and the numerous possibilities that it could be used, as people often said at that time, "to help the truth come out to the world."

But suddenly, as if the topic no longer interested him, Mr. Panic interrupted this speech and turned the conversation to the theme of business and banking. He did it briskly and angrily so that it was clear that this meeting would have another side as well. The more, the fiercer and the louder the premier expounded his vision of the economic situation and the business possibilities under sanctions, the more persistently Big Daddy Jezda contradicted him. As the situation came to a climax, Bobby, completely disinterested in this topic and in spite of the loud argument, leaned his head on his hand and dozed off. However, when Mr. Panic, ultimately frustrated, shouted in a falsetto that "Jezda and his savings banks are a black mark on the country, that nothing like that exists anywhere in the world", Bobby shuddered as he woke and thus became a witness to a great verbal business showdown.

"But anyway I am special and unique," Vasiljević answered him calmly, with a smile.

---

doing business with a country under embargo, because in such circumstances he made a profit (his prize money, the TV rights, the income from his clock...).

"Monthly interest of 14%?! Unheard of! Scandalous! How is that possible?" the premier roared from his armchair, waving his hands about and writhing.

"It's quite easy. I'll teach you," Jezda answered slyly.

At the moment when, as he would often repeat this anecdote later, it seemed that they would start throwing chairs at each other, Vasiljević stood up. At almost the same moment Mr. Panic did the same and that meant the meeting was over. As opposed to the welcome, the departure was quick, with but a brief and courteous shake of the hand.

The atmosphere in the car home to Dedinje was exceptionally good. Details of the conversation were retold with a laugh, along with the firm affirmation that no kind of pressure would be able to threaten the plans of "the great Serbian businessman and the legendary American chess player."

*

Just when it seemed that Fischer's team, after almost two weeks of familiarization and synchronization together with the grandmaster himself, had reached the first phase of the ideal degree of cooperation and the optimal daily schedule, the first more serious incident occurred which would be another warning that things with Bobby would not go easily and smoothly. In the early afternoon, while Mr. Kubat and I were chatting in anticipation in the downstairs salon for the arrival of Mr. Vasiljević, we suddenly heard a loud thumping noise from the room upstairs, accompanied by the typical sound of things falling to the floor. This was followed by slamming doors which shook the whole house, and finally we heard a something that sounded like the rush of an avalanche barreling down a mountainside.

As we quickly, Mr. Kubat and I, reached the first step in a couple of strides, we were faced with a horrifying scene. From upstairs, directly at us, at high speed and skipping steps, Bobby's massive figure was rumbling toward us. For an instant I managed to catch the expression on his face which did not look very promising.

He ran past us as if he did not even see us and headed out the front door into the yard. We looked at each other because we did not understand what was happening, but we followed him, quite aware that we had to act quickly. Bobby had already disappeared around the corner of the house and in long strides was heading purposefully toward the gate that was still some twenty yards away. Mr. Kubat and I caught up to him as the other security guards took their places in the yard. In the next few steps, we poured out questions to him from both sides, trying to figure out what had so dramatically affected his mood. His head lowered, as if to himself, Bobby mumbled that "it can't go on like this, maybe I made a mistake." The depression that obsessed him was so obvious that it seemed to me that we would first have to drag him back from the abyss of negative energy so that we could communicate with him. As if Mr. Kubat also sensed this, we started almost shouting at him that "everything will be all right and we will do everything possible to solve the problems, whatever they might be."

But Bobby kept striding toward the locked gate which was manned by a guard with a key in his hand who was waiting for a sign or an answer to the question of what he was to do, because it seemed that the furious grandmaster had certainly decided to either jump the gate or walk through it, even it if were locked. Our loud questions and words of comfort seemed to get to him at that moment and he said clearly "I'm too isolated here and I feel like a prisoner."

By then we had already reached the high wrought-iron barrier, and Bobby made a movement to suggest that he would start climbing it, when Mr. Kubat exclaimed, "Walking, recreation, that's what we're missing and because of that we're nervous. Let's walk around this beautiful garden for a while and talk everything over." As the match organizer said these words, I took an energetic step toward the path that led along the fence, through the bushes and flowers that edged the garden. From the corner of my eye I saw that Bobby was following me, I knew that the "storm" had passed and that Mr. Kubat and I, with our synchronized approach – as if we had practiced it – had reached our goal.

The Greatest Secret of Bobby Fischer

After a few minutes of fast walking, we began to explain to Fischer, by now much more in harmony, that he "could go anywhere he wished day or night, and that we were there to help him do whatever he wanted." As we tried to convince him, we made a complete round of the garden and came back to the gate. Then Bobby, as if he wanted to check out what we said, asked, "Does that mean we could go out right now?"

"Of course," I said, and gave the guard a signal to unlock the gate. So, we all stepped out onto the sidewalk and went for a walk down Užička Street, where there was almost no traffic anyway. After an hour of walking, during which Bobby looked at the villas and residences in our neighborhood, we went back "home". But then, probably as a final confirmation that he had freedom of movement, he asked if we could take a drive around town. When he had fulfilled this wish as well, and now in a very good mood, he looked at his watch and realized that it was lunchtime and that the next destination should be a nice restaurant.

After we had fulfilled all of his wishes, when we arrived back at the villa we found Mr. Vasiljević and his entourage, along with Mr. Gligorić who was waiting for a now long overdue continuation of their work and preparations. Bobby, now mellow, said hello to them all and withdrew straight upstairs with Gliga, ready to take on new chess challenges.

Mr. Kubat and I related to Big Daddy Jezda the experience of our afternoon adventure, and we both agreed that such excesses were certain to occur again. After all, Bobby knew very well from the first day of his stay in Yugoslavia that he had freedom of movement to go wherever and whenever he liked, even though, truth be told, we had been synchronizing his excursions with Mr. Vasiljević's schedule. It was clear that the reasons for this incident were primarily in Bobby's character which, stricken by a huge stress attack, was seeking a means of expression. Among other things, this stormy and fortunately short-lived episode was a sign that the time had come for Zita Rajcsányi to come back to Belgrade, so Mr. Kubat set about that task.

From the very first moment when the news of Robert Fischer's comeback had traversed the world, much had been written and spoken about his lady friend, the young Hungarian chess player, Miss Zita Rajcsányi, about her place and significance in the life of the American grandmaster. Immediately it should be noted that her influence was enormous, and that it was even crucial and decisive for Bobby's new beginning.

It was enough for me to be present two days later when Zita appeared in Belgrade again, at her meeting with her friend who was much older than she, for me to understand the incredible depth and strength of their relationship. The power of their feelings was not manifested in stormy public expressions of affection. To the contrary, I never saw them even touch each other, much the less hold hands, hug or kiss in a conventional way. The perfection of harmony and understanding they had achieved, which was so visibly evident, manifested itself like a myth about a romantic relationship and the predestination of two souls to be happy together. In those days, the two of them left exactly that kind of impression. They seemed to be a harmonious and self-satisfied completeness which related as such to the world and the events in it. However, it was immediately clear that Zita was the one who gave the tone, character and emotion to that symbiosis. She did not do this with her appearance, nor her feminine charms, which journalists placed an emphasis on by widely using the catchphrase "young Hungarian girl", which by itself conjured up such associations, but rather with her personality which was dominant and with which she definitely showed who was the real *spiritus movens* of that "coxless pair."

Carefully hidden behind an enigmatic smile and large glasses, at a personable distance from everyone, Zita would only make a dramatic scene when it seemed to her that someone had forgotten her importance in what was happening, to remind us all of that (this did not pertain to Bobby, of course, because he always kept that in mind those days). Most often she would resort to dramatic escapes, directed by the mindset of a nineteen year-old girl,[14] which we would solve while still in the yard, or later at the hotel.

---

[14] Zita celebrated her nineteenth birthday on September 1 on Sveti Stefan. Marked by the huge press conference, the Fischer-Spassky match began that day.

But these "happenings" almost always achieved her goal. In those ten minutes, the time they usually lasted, frantic Bobby would raise the alarm with everyone around, simply demanding an all-encompassing and, of course, unnecessary panic.

When smiling Zita would come back in our company, once again with a confirmation of her importance, the message of which was that we should always keep that in mind, Bobby would, with a look of relief, immediately take her upstairs to his room and they would stay there for a long time. If we ignore these situations and their excesses, because everyone on Fischer's staff and the entire organizational team of the match knew very well the strength of their relationship and thus maximally respected Miss Rajcsányi, she always showed a special maturity and soundness during the whole period of their time together.

As the crown of the description of their mutual relationship, I should emphasize the strong impression I got that the basic motive which Zita used in her relationship with her much older friend and chess idol was pure and honest love, even adoration for him, feelings that Bobby had longed for his whole life, and when he experienced them in the later years of his life, he was unable to recognize them completely and to keep them with himself.

*

Although the preparations for the upcoming match were progressing well on all fronts, they caused Bobby a lot of stress which, despite his very best wishes, because of his age and the long period when he had lived without any responsibilities, was harder and harder for him to take. As a result, he was a bit nervous and moody from time to time, so that Zita's arrival was just in the nick of time.

She showed up at the house on Dedinje this time accompanied by her family which she arrived with from Budapest in their old Lada.[15] In addition to Zita, there was her father Peter Rajcsányi,[16] a

---

[15] Lada - a well-known Russian automobile.

respected man with a career in diplomacy, who entranced everyone with his stature and manners. The family appeared to be harmonious, and their relationships seemed to be in concert, so that there was not a trace of any sort of parental objection to the relationship one of their daughters had with a man whose date of birth was nearly the same as her father's. Their arrival introduced quite a bit of liveliness into the overall atmosphere, while Bobby, who did not hide his satisfaction with the return of his dear friend, got an additional injection of energy for the upcoming challenges and efforts.

The uproar in the media, both domestic and foreign, did not die down. After the initial euphoria, caused by the news, the texts and commentaries, became ever more analytical in their search for answers to a wide range of questions that dealt equally with sports and politics. Our attention was caught by the information first given to us by Mr. Vasiljević, and the next day reported in the papers that, after the large American media corporations, the first in line for journalist accreditations had been sought by representatives of the "fourth estate" from Croatia and Slovenia. Likewise, interest was aroused by newspaper articles like the one from the Swiss *Tagesanzeiger* which connected *Jugoskandic* and its owner directly the president of Serbia, Slobodan Milošević. Public denouncements followed quickly, with the statement from Mr. Vasiljević that he had never even met the president.

The chess related news slowly began to appear in public. Those days it was announced that Fischer's second at the upcoming revenge match offered to Spassky was to be his long time friend, the Philippine grandmaster, Eugenio Torre. Bobby actually claimed that he had never really had a real second nor, in his own words, had he ever really needed one. He believed that in the game on 64 squares he could do it all himself, and that "because of common chess practices he had sometimes been forced to choose for that role a friend who was not a championship chess player

---

[16] Bobby himself was enthralled by the eloquence and education of Petar Rajcsányi. Many times he was quite surprised when, in conversation, he realized that Zita's father knew very well the titles and contents of books that Fischer believed were exclusively in his sphere of interest.

(Lombardy), or a strong player who hated him (Larsen)." One of the best grandmasters coming from Asian soil, Eugenio Torre, a long time friend and most faithful companion to Fischer, was the ideal solution for this position because of his character traits and personality.

On the other hand, in the expectation of Boris Spassky's arrival, the media announced that Yugoslav grandmaster Bora Ivkov was to be on his team. The lively "political" activity went on with the visit of Mr. Vasiljević and Mr. Kubat to the Yugoslav foreign minister of the time, Mr. Vladislav Jovanović, who himself was a great fan and avid player of chess. During this period, again in a good mood, Bobby easily carried out all his daily responsibilities and trained with great enthusiasm, often all night long.

The arrival of the second player, necessary for the "replay" of the Reykjavik match, once a Russian but now a French grandmaster, Boris Vasilievich Spassky, was announced for Thursday, August 6. Originally it was agreed that he would fly to Budapest but, because of the huge interest of the journalists and the possible tumult it would cause, the plan was changed at the last minute and a special team went to pick him up in Sofia.

The excitement gradually grew all day that day, into the early evening when we left the house in Dedinje and headed for the heart of old bohemian Belgrade and the romantic quarter of Skadarlija, to the restaurant "Dva jelena", to wait for Boris Spassky there. The whole atmosphere, magnified by the very ambient of the place, was solemn and lovely, but with a patina of nostalgia which lent the night a special tone.

As he waited for his competitor from long ago for the FIDE throne, Bobby played with a pocket chess set and chatted merrily with those around him. At one moment Zita disappeared for a few minutes, attempting to take over the role of "star of the show", but this did not work because we quickly found her and brought her back to the table. The story, which became a myth and the heroes in it, thanks to the whirlwind of time and events, was to take on the epithet of legend during their lifetimes, was continued at 10 p.m. when Boris Spassky walked into the room.

The Greatest Secret of Bobby Fischer

It is certain that in the life of every person, there are moments when, with his entire being, he becomes aware that he is participating in something quite different and special. That realization, which surpasses all boundaries of the mind, elevates the event to a significance which is not defined by temporal definitions and which remains permanently marked on the map of the collective memory.

For, when they write the history of the twentieth century, there will be mention of many individuals and facts in every segment of human activity and pursuit. From each of those areas, one name will stand above all others, shining more brilliantly than them, whose importance will be ensconced in the title of the chapter where it belongs. By the will of God which is transmitted into their talent, a harmony or note will resound which no one else will ever create or play, a light will shine forth from the picture on the wall and land on you, even though thousands of days and nights will have passed from the moment of that creation, or when a writer describes his childhood and you actually smell the scent of the quince in his grandmother's closet. Such people have fought to occupy their special place in honor of the creator of their talent.

In the encyclopedia of uniqueness for that century, the chapter entitled "Chess" will be illuminated by the name of Robert James Fischer, and the subtitle *Events* will note his triumph in the battle for champion of the world with Boris Spassky in Reykjavik in 1972. Whether certain people like it or not, Bobby was the watershed of the epochs in chess. He entered the new era on the wave of his own ideas about the overall improvement of the position of the game and the status of those involved in it, of those who contributed to its advancement with their enormous talent and refusal to compromise. And ultimately, with the publicity that he attracted to himself, he made it so that chess became a planetary media attraction, thus recruiting millions of new players and fans.

That is why it seemed to me that, at the moment when Spassky walked into the "Dva jelena", that whole piece of history entered with him, that part which will definitely be used to complete the mosaic, and with which will perhaps begin a new story predestined to become a myth. The encounter was more than cordial. Sincere kisses on the cheek, hugs and handshakes. In the days previous, I had clearly come to understand through my talks with Bobby that he truly respected and liked Boris, both as a man and as a fellow player. Since the days of Reykjavik and their rivalry, which had been elevated from a sports competition to "a battle of cultures" and a war of two systems, he had somehow differentiated Spassky, though not quite entirely, from the "other Russians." During the period of Fischer's isolation, they had met up four or five times and talked "about the good old days, but also about modern chess."

Fischer expressed his liking through his choice of Spassky for his comeback, even though the names of other famous chess masters also popped up during the negotiations for it.[17] In all honesty, it was obvious that it was to be easier for Bobby, after two decades of public inactivity, to play against someone of his generation than against one of the myriad of "young lions" out there, especially in a match whose very title precluded the possibility of him going on if he somehow lost. But the "undefeated world champion" did even more than that. At his express request, the prize money was divided into a part for the winner, a larger sum of course, and a part for the loser. From the very beginning of the negotiations, Fischer was offered the possibility of pocketing practically all five million dollars because Boris Spassky, who was on the downhill side of his career and barely holding his own against the hundred best players in the world, would probably have agreed to a sum of a couple of hundred thousand dollars. This surprise event certainly was an unexpected gift from heaven for his bank account.

However, in accordance with his principles, Bobby sought for fair-play conditions by which he gave up his right to about a million dollars, and ventured another two million. He also demanded that Spassky get a significant percentage of the television rights and a part of the marketing income.

---

[17] As potential candidates to be Fischer's opponent, mention was made of Gligorić, Ljubojević, Judit Polgár, Anand, and even Karpov.

The Greatest Secret of Bobby Fischer

The crown of Fischer's almost incredible beneficence was his wish to concede to his opponent and colleague fifty percent of the profit on the future sales of a new type of chess clock, the creation of which Spassky had absolutely nothing to do! Thus Bobby made it possible for Boris to quite unexpectedly become a millionaire and, at the same time, secure for himself a worry-free retirement. It would be logical to expect that all of these gestures by Fischer would be met with gratitude and respect, but outside of the spotlights in the press conferences where Spassky did make some effort to show that, his behavior was surprising, to say the least.

That first evening together in Belgrade after Boris's arrival unwound in an excellent atmosphere which was dominated by the recalling of old times and also by the exchange of ideas in chess, played on Bobby's portable board. In the wee hours, everyone went their own way. We headed for Dedinje, and Spassky for the Intercontinental Hotel where he was staying and where a new meeting had already been set for the next day at lunch.

*

The initial preparations were drawing to a close with the arrival of the other figures for the upcoming match in the capital of Yugoslavia. We had already packed our suitcases because the next stage would last more than two months and we were to spend that time far from Belgrade, in the most beautiful area of the Montenegrin coast in the resort of Sveti Stefan.

After that unforgettable night, a night in which history and the future came together, a steamy August day followed with us turned to focus on reality and hard work. After having lunch together, Fischer and Spassky decided to spend the afternoon and evening at the chessboard in Bobby's practice room. Because of the heat and their hard work, they ordered dozens of liters of locally produced mineral water, enthralled by its quality.

In spite of the fact that the program for the following day included the journey to Montenegro which was to be quite stressful, they did not part ways before midnight. At Bobby's insistence, we started packing his things that very same evening.

The Greatest Secret of Bobby Fischer

Like everything else that was done with him and for him, even this activity demanded a special procedure. Each thing had to be put in its own special place, precisely arranged in a bag or suitcase, everything had to be carefully closed up and fastened shut, and certain especially important elements had to be tied up with string or special small chains and locks which Bobby already had in great number. The luggage that was secured in that way was then placed in the center of the room. Then Bobby and I would check out in detail all the rooms where he had spent time to make sure nothing had been forgotten.

During our time together, I would have the chance to pack his things with him several times, repeating this exact same procedure every time. It would be finished at the moment when we set off, when I would put Bobby in the car and then return one more time to check everything out. This was followed by the equally demanding transportation procedure.

To some, perhaps these security measures we took over such simple things might seem like overkill but, as I already said, there was no detail which was so small it could not have enormous consequences for Fischer. Aware of that, I always approached this procedure with the greatest of attention, because there was the constant concern that some misplaced, or God forbid lost, thing could cause a catastrophe. One such dangerous moment occurred suddenly during the second part of the match in Belgrade.

The calm and quiet day off between two games offered not a hint of the oncoming storm. Then, unexpectedly, I heard Bobby's voice, the way it sounded when he was upset, Bobby's figure at the wide open door of my room (I could see directly into his suite through it), letting me know that something was wrong.

"Nesh," he said, "some things are missing!"

Even though I knew that the security measures I had set in place with my team absolutely excluded this as a possibility, I realized just how serious the situation was when I saw Mr. Torre's face as he nervously paced about Bobby's room. His hands shaking, stuttering, Bobby showed me the open wardrobe, saying,

"My favorite suitcases are missing. You know that we put them here!

The Greatest Secret of Bobby Fischer

Since I knew the list of his things by heart, along with the exact place where we had placed them when we moved in, I immediately realized that those two old bags, so dear to their owner, were indeed missing. When I confirmed this, after a detailed search of the two-room suite where all three of us were situated produced no result, Bobby blurted out, "Nesh, you know what this means?" his eyes wild, he got right up in my face. "This is a message that They can get to me at any time, whenever they want. Just like they took my bags so easily, they could just as easily take my life!"

"But, Bobby," I tried to calm him, "I'm sure that there must be a rational explanation, and I will find it for you in the next ten minutes."

"Explanation?!" he mumbled nervously under his breath. "I don't want to play anymore. This is the end. Now we will pack up and leave this place. You, Nesh," he pointed at me, "will take me out of this country. Where and how is up to you."

Furiously and loudly he went on talking about this. The whole time, Mr. Torre sat with his head in his hands listening to the tirade, while I hardly managed to get word in edgewise and repeat that I would solve this terrible problem, and that there was no need to interrupt the match. At that moment I was not absolutely sure that my suppositions about the solution to the mystery of the missing things were true, but I was completely certain that I could claim that they had not been stolen, especially not with the motives that Bobby attributed to the event.

It was impossible to reach his suite without passing several checkpoints and without an invitation, regardless of whether Bobby was actually there or not. The maids were supervised when they did their jobs, and no one could come near Bobby without me. If I was with Bobby, guests were accompanied by one of the other bodyguards. Therefore, the solution must be sought with one of the two privileged people for whom none of this was true.

Now, I had seen that Mr. Torre was already desperate because of this problem, so it was clear that he was not "suspect" and that he knew nothing about the enigma. However, a few minutes later I saw the ever merry Mrs. Torre and her little daughter Nichol happily returning down the hotel hallway after a walk around town, headed for their room which was right next to ours, and my suspicions took on a concrete form.

It did not take long for the wife of the Philippine grandmaster to "confess" that "she had wanted to borrow a large bag from Bobby so that she could use it for the shopping she planned." With Fischer's permission, while he and Eugene worked on their chess, she chose a large backpack but, surprised by the mess in his wardrobe, she decided on her own to make a little order there by shoving the two folded, missing bags into it, and putting them all in their suite for temporary safekeeping. She had not mentioned this to the bags' owner, nor her husband, and especially not to me, because she did not think it was terribly important.

Not imagining for a moment the enormity of the drama she had caused, she sheepishly and apologetically gave back the "incriminatory" objects, and I quickly took them back to Bobby. While this was going on, he was considering all the aspects of the consequences that would arise because of the interruption of the match and was analyzing all his future moves in the light of the newly arisen situation and "the high degree of the danger to him."

However, when I showed him the "treasure" I had found, his moodiness instantly turned into an eruption of joy. Now, when he was again safe and sound, everything could go on normally, while only ten minutes before it seemed that everything had ended forever.

After such situations, Bobby usually did not admit his mistake, nor would he apologize because of the problem he had created because of it, as if it was quite by accident that what he had claimed to have happened actually had not, but he would rather just smile and say "thank you."

Those are the reasons why Bobby setting off on a journey was always a high risk event. Thus, on that sweltering Belgrade evening Bobby and I, with a little help from Zita, pedantically packed everything up so that he would have time to rest up before our planned departure at 2 p.m.

That Saturday, August 8, everything started in a whirlwind because there was still plenty to do before our afternoon departure. In the morning, a press conference was held with the match's coordinator, Mr. Kubat, in the main role, and he announced the chronology of the upcoming events and making special note of September 1 when a press conference was to be held in Miločer at the hotel where the match was to take place, and he said that Fischer and Spassky would appear then before the accredited journalists to answer all their questions. The opening ceremony was to take place that same day, at 8:30 p.m. in Sveti Stefan. He also announced the list of invited guests who were supposed to come and celebrate this event. The list contained almost all the important names in world politics, former and contemporary, including the accredited diplomatic corps in Yugoslavia, top athletes, and people from the world of show business. Invitations had been sent all over the globe to the addresses of the President of the USA, Bush, Yeltsin, the President of Russia, Mitterrand, the president of France, but also to former presidents Richard Nixon and Mikhail Gorbachev. Also expected were Juan Antonio Samaranch, President of the International Olympic Committee, Melina Mercouri, the Greek minister of culture, and the athletes Carl Lewis and Sergey Bubka.

Of special interest to the journalists at that press conference was the information that had just arrived from the USA, stating: "The American government will not interfere in the match. The entire case has been turned over to the IRS, which will determine the income tax on Fischer's winnings." This news sounded quite different from the other announcements that had been arriving, all of which had been biting and full of warnings.

Since we did most of the preparatory work the night before, Bobby woke up around noon, ate a slow and bountiful breakfast, and then took a walk in the garden with Zita. The rest of the Rajcsányi family had left for Hungary the previous day, and they were to rejoin us later on Sveti Stefan. Around 12:30, when Mr. Vasiljević came to collect us with his family and entourage, everything was set for us to move out. After following the procedure mentioned above, Bobby came down carrying hangers with his two new suits and a bag full of newspapers, magazines and books slung over his shoulder; he took his place in the car, the final sign that it was time to go.

Thus we said farewell to the villa in Dedinje where we had spent an exciting fifteen days or so. Bobby's cheery mood was amplified by Jezda's explanation that we would not be making our journey from the commercial airport at Surčin, which was used only for domestic flights in Yugoslavia at the time because of the sanctions, but rather that we would depart from the military airport at Batajnica, and "in a plane not meant for ordinary mortals." Mr. Vasiljević said this because of his custom of adding an exclusive element to everything, which made Fischer quite happy, but when the situation changed from the bottom up later on, he would learn to interpret this fact differently.

At the airport, Boris Spassky was waiting with his own entourage which was finally completed by the arrival the day before of the grandmasters Balashov and Nikitin, who were to be his seconds. Already with his polite handshake Bobby clearly showed his lack of patience toward both of them, a powerful antipathy which was to culminate during the match and cause a lot of difficulties and problems. In those moments the first incident occurred caused by photographers and journalists, though there would be dozens of them in the days to come.

As we arrived at the entrance of the base, when we got out of the car I noticed two people whose faces I had never seen, and from their appearance it was clear that they were not military personnel. In spite of the fact that the place and time of our departure was known to a relatively small number of people and the fact that a military base was close at hand and guaranteed a certain level of security, these two immediately seemed suspicious to me.

At the moment when it seemed to these two "bystanders" that the mood was right and that the travel atmosphere had diminished our alertness, a camera lens flashed under one of their jackets. But since I was expecting something like this and had alerted the whole team, we intervened discretely, so that the journalists from *LIFE* magazine, or so it turned out, did not manage to do their jobs. The secret of their "mysterious" presence

I would uncover soon after, a few days later when I ran into them again on Sveti Stefan.

The airplane which "was not meant for mere mortals" was actually a re-outfitted military transport with propellers, not really to be noted for its comfort or luxury. Still, it served its purpose and took this group of people to the airport in Tivat, people who were there from various parts of the world, seemingly almost from various eras as well, all in order to play their roles in the media-financial-political drama that was about to unfold.

CHAPTER 5.

THE BOY BEHIND THE MASK

Through the mist of the past, from childhood, a painful memory can be discerned in the grimace on Bobby's face, stopping words on his lips just before he says them. A long silence between us would ensue at the beginning of every conversation about the man whose name, Gerhardt, would not really be of consequence to anyone, if it were not for the fact that his son would make his last name, Fischer, so famous.

Indeed, Bobby never wanted to talk about his father, nor did he ever allow anyone to ask about him. The careless person who, driven by his own curiosity, would dare to turn the conversation in that direction would be "punished" with the immediate interruption of the dialogue, with the abrupt warning, "I don't want to talk about that."

From this alone, it was not difficult to conclude just how much the wound of the trauma of growing up without a father had an overall influence on the development of the future chess champion. Because Gerhardt Fischer, a German immigrant, born in Berlin at the turn of the century, a biophysicist by occupation, left his family when little Bobby had not yet turned two. He sought his fortunes somewhere in the wilds of South America, in one of the countries of that continent, far from his family and his son, whom he never met till the day he died, nor did he ever try to contact him.[18]

It is quite clear that in that first misunderstanding with the real world, which his hypersensitive boyhood soul could not possibly explain or understand because his father's departure and the loss

---
[18] Fischer's sister Joan once told me that she supposed their father went back to Europe from South American and that he lived somewhere on the Old Continent.

of one part of parental love was surely not his fault, lay the roots of all the later problems and misunderstandings that were to become the leitmotif of Bobby's life and career. I was quite surprised by the fact that all the experiences and events from childhood were actually that way, traumatic and painful; he remembered them well and told me of them in our long talks.

Suffering could be seen on his face when he talked about them as if decades had not passed since then, his being would tremble with horror, as if he were going through them at that very moment. "You know, Nesh," he would say, "I always knew that something wasn't right with this world and the way it is." Leaning over the table, his eyes wide open and staring, it was as if he were listening to the echo of his words and waiting for a reaction. After several seconds, when it seemed to him that my facial expression showed the maximum of readiness to listen to his confession carefully, he went on, "I remember one fine day when my mother took me for a walk in the park. There were a lot of children and I started playing with them. We were running around until we saw a beautiful flying creature. It was a large insect with a peculiar sound and marvelous colors that fluttered in the sunshine and caught our attention. All the kids ran after it and were waving their hands and feet around trying to swat it. I also ran and cried at the top of my voice, 'Leave it alone, leave it alone, it's so pretty, so pretty.' After several minutes of unsuccessful chasing and my cries and shoving, I managed to stop them from harming it. They all went back to playing, but I kept on following it. When I finally managed to draw close, right at the moment when it landed on a flower, I reached out my hands because I wanted to admire it some more. But my small flying friend rewarded me for saving its life by stinging me and causing me great pain. Over the next days my palms swelled to the size of ping-pong paddles. My mother's scolding and the ruthless teasing of the neighborhood kids was all I got."

After a couple of seconds of silence, he added, "Stuff like that happened to me my whole life. My sincere and honest intentions were answered by the world with stings and pain."

The Greatest Secret of Bobby Fischer

Sitting in his chair, posed like a groggy boxer before the start of the last round where he will face powerful attacks from an opponent in better shape, with his legs stretched out under the table and his arms stretched out on the back of the chair as if over the ropes on the ring, he fell silent and his thoughts wandered.

On several different occasions, Bobby told me of a similar event from his early school days. "During recess, all the children from my class were having fun drawing with various colors and paints on the freshly painted school wall. I was standing aside watching, disapproving of what they were doing because I actually liked its whiteness and cleanness more than their attempts at creative expression.

"Still, after ten minutes or so, when my classmates' enjoyment reached its climax in chattering and laughing, I started also wanting to draw something. I had just picked up a piece of colored chalk and reached for the wall when I got a hard slap across my backside and I heard a thundering voice, 'You've been caught, Bobby!' Then I looked around. All the other children had seen the teacher coming, so that I was the only one standing in front of the ruined wall. I was just about to say something in my defense when I got hit again, this time a slap that dispersed all my illusions that I would be able to explain anything. 'You've been caught, Bobby,' the teacher repeated. 'Have your mother come by the school tomorrow to have a talk with me.' After all that, I got a scolding from my mother and punishment for vandalism and the damage caused."

To the rhythm of our steps as we walked, he repeated,

"You've been caught, Bobby, you've been caught, caught..." as if to that very day he felt some sort of invisible power haunting him, one that was always ready to punish him though he was not guilty, and to shame and humiliate him in front of an already disparaging world. This event at recess was not decisive in Bobby's attitude toward school.

"Even before that, but also later, I didn't like school," he said. "There was never anything for me in that institution."

On the other hand, a visit to another type of institution left an erasable mark on him.

"My mother worked for a while in a psychiatric hospital, or more simply said, an insane asylum. Since she didn't have anyone to leave me with, she took me with her to work several times. I will never be able to forget that horrible place. It was almost like an entire town. The multi-storied, cinder-block buildings were packed with people whom someone else had declared mentally ill. It all looked much worse than the worst of prisons, horribly depressing and terrifying. I only saw something like it much later on a visit to the USSR, the only difference being that in Russia those were 'normal' residential areas."

Throughout his life many people, especially journalists, trying to describe and define Bobby, using a variety of epithets, quite often even declared him to be crazy. As time went on, that primary disconnect between Bobby and everything around him grew more and more profound, and he became ever more difficult to understand and interpret.

In addition to the fact that he never met his father, there was also his realization that he did not have much better luck with the other two members of his already fragmented family. Bobby mentioned his mother relatively often in various connotations and situations but with an almost unbelievable range of feelings and emotions.

On several occasions he told me of her will, energy and intellect with unbridled enthusiasm.

"My mother Regina is a woman of fascinating life energy. Even today in her waning years, she's learning languages, though she already speaks five or six, she uses a computer, she keeps up with new things in the bookstores and reads a pile of newspapers every day. She really is a great fighter. She comes from a relatively poor family which was never able to afford an adequate education for her. So, when she was only nineteen she went to the USSR, because college education is free there. In 1939 she finished medical school in Moscow. Since she had trouble validating her diploma in the US, she did all kinds of jobs to support us."

While talking to her on the phone once, smiling, he covered the mouthpiece and whispered to me,

"Come listen to her voice." Later, he asked me,

"Could you feel the strength?" When he was in a really good mood, he would shout,

"Nesh, come talk to my mom!" On the other end of the line, I would hear the melodic and soothing voice of Regina, asking warmly about her son's stay in a faraway Balkan land.

Once when Bobby wanted to send her something nice from Belgrade, we spent days walking around downtown to find her an adequate present. We invested a lot of effort and care, desiring to choose something special that would make her happy. As a result of those efforts, a package was sent over the ocean in which there was, you can already guess, a hand-carved chess set.

Yet, if we put aside these rare idyllic moments in their relationship, Bobby would speak quite often rationally and mostly negatively when appraising her role in his life. "She did sort of take care of my sister and me, but her own life always came first. She followed her own ideas and desires without compromise, not caring about other people, not even me. She often left our apartment in Brooklyn, leaving me alone, which you'll have to admit was not the ideal of motherly love." Then he went on, "The methods she used to help me in those early years, if you ask me, were far too aggressive. She hounded everyone whom she thought might have a positive influence on my career, she shouted, protested, marched and carried banners, chained herself to the fence of the White House, in order to collect money for us to go to tournaments, and a lot of other things. Sometimes I felt ashamed because of the stuff she did. I can't deny that she had good intentions and that she wanted to make people aware of my talent, but the louder she got, the more I withdrew into myself."

Over the years the relationship between Bobby Fischer and his mother Regina Wender Fischer (later she would change her name again when she got remarried) went through a variety of phases, ranging from superficial closeness, through tolerance where it usually stayed, and down to not so rare periods when there was no communication between them at all. The extent of the icy depths to which their relationship could sink can best be seen in the following case.

The Greatest Secret of Bobby Fischer

Even though he knew that after the match was over he would not be able to return to the USA for a long time, Bobby, for reasons known only to him, wished to hold onto his humble apartment where he had been living for years before and from which he headed off into a new life in chess. So, in order to pay off his debt to his landlord, he sent his mother a check asking her to send it to the right address.

After a month, news came from the other end that the rent had not been paid and that the apartment would be rented out. In spite of the fact that Bobby had brought almost everything with him to Yugoslavia, except his chess library and part of his personal archive (the most important things were anyway stored in a safe deposit in a Pasadena post office),[19] this made him really angry. He called his mother and she answered that she did not dare to send the check because of her fear of the fact that her son was under a threat of prosecution by the Treasury Department for participating in a match organized in a country under strict international embargo. But Bobby had no understanding for his mother's worries. Trembling with anger, he shouted into the telephone,

"Damned bitch, you always were and still are a bitch! I hate you! Oh, I really hate you!" After he repeated this several times, he slammed the phone down angrily and hurried off into his suite (he had called his mother from my room) from where he did not come out until the next day.

Bobby's relationship with his sister Joan is seemingly easy to describe,[20] because throughout most of their lives there was almost none. Such a characterization was best given by Bobby himself just before she arrived in Belgrade to visit her younger brother who, by then, had just triumphed in his match with Spassky. That day, Bobby knocked on my door unusually early and asked me to come to his room. With little introduction, he stated decisively,

---

[19] Bobby Fischer's postbox in Pasadena was under a pseudonym for security reasons, one he chose himself: R.D. JAMES P.O. BOX 50917 PASADENA CA. 3115 USA.
[20] Joan Fischer-Targ was born in the USSR in 1939; she was four years older than Bobby. Bobby Fischer was born on March 3, 1943 in Chicago.

"Next week we will be visited by a person who by pure accident happens to be my sister. You have no obligations toward her, I will just ask you to pick her up at the Budapest train station and bring her to Belgrade because she is quite afraid of making the trip down here because of all the things in the western media are saying about the situation. She's coming in from France where she's been visiting a friend." With a wave of his hand he went on,

"Please understand that this person is a complete stranger to me and that I will act accordingly. We have never been close at all, and I haven't even spoken with her for the last ten years. I've decided to see her, even though I'm sure that the only reason for her coming here is that she caught the scent of money. Even though she is fairly wealthy because of her marriage, it seems that even that is not enough for her. I'm asking you that no one, absolutely no one connects that person with me and that her presence here remains a secret to the media, since you will take care of her bills and find her a place in one of the less expensive hotels. After all, a guest is a guest," he added with a grin.

This statement alone by Bobby, spoken all at once, was a clear indication of the nature of their relationship. If it is considered from this perspective, then his answer was not strange when I asked him about any possible homesickness he might feel when he thought of his homeland, especially when his return to it was no longer possible. In a quiet voice, he answered, "You know that I consider myself to be a great American patriot, but at this moment there is nothing on American soil that I could possibly long for."

At that time his mother and sister still lived in the USA. Using a play on words, Bobby said of himself,

"I grew up in a cold family, in a cold American society, during the Cold War."

Thus it was not strange that his sensitive and lonely child's heart froze so long ago, surrounded by all that coldness and the impossibility of understanding and interpreting the people around him.

In such surroundings, chess appeared at one moment in the life of young Bobby Fischer. Or had it perhaps always been there? I asked him,

"Bobby, what about that old story that Joan brought chess into the Fischer home, and that it was she who taught you the first moves?"

"I wouldn't pay too much attention to that story. I'm convinced that chess would have come to me at that age in one way or another, and that she was only the means to an inevitability."

Bobby believed in a kind of predestination for everything that he would achieve at the chess board. He claimed, "The basis of success in chess is talent. It is the necessary foundation which one must build onto with enormous, persistent, and everyday studious work. But without that foundation there will be no special results and all the effort is in vain. I don't know where that predisposition comes from, whether it is a natural talent or a genetic code we get at birth,[21] but I felt that intellectual and mental energy from the very beginning, when I was seven or eight, when I first came into contact with chess." Bobby thought that the reasons for his future success in chess should be sought for in that very fact.

"That is why," he said, "I have dominated in my generation. I was simply more talented than the others."

He had very tough convictions about his contemporaries,

"Some of today's 'champions' are the best example of untalented individuals with whom entire teams of experts have persistently worked on chess for years, but unfortunately on some other things as well. That's why everything possible should be done to return the game to the basis of talent. That's what causes excitement and beauty." Describing his own path, he went on.

"This must be accompanied by fanatical work. In those early years, of course, this was not a conscious decision for me but an insatiable hunger that simply drove me to spend days bent over the chess board. After those first few games I played with Joan, I played countless matches against myself. I would make a move as white, then put all my mental energy into outplaying that move as black. This lonely playing against myself contributed to my

---

[21] Bobby did not believe much in this hypothesis because, "if it were true, one of my ancestors certainly would have already been world champion." In his wider family, in fact, he had only one fairly good chess player (it was the brother of his mother's father, whom Bobby never met).

analytical and creative ability and formed me as a player as I cleared the paths and roads through the primeval forest of chess variations and possibilities. Since there were no computers at that time, and if there had been I probably would have been a grandmaster at seven and world champion at ten, chess books and brochures were my only sources of information.

From the owner of the store where Joan bought the chess set, right there in our neighborhood, I got my first introductory chess book as a present. I took it everywhere, and I paged through it hundreds of times and soon learned it by heart. My desire for new knowledge very quickly brought me into contact with people who were interested in chess, or who actually played it, and I was able to use their chess libraries. All of that time I had the impression that I was being led through that new world, where I had been invited, by a confident hand that would not allow me to stray from the right path."

Bobby claimed that, in his beginnings nor later, there was no one who could be called his chess teacher.

"You'll hear from various sources or perhaps read somewhere that my name is mentioned by some people who were purportedly my teachers in chess. I never actually had someone who could claim that. Certainly in my younger years I had to play against someone and they were mostly older players, it would have been hard to find someone younger than me," he added with a grin, "but I beat them most of the time. I never had a real second in my career, while the influences on my style, which might have come from my forerunners or contemporaries, can be a matter of discussion."

Young Robert Fischer thus found his real home, his one true homeland and religion to which he would be faithful his whole life there among the black and white figures that were to become synonymous with his very being. He was much more than a devotee to this game that defies definition, because many people call it an art or even a science.

In his early sixties, when his career and personal destiny took on real contours after his return to public life, Bobby experienced himself and expressed his personality through his own sort of hesychasm.[22] Because everything he worked on and did was chess, or it could have become chess. Many times I saw him sitting at the table in his usual pose, his head lowered onto the table with his hands under his chin. He would remain like that for a long time looking at the black and white spaces from the perspective of the figures themselves, or as if he were one of them. His eyes wide open and his forehead wrinkled in a frown told me that a great battle was taking place between wooden warriors standing at attention in their starting positions, but that the battle's action and outcome was known only to the leader. After an hour or two he would suddenly get up, often with his shirt soaked in sweat as if he had been doing hard physical labor, and then he would look at me as if awakened from a trance and smile, letting me know that he was ready to talk about anything and everything.

While he was playing or analyzing with one of his colleagues, Bobby demonstrated a fascinating ballet, the protagonists of which were his long fingers and his hands. At lightning speed he would set up a position, change it and move the figures about the table with a certain type of movement that had been brought to perfection, always leaving the impression to the observer that his entire body was involved in the game, involved in winning.

If one could describe the vision of Fischer going full tilt as he played a chess game, if that energy could be sublimated to the shortest form, then that would be the drive for complete and absolute CONTROL. No matter how we turn it, from the past, or from the future we now know, from the north or south, from New York or Moscow, all of the winds in Bobby's heart and mind came from a thought which, spoken through the sound of voices or written on paper in ink or blood, it must sound and be read in the same way—CONTROL. In Fischer's understanding of the world, in the relation of cause and effect, everything and everyone must

---

[22] The term originates in the Greek HESYCHIA, or (EN HESYCHIO); in Orthodox Christian practice it signifies a monk in solitude (or among people) who has an affinity toward constant prayer, the peak of which is that every thought, word, movement, and breath be dedicated to God. Although he went through a religious, or rather quasi-religious, phase, Bobby was never a believer, nor did he ever believe in God. He put chess on the divine pedestal.

be under some kind of control by someone, or a person or a thing must control someone or something.

Since in Bobby's collapsed reality all the roles of controllers had been handed out long ago, he could and had to put up with all the consequences, except in one exceptional and special place, at the chess board. There, and only there, he was the great creator, the owner, the master, the ultimate king who had power beyond limits or borders. His thoughts pulled the threads and strings in the world beneath and before him, on 64 squares, in his real and only life.

Accordingly, it is quite clear that the choice of chess sets for Bobby Fischer was a tortuous and long-lasting process that demanded a special procedure. In order for this grandmaster to want to own one of them, it had to satisfy a whole series of criteria, and they had to include: the highest quality wood, first class green felt for the base of the figure, and stylistic perfection which meant certain dimensions. His army did not dare to be of any other kind of material besides wood, and they had to be classically simple and ideally they had to adhere to the board. These were just a few of the dozens of demands which made the job of choosing a set equal to the task of Sisyphus. On one such occasion of making a more narrow selection stretched out over several days, and the finale of choosing between two sets lasted a full eight hours. Just how long it took for Bobby to finally establish which of the two knights had a prettier mane.

The exception to this rule was a special type of plastic set of larger dimensions whose board could quickly and easily be rolled up and, of course, his pocket set that he never parted with. Dozens of times a day, whether we were at a meal or walking, at times at the movies, regardless of the place or circumstances, he would start using it with lightning fast motions. When he would finish and visually define his chess idea, he would put it back in his pocket and once again be present in the real world.

From a series of such details it is clearly seen just how Robert James Fischer's entire being was obsessed by chess, and just how much this game was the essence of everything that the undefeated world champion actually was. It is from that perspective that one should view everything that happened in his career, that which many of his chess colleagues, an army of journalists and analysts, and millions of fans of this ancient game often called eccentricity, arrogance, disregard for social custom, and quite frequently even more vulgar names. That is why, during his career, Bobby so longed to outplay his opponents, to crush them and destroy them at chess, until the point when, as he said so often, he saw fear in their eyes. But to be honest, sometimes he himself, fleeing from certain defeat, making nonsensical moves for hours, putting off a certain tragic ending for himself which certainly was not pleasant for his ego.

To a great extent all of that contributed to the fact that the hero of this story became the greatest player in the history of chess but, on the other hand, led to his loss of touch with reality in many segments of life and with those things understood as the concepts of reality and objectivity.

He said, "All I ever wanted in my chess playing was for people to appreciate me, and through that to respect my knowledge and talent. I wanted to achieve that in two ways. First, I always demanded ideal conditions for match play, and second, since this world functions on material principles, I tried to make the organizers show their respect toward me and the things I do through the amount they paid me. Naturally, I asked for the same things for other chess players but most of them just accepted the positive results of that struggle, without supporting my efforts. It's completely clear to me why that is so, but they all have to admit that their limit would have remained a couple of hundred, or a couple of thousand dollars per match, which is what they earned up until my time and probably what they would still be earning today if it hadn't been for me and my mission."

"Some people," Bobby went on, "thought that one could come to chess matches with popcorn in one hand and a bottle of Coke in the other, take their place in a small smoky room and then cheer and make comments out loud. Journalists and photographers would pull on the players' sleeves and blind them with their flashes, while cameras with spotlights buzzed over their heads raising the temperature on the podium to dangerous levels."

The Greatest Secret of Bobby Fischer

Intentionally exaggerating, he wanted to emphasize and clearly illustrate the miserable position of chess and chess players in the past. "In such an atmosphere that reminds you of the devil's garden, is it possible to play matches for the title of world champion and to fight for prestige? No, no, no! Maximum respect, dear sirs, for the most important thing on the planet. Is there really anything more important than chess and the people who play it?" Bobby exclaimed in his excitement and inspiration. Summarizing, he added, "Finally for myself, but for chess as a whole, I got this rematch which I offered to Spassky here in Belgrade, under conditions that could be called almost perfect. That means that my struggle was not in vain!"

It is an undeniable fact that the root and primary source of everything that happened to Robert James Fischer during his career lay in childhood and early childhood. That was when all the important events played out that had such a significant influence on forming his spirit and character, both in positive and a negative way. It is commonly known that childhood is significant in the forming of every individual, but in Bobby's case it was so clear and obvious, perhaps also because he experienced everything from the position of a child who refused to grow up, even though he was in his fifties. From those days so full of unexpressed suffering and suppressed pain, he got enough confirmation of the beliefs that would mark his entire lifetime, which would lead and direct his life, his career, and play a decisive role in all his decisions.

In moments when he was suffering heavily because of his personal, emotional worries and because of the confluence of circumstances, for him unfavorable and objective, during his last months of residence in Yugoslavia, after the match with Spassky, Bobby was to admit something which would largely define what I already knew about his most carefully guarded secret. In those weeks, under the influence of everything he had gone through and in addition to other manifestations, psychological problems and suffering, he was practically unable to sleep. It all started with nightmares and terrible fears that overcame him completely and because of which, on Bobby's request, I moved from my own apartment into his living room, so that we were separated only by the hotel hallway and not more than ten feet. Since he could not sleep, we spent the nights in long conversations which often turned into the champion's monologues on a variety of topics.

Sometimes he would sit for a long time in silence on the edge of his armchair, with his elbows on his knees and his face buried in his hands. Only an occasional deep sigh would testify that he had sunk into himself and was suffering horribly. At one such moment, when I felt that night was breaking up in the dawn of a new day, and when EVERY BEING, his very being driven by his own destiny up until that moment had not found peace, and when the quiet caused him to give a gentle shudder caused by the cool of the coming morning, he said, "You know, I knew from my earliest childhood that something was wrong with THEM.

Although I could suppose from Bobby's earlier stories who he was talking about, I asked anyway,

"With whom, Bobby, and what's wrong?"

"With THEM, damn them all," he said in an icy voice.

"With whom, Bobby, with whom?" I repeated.

As if he had not heard my repeated questions, or no matter what it was or what else it might have been about, he was about to finish the thought he had started and nothing could stop him from saying it.

"They were standing in the door of our Brooklyn apartment. Their voices reached me in the dark of my room where I was ready to sleep. I was afraid of that sound coming to me and I hated the way they spoke, because I knew that this evening, too, the same thing would happen that happened whenever THEY were there. I wanted so badly to see my mother once more before I went to sleep, to give her another hug and a kiss. But THEY were always asking her something and kept talking with her, right at the moment when it seemed they were about to go. And as if they were playing a cruel game with me, just when I thought that they had left and my mother was coming, just then came that nasal voice asking or saying something, and they kept on talking. The more THEY drew it out, the more I longed for her. But sleep always tricked me and I never waited long enough to see my mother again before I went to sleep. That always happened when THEY came to see us."

"Who were those people, Bobby?"

He shook his head for a moment to come back to reality and gave me a look that asks,

"Don't you know that by now?" Still, in a slightly quieter voice he added, "There were a lot of them in our neighborhood."

"Who, Bobby, who are you talking about?", risking his scorn, I went ahead and asked him in a whisper.

Exhausted, he sank into his armchair and let out a shout funneled into words that almost knocked the walls of the room down.

"The Jews, the damned Jews!"

However, after several moments, that voice whirling around us echoing off the edges of the room and slowly losing intensity, gathering vibrations clear to my senses and my hearing, that voice turned into the distant, aching cry of a betrayed little boy.

CHAPTER 6.

WAVES AND STONES

After more than a month of sojourn at the gem of the southern Adriatic, on the exotic and exclusive isle of Sveti Stefan, in a moment of poetic inspiration uncommon for him Bobby would write in the guestbook: "I would like to thank Mr. Jezdimir and the hotel staff for giving me one of the most beautiful times of my life. I will never forget the sound of the waves and the brightness of the white stone. Sincerely, Bobby Fischer."

And indeed, those days he seemed to be the most satisfied man in the world. As if a long awaited reward for the suffering he had experienced had arrived in the form of a deserved heaven-on-earth just for him. The isle of Sveti Stefan is like a heavenly tear that dropped a hundred yards from the shore and turned into a lovely open shell, where human will created a fishing village and then a tourist attraction, a cluster of houses-apartments, a conch emerging from the deep blue sea toward a heaven of the same color. Just beyond the gorgeous sandy beach rise enormous mountains and woods of the Pastrović clan from where a fragrant cypress breeze brings freshness after even the hottest of days. Without any sort of poetic exaggeration, if you fall asleep stunned by the fresh air on one of the hotel terraces, a sudden waking will confuse you as to what is up and what is down, and where the heavens and water meet.

The famous villa 118, on the far southeastern part of Sveti Stefan, took in its new guests who would, without doubt, remain unsurpassed by the length of their stay in that prestigious place. This prominent cell, separated from the sea by high sheer crags and isolated from the other apartments by its location and a stone fence which fits ideally into the surroundings, played home to world famous movie stars, presidents of countries and other famous guests. While those who were richest enjoyed that Mediterranean wonder for a week or two, Bobby and I were to stay there for almost three months. The man in the leading role took his customary room upstairs, while I stayed downstairs, where we turned the large sitting room into a training and analysis room, and a small office for everyday work.

At the moment when we arrived on Sveti Stefan it was still open for visitors. A varied and unusual crowd could be found there those first days. Generally speaking, that picture was also a sketch of Serbian-Montenegrin reality in those times. *De facto* and *de jure*, this world famous tourist destination was already owned by the main financer of the match, the owner of *Jugoskandic Bank*, Jezdimir Vasiljević, who had rented it out for decades in advance, though it was once communally owned. That was how we got the right to move in.

Although we were thus practically "at home", it quickly became clear that the resort would have to be closed to "normal tourists", to their visits and sightseeing. Most of the guests at the time came from the milieu of the "grey areas" of Belgrade, the wide reaching underground, who were exposing their tattooed bodies to the wonders of summer. However, the position where we were located gave us a perspective of the absolute authority which, like the whistle of the main arbiter at the end of a soccer match, cleared out the rooms, the promenades, and beaches of the southern part of Montenegro, clearly showing who the lion was in that jungle and whose word was important and whose will was dominant.

If a group photograph existed of most of the guests we moved out, today we would not be able to find a single one of them. Pale figures executed in showdowns or liquidated on someone's order, on the road, in the streets, in the forests of "the mountainous Balkans", memories, shoved into insignificance – unknown, silenced voices, they no longer call out to anyone, traces in the sand whisked away by the tide. It was a time when everything seemed possible, except for the impossible to occur. But Bobby Fischer did not notice any of that because that was the way it was supposed to be. From the first moment on, he relaxed and enjoyed his newfound freedom and security.

The daily schedule and everyday rhythm changed quite a lot in comparison to our life in Belgrade. Bobby got up a lot earlier, already at 9 he would be ready for breakfast. A special place was set up for him to take his meals. It was a small terrace in immediate proximity to the central restaurant on Sveti Stefan, with a lovely view of the sandy hotel beach and surrounding landscape, but still shaded from the sun's rays and the curious looks of invited and uninvited guests. Bobby and I ate there, later often in the company of Mr. Gligorić and Mr. Torre.

Local teams took care of the external security of the island and nearby places, coordinated by Brano Mićunović, an influential businessman who was quite involved in events in Montenegro at the time (and even today). Members of these teams wore uniforms of sorts, with white t-shirts bearing the emblem of the upcoming match; they were calm and kind, physically fit, responsible in their activities and they were excellent support for Fischer's personal security team. It consisted of a dozen people, but only two of them who were at the top of their profession had any direct contact with our ward. They were my friends, my right and left hands those days, Mr. Dane Filipović and Mr. Voja Delibašić, experts in security in the Federal police.[23] I also had available two young men from the special forces of the Serbian Ministry of Internal Affairs, but they were not involved in concrete activities and soon after the opening of the match they were sent back to Belgrade.

Were such measures really necessary? Of course they were set in place because of Fischer himself who demanded, expected and certainly got a real feeling of complete protection. On the other hand, we were crisscrossed by a multitude of various, and above all serious, political and financial interests, so that this seemingly commonplace element certainly dared not to be neglected.

There was direct opposition of certain quite powerful foreign circles, the proximity of the war zone, the express motives of

---

[23] For a period, Goran Simić, my friend from the basketball courts and some earlier jobs, also made a great contribution to our work.

individuals and groups who wished and tried to prevent the event from happening at all for a variety of reasons. The fact that Bobby was a good target for blackmail, kidnapping or as a potentially unlimited source of income for those circles of criminals who, with their "creativity", might try to find a way to make an enormous financial gain by controlling my ward – all of these were valid justifications for setting such wide-reaching security measures in place. That all of this was not baseless, the further development of events would show.

There was one more especially important reason for this kind of approach. During his career, Fischer had quite an ambivalent relationship to journalists and the media in general. He was and remained desirous of their good will and attention, completely aware of the significance of publicity for his personality and work. On the other hand, if I were to channel into written form all of his disappointment, hurt and anger toward the members of the fourth estate as he expressed them to me in our endless conversations, I would have to fill volumes of books full of bitterness. Fitting right into his vision of the world and the order of things, the pen and camera which wrote about or testified to his brilliant career were also actually an instrument of the repression of his persona in the hands of "big brother".

From past times, Bobby separated out as an exception a shining example of the honor or, in his words, disgrace of this profession. Once, he told me, "I never read anything honest or well-intentioned about me. Even when they praised and edified me, journalists did so in order to knock me down later from the greatest height possible, so that the fall would hurt as much as possible and break my spirit to the point that I would never rise again. The flashes went off even when I didn't want them to, cameras were humming at moments when I was preparing to make a decisive move in games which were 'life and death' for me and degraded those moments, destroying my privacy and attempting to have an influence on my creativity. In doing so, those blood suckers never paid for using the facts and the solved puzzles they gathered in that way. I remember just one shining exception which confirms this rule. Long ago," he went on, "I got a phone call from a journalist at *Esquire* magazine. I agreed to a conversation and so I met the gentleman in question at a small restaurant near the place where I lived at the time. I liked the young man from the outset. He asked, I answered, we chatted. At one point he threw his pen onto his open notebook, wiped his forehead with one hand and slammed the other down on the table with all his might. 'Damn, damn, damn, I just can't do this. Certain influential people have given me some very specific instructions that whatever you say in the article we are printing, you have to come out as a bad guy. They didn't tell me why,' I'm citing the journalists words from long ago, 'but everything I write about you has to be negative. But, you,' the echo from long ago can still be heard, 'Bobby, I like you. You are an American hero, you're my hero.' We talked long into the night," the chess master went on, "the interview was never published, I met an honorable man, whose name I have unfortunately forgotten, but I will never forget that on that occasion I met a real JOURNALIST."

From this small digression we dive directly into the events in Yugoslavia and the mentioned fact that Fischer was photographed without his permission as he got off the plane at the airport in Budapest, and somewhat later there was the "secret" video recording in the studio of Mr. Vasiljević. With the experience of Fischer's reaction at the time which almost sent him back home, a month and a half later the investment was even larger and thus there could be no mistakes. Journalists had to be kept at bay, cameras kept even further away until the first scheduled press conference. For all of us that meant there was no difference between the assassination of the greatest chess player of all time and his photograph appearing in one of the world's newspapers or famous magazines.

From early in the morning, in accordance with this, all the surrounding hills were searched, places from which a skilled paparazzi could "shoot" my protégé, the path between suite 118 and the restaurant was cleared, all the beachfront approaches were guarded. This was a very serious, everyday job that demanded a lot of thought, careful preparation and a large number of people. The attempts were rare because the readiness and responsibility of the organizers was a well known fact, and the attempts of the bravest who wanted the exclusivity of Fischer's image on celluloid were quickly and efficiently thwarted.

The first "victim" was a German photographer who, disguised as a local fisherman in a blue and white striped shirt, cap and shorts, tried to catch a moment from his boat near our favorite sunning spot on the hotel beach, to take a photograph that would bring him a lot of fame and certainly a bundle of material satisfaction.[24] Noticed by one of my team, it gave me a chance to stage a little exhibition. Without wanting to frighten the "unfortunate" but certainly brave member of the fourth estate, we set up a dramatic scene of the action of him getting "arrested". He was brought to the terrace of the suite which was the main security center so we could talk with him, we made it all look pompous and serious so that all the journalists would be clear about the fact that jokes about our decisiveness were certainly not going to tolerated. The film was taken from his camera, our "friend" was briefly but thoroughly questioned up to the moment when it seemed that he was getting really frightened. We led him out, smiling after all, because he got a glass of juice and a couple of hundred dollars as a reimbursement for the film, and he felt free and saved from Fischer's "cruel" security team.

To be precise, those days the Croatian newspapers gave exhaustive descriptions of the extent of Fischer's security and directly implied that it was made up of members of the Serbian Volunteer Guard of Željko Ražnjatović Arkan,[25] and that Mr. Vasiljević was paying 50,000 German marks daily for these services. This certainly added a negative connotation to the whole

---

[24] During the match there was a multitude of "indecent offers" by many of the international magazines, their photographers and journalists, to help them in their intentions to get any kind of exclusive photograph or information. Naturally, all of them were rejected, and as a parameter of the "possibilities" it is a fact that I was offered 5,000 dollars for Fischer's autograph (even if it were on a hotel napkin).
[25] Although, as I have already mentioned, the match attracted many people from the social sphere primarily with its financial potential, this also included those whose roles in those years was later to be signified with negative epithets; the sports (chess) event itself was protected from such influences, interests and negative publicity through our enormous efforts.

match and tried to highlight the connection between the political and military events of the time. In any case, there were no sort of paramilitary, military or other formations in our vicinity, although Fischer was confused by the strange Montenegrin micro-climate, because he would ask me from time to time how it was possible that thunder could often be heard in the middle of a calm and sunny day. I explained it to him as the proximity of the surrounding hills and mountains, while the thundering sound, softened by the distance, was actually coming from the Dubrovnik front.

Whatever the case, our "performance" produced results because it sent a clear message that no one and nothing was going to menace the upcoming match, including all the wishes and plans it presupposed. So, from the ramparts of the Sveti Stefan fortress, we watched the walk of the "lost fisherman" who departed from the place of the incident with knocking knees, convinced that his experience would echo throughout the world of journalists. However, even in this element everything was not always clean and clear. I have already mentioned the event that occurred just before we took off from the military airport near Belgrade and the incident with the journalists from the famous *Life* magazine. After a couple of days I again noticed those careful and elegant gentlemen, walking the paths and streets of Sveti Stefan, having supper in the central restaurant or sunbathing and swimming at the same time as we were. I kept an eye on them as I waited for official confirmation of their identity. My interest soon received its epilogue when one morning I saw them at our headquarters talking over breakfast with Mr. Vasiljević. I joined them for a moment and thus through the mediation of the head organizer I officially met the journalist and reporter from America's *Life*. When they left, Jezdimir confronted me with his desire that the new guests should be allowed near us for a while. "And if they get a chance to interview Fischer, let them do it." He also informed me of the agreed plan that, in the early afternoon when it was time to go to the beach, I was to take Bobby down the usual path but that I should stop at a small widening of the path near the hotel terrace so that photographs could be taken.

The Greatest Secret of Bobby Fischer

This was one of the rare occasions when Mr. Vasiljević asked me to do something that was in conflict with Fischer's wishes. Even though I was promised that the photos would be published only after the match was over, which I believed completely because bad timing would have jeopardized everything, I had to react properly and wisely so that the achieved balance would not be disturbed. I knew that Jezdimir truly respected and liked Bobby, and that he would never do anything to hurt him intentionally. All of this seemed to me to be a little favor that would mean something to someone, or the return of some sort of private debt the banker had with someone. The solution was actually simple and was hidden in the magical concept of loyalty which is pronounced "THE TRUTH".

I told Fischer everything, not fearing the consequences, certain that the risk was small, because he was already showing that he had absolute confidence in me and the work I was doing for him. Thus, the visit to the beach that day and the next few days never happened, with the explanation to everyone around us that Bobby wanted with Mr. Gligorić to go through as many analyses as possible and thus expedite his readiness for the match. Carried away by his responsibilities and the speed of events, Mr. Vasiljević never mentioned this situation again and everything went back to normal. But beneath the seemingly quiet landscape, a volcano full of lava was pulsing, ready to erupt into the heavens at any time.

The first above-mentioned reactions of the US administration to Fischer's decision that the match be played in Serbia and Montenegro had been more like gentle warnings than a real reason for concern. However, at the end of August, the spokesman for the American Treasury Department, Bob Levin, made an announcement carried by the world agencies:

"THERE IS A REAL POSSIBILITY THAT THE PARTICIPATION OF ROBERT FISCHER IN THE MATCH AGAINST BORIS SPASSKY WILL BE DETERMINED BY THE ADMINISTRATION OF THE UNITED STATES OF AMERICA TO BE A VIOLATION OF THE UN SANCTIONS, WHICH COULD, ACCORDING TO THE EVALUATION OF WASHINGTON, BE CHARACTERIZED AS ILLEGAL ACTIVITY. IT IS

ABSOLUTELY UNIMPORTANT WHETHER FISCHER WILL MAKE MONEY ON THE MATCH OR NOT. BY HIS VERY ARRIVAL IN YUGOSLAVIA, WHERE HE IS PLAYING THE MATCH, HE HAS VIOLATED THE REGULATIONS WHICH FORBID TRANSACTIONS WITH THE ENEMY. WE HAVE ALREADY WARNED HIS LAWYERS OF THIS FACT. THE PEOPLE IN OUR ADMINISTRATION WHO ARE REPSONSIBLE FOR CONTROLLING THESE REGULATIONS ARE FOLLOWING MOST SERIOUSLY ALL THE EVENTS RELATED TO THIS. MOST PROBABLY WE WILL BE TAKING ACTION IN COURT,"

Bob Levin said at the press conference and he would add:

"THE LAW ON FORBIDDING TRANSACTIONS WITH THE ENEMY FORESEES A PUNISHMENT NOT EXCEEDING 250,000 DOLLARS OR A PRISON SENTENCE OF 10 YEARS FOR OFFENDERS."

When I read the fresh news to Bobby, who had just gotten out of bed, he just roared with laughter and waved his hand. I actually expected such a reaction, because I knew the fact that one of the most important motivating factors of this chess champion for his comeback to public life was precisely the geographic coordinates of the entire event. For him it was an ideal chance to show his spite toward everyone and everything he despised: resistance to the government of his country who had rejected him (at least that was how he felt), the new world order (personified by the United Nations), to stand on the side of those who were in "unjustified isolation" (Yugoslavia – Serbia and Montenegro), and who, like him, on the personal, global, planetary, political and geo-strategic scenes collectively said "No".

The chess player chose for the millionth time in his exciting life, without a moment of hesitation, the role of a rebel who was ready to go all the way to his end. The extent to which that would be good for him, how good for his host country, would be proven in the years to come, in the period which is now the past or history.

Thus the stamp was placed on the dilemma which circled among the organizers of the match after the middle of August. Indeed, the director of the upcoming event, Janos Kubat, at a press conference on August 15, publicly offered his opinion that for political-security reasons, and because of the difficulty of disseminating information, there was a chance that the venue for the chess event of the century might be changed. As an alternative solution, Budapest was mentioned. From a legal standpoint this idea was legitimate because that option was included in the contract the participants had signed. Pressure to withdraw from participating in the duel with Spassky also came from the other side. The most agile was certainly the above-mentioned Charles Pashayan, the doyen of American political life, a congressman and, as he presented himself, a friend of Fischer. He contacted us already in Belgrade, two or three days after the famous chess player arrived, and his insistence and persistence continued during our stay in Montenegro.

Since Bobby did not want to have direct contact with him, except in one case, I was to listen for hours to the advice, requests and wishes this influential man expressed, which I was supposed to relay to my protégé. Despite all the reasonable arguments that arrived from across the Atlantic over the red-hot telephone, they were to have no influence on the decisions the champion had already made. It was already completely clear that that pressures and threats, at least in terms of Fischer, would be absolutely counterproductive for those who had such wishes and expectations, and that every one of their words, even if they were ultimately well-intentioned, would only strengthen Bobby's uncompromising desire to meet his goals.

The technical preparations for the match, which was announced to start on September 1, were moving at full speed. The organizer promised to set up the game hall, a press center, access and an entire infrastructure to the tune of one million dollars. In the offices of the Montenegrin government, Mr. Vasiljević discussed improving the technical conditions so that the pictures and sound sent out to the world would be of the highest quality. The Maestral Hotel, which was to be the center of the chess event, where the match would be played, underwent significant adaptations, and the small hall was completely reconstructed. For the purposes of mobility, an impressive fleet of over thirty of the most exclusive automobiles was procured. Everything in us and around us was in motion and full of excitement.

That kind of feeling and energy drove Fischer in a positive direction. A regular and healthy life, food of a quality, taste and means of preparation which Bobby spoke of in the superlative, the care and concern he was surrounded by, the pleasure and wonders of late summer, made him feel, so he said, mentally and physically stronger and more prepared to play chess than ever. Full of enthusiasm, he worked with Mr. Gligorić during the day, but even more so in the evenings and at night. Gliga himself expressed satisfaction with the developing situation and concisely but concretely he praised his friend's mental and athletic condition.

Those days also saw the long awaited arrival of Eugenio Torre who was to be Fischer's second in the match. Even before I saw him the first time, I was quite familiar with this man with whom I would also establish an excellent relationship in the days ahead. Philippine grandmaster Eugenio (Eugene) Torre was forty years old when he wished me good morning through the gate at villa 118 in strongly accented English. I returned the greeting and squeezed the outstretched hand of the young looking man, medium height, well built, in a colorful short-sleeved shirt with an intense red as a background. Light brown pants and sandals of the same color lent an air of nonchalance, of someone adapted to life in warm climates. In the preceding days, Bobby praised Eugene's thoroughness, sincerity and honesty. It was as if I immediately saw all of that in the eyes of our new guest who, with his rational eastern wisdom, was to be a valuable partner in conversation and an inspirational cohort for the good of our common task.

A special lightness and dearness would be brought to the team with the arrival of the wife and daughter of Bobby's friend and second, who were always bright and merry and brought smiles to our faces even at moments when we did not feel like smiling. Cordial hugs and slaps on the back turned the encounter of two old friends into a long and heartfelt conversation. While the training and work with Mr. Gligorić had a certain measure of reticence, Torre and Bobby looked like two boys who were enjoying a newly discovered passion for the game. Roaring laughter, loud commentaries, a joke or two but everything was, of course, very detailed and serious. Two days after Eugene's arrival, popular Gliga would return to Belgrade for a well-deserved rest.

Boris Spassky's team also became complete at that time. Seconds Nikitin and Balashov were already there when they were joined by Serbian grandmaster Bora Ivkov. During those days, every meeting of the Russian-French and American chess players, which happened on the paths of the hotel and the beach, always ended up in an exchange of polite sentences and forced smiles. However, Bobby soon publicly and loudly showed enormous animosity toward Boris's seconds. To the greatest extent he demonized Balashov, who had incidentally graduated on the theme of Fischer's contribution to chess, because he was convinced that Balashov was constantly giving him looks to affect his psyche and concentration. Bobby asked me to make sure that our paths never crossed with theirs, and that all possibilities for the two of them ask him anything or approach him be decisively nipped in the bud. We thus got one more difficult assignment which would culminate in the express wish of my protégé to never see their faces at any time on the way to the hall or during the games once the match had begun.

Just before the beginning of the rematch of the two grandmasters in Montenegro, Boris's wife Marina and son Alexander would also arrive. The schedule of upcoming events was already known and it was a creation of the charismatic, somewhat mysterious, but certainly exceptional uniqueness of Janos Kubat.

It certainly must be said that one of the crucial people for Fischer's comeback to chess and for the entire event which is the subject of this text was actually the match director, Mr. Kubat. With his life, athletic and managerial experience he was the missing link, the very note that makes a symphony perfect and complete, the word that drives the point home at the end of a verse. A figure in the complex structure of a work of art showing a battle with a thousand participants will not be noticed at first, but as soon as a careful observer takes a closer look, he realizes that the painter has drawn himself into the painting. He always showed up according to his instincts, whenever it was necessary, but without having anyone telephone or contact him in some other way; he was not there when he knew that everything was under control, because there was simply too much else to do in organizing the match, and he elegantly, nobly cruised on the sea of his self-confidence.

During the match, like a pine stretching above the forest, Janos suffered the animosity of individuals who somehow wanted to make their own role in the event be more important than it really was, usually insignificant jobs, and of those wanted to appear to be cosmopolitan but were still trapped on the roads of their village. This interesting man, born in fabulous [26]Senta, skillfully overcame all of that with noble ease, without raising his voice, without wild gestures demonstrating anger. Of course, he knew what was important and what was not, he kept his distance, just as far as he wanted others to be distant from him. Even today, when the years have not spared me either in experience and the inescapable beating of my heart, I still remember a compliment I once got from him.

Several weeks after the end of the match, Mr. Kubat showed up in my suite where there were a dozen people who were close to us in one way or another, saying farewell to the still bubbling activities which were slowly disappearing after the curtain went down on the event. As elegant as always, he greeted everyone present, sharing a word or two with each of them. Then a voice from the crowd said, "Here's the man who knows everything about the match. Our director."

He gently ran his hand through his hair, looked out among the guests and said, "I know almost everything, but this man," I was standing right next to him and he put his arm around me, "he really knows everything." Perhaps Janos, aware of his importance, wanted to praise me in front of our colleagues who already respected me and to verbalize his satisfaction that everything had gone well, but I remember those words and carry them within me

---

[26] Senta – a small town in northern Vojvodina, the part of Serbia that borders Hungary.

The Greatest Secret of Bobby Fischer

since they came from a man who was so radiant in every possible way.

But who Mr. Kubat really was and is can best be seen in the following scene. After Mr. Vasiljević left the country,[27] when I was thinking about where I could "hide" Fischer, because there were few possibilities and a lot of dangers, I naturally wanted to consult with someone I trusted.[28] The next evening, Mr. Kubat showed up at the Intercontinental Hotel in Belgrade. We discussed all the modalities of that very risky business and our choice narrowed to two countries, Hungary and Greece. Our northern neighbor had many advantages, and in the end we chose Budapest as the best destination, but when we wanted to analyze the other possibility which led us straight to the Ionian Sea, Janos picked up his telephone. Without an intermediary, without a second thought, the phone rang and we had a direct connection to the famous Melina Mercouri, at that time the Greek Minister of Culture.

The basics of the game rhythm and the rules of the match were already established in the contract. They would play until one of them won ten games. "Working days" were Wednesday, Thursday, Saturday and Sunday, thus making days off on Friday, Monday and Tuesday. The games would not be interrupted, and if a quick draw was achieved, in less than an hour, a new game would be started immediately. So that the symbolism would be complete, the organizer arranged it so that the match arbiter was Lotar Schmidt, the same man who had refereed the game in Reykjavik in 1972, while he would be assisted by his Serbian colleague, Nikola Karaklajić. In this segment as well, Fischer's wishes were completely fulfilled.

---

[27] Although I knew the fact that Mr. Vasiljević was to leave the country almost a week earlier, I must say that the newfound situation still confronted me with a whole series of trials and difficulties. One of the biggest was related to Fischer's future, because at that time his prize money had still not been paid.

[28] Because of the UN sanctions, the airports in the country were out of service, the war in the surroundings certainly closed certain possibilities, so that our options were reduced to land routes to the north, east or south, again with the emphatic uncertainty of how the border guards of those countries would react when they saw a person who was under suspicion by the government of the USA, because it might "just come knocking".

The Greatest Secret of Bobby Fischer

Everything had fit together nicely so that after twenty years of self-imposed isolation the American chess genius could start his new life, turn destiny around and perhaps experience complete personal satisfaction, equal to that of the achievement which had reached its zenith in far away Iceland, when the crown of world champion was given to the only officially undefeated champion. We were thus in Fischer's heaven where he got everything he wanted and all the things he had hoped for through all the years of darkness. The backdrop had been painted so that the primordial biblical picture could be funneled into chess reality. And of course, Eve was also there.

A lot was said at the time, and certainly even later, about the role of Miss Zita Rajcsányi in Robert Fischer's return to chess. It is certain that her entrance, shining bright like a comet, into the life of the hero of this story was indeed decisive in the fact that it happened at all. She was the one, with her unbelievable calmness and restraint (we should not forget that Zita turned only nineteen on September 1, 1992), who was the center of new hope, the wind in the sails of an aging ship, an oasis of peace and newly acquired certainty who created the inspiration and strength for the new beginning to a man who had already given up.

This delicate girl had quite a special status in the event that was just about to take place. She and her wonderful family were staying in a suite in the central part of the island. I remember her appearing unannounced at the door of villa 118, as if she had surfaced from the ramparts, her silent steps going up the stairs, and later after midnight slipping out through the bathroom window and heading down the path leading into the night. Of course she could have exited through the front door, but Zita liked to play, to enjoy her nonchalance, but also show and demonstrate her influence and importance when, in her opinion, it was necessary.

At the time she was preparing to participate in a qualifying tournament of female Hungarian chess players for the junior championship of the world. She worked on her chess skills whenever Bobby had time. She got the very best possible help in developing her talent, which bore fruit and materialized when she placed high at the competition. That was to secure her a place at the world championship in Argentina. We were all very pleased with her success, because we considered it to be our own as well, and Mr. Vasiljević announced to joyful Bobby that he would sponsor the travel costs and sojourn of Miss Rajcsányi in the land of the exciting tango.

Whenever Fischer spoke to me about her, he always softened his voice, his sentences grew shorter and became clearer. "I got her letters at my post box in Pasadena. I think I didn't answer them for a long time, maybe a year, because I was in Germany at the time. But they were somehow different from the others that arrived. So I also started to write, until we met the first time," almost a shy facial expression. "You know, Nesh, she's incredibly mature and wise."

Everything was clear. A man well along in years had met the woman of his life by the whim of predestination. Her maturity was attractive, needing a family, and it seemed to Fischer that he really wanted that for the first time in his life. Even though the difference in years was large, they were contemporaries in the mental coordinates of real life, where it was Zita who dominated after all. When she would disappear for a moment, he would cry "Where is she, where is she?"

The newspapers kept repeating, "Young Hungarian Girl". A cliché that rouses the imagination. Young – exciting, erotic, explicit or seductive; Hungarian girl – she must be beautiful because, as anyone who has ever heard of a *czárdás*, seen the Danube or been in love in Budapest, the female portion of the population of this central European country is certainly a decoration in the European bouquet of womanly perfection. But Zita won hearts above all with her intellectual domination. Always wearing comfortable pants, a simple t-shirt, canvas All Star tennis shoes in a variety of colors, and with her glasses on the tip of her nose, always smiling gently and rarely saying a word.

Only occasionally loud talking upstairs. Arguments and disagreements. Zita heading off into the night. In public they never touched, much the less held hands, kisses were unthinkable, it all looked more like a strong friendship than...

Someone might say: Fischer went public, started playing in the chess arena again – because of love! For love to become reality, for a family to be made, poverty and hardship are not a good frame for the picture of harmony. Of course, it can be done without money, but when it is right at hand and especially when there was so much available... Why not? However, here I must disappoint all those who would like to take the emotion out of it. The idea of love is what drove Bobby, but not love itself. Cupid's arrow had struck his heart, but he was not intoxicated by it, his heart would begin bleeding in pain only a year later. Zita was a missed chance for Fischer, a train toward happiness that he missed on purpose because of the vain belief that another one would come, just like the lie that there are other railways. The voice from afar: Robert Fischer, can you recognize a friend when you see one? In your soul do you feel the soul of a woman who wants to do you good?! It is late for such questions, the years have consumed the time when that was a reality. We kept working, waiting for the start of the match and the first moves of the black and white figures that would change history.

In spite of the wishes of many political and chess circles to minimize the significance of the upcoming events, even in those days it was clear that such attempts would not produce the results they desired. Namely, the enormous media interest in "the revenge match of the 20th century" had already materialized in the fact that two hundred requests for journalist accreditation from all over the world had arrived at the organization center. Special interest prevailed in the opening press conference scheduled for September 1.

The focus of the organizer was certainly on preparations for the festive opening ceremony which was announced as an event never to be forgotten. It was known that the directors and choreographers had intensively been working with 650 artists who were to make the eve of the beginning of the match into the crown of all the effort and investment.

Invitations had been sent from Belgrade to various addresses of high reputation and importance, people whose presence would beautify and highlight the significance of the spectacle, above all because of the UN sanctions and the "adventurous" and risky connotation it might have on their status, the result of which was that there were few positive responses. Still, even without them, the majesty to be remembered was a certainty. A special invitation, not without sarcasm, was sent via the American embassy to the American Sixth Fleet which was already in the Adriatic, some fifty miles from the venue, nearby the flaming Balkan war drama.

Pulsations from the roiling world of chess were reaching us and could be felt strongly. The media clearly maintained that image, broadcasting the statements and comments of many of the greats of the game, Kasparov and Karpov in the first place. All of the well-known Serbian and Montenegrin grandmasters were somewhere nearby, waiting and looking for details. Eighty-two year-old Andor Lilienthal, the oldest grandmaster in the world, came for a short visit to Sveti Stefan to express his respect and satisfaction. He had won the highest title in chess long before in 1940. With a trembling voice he talked of his memories of legends who had not been forgotten such as Capablanca, Lasker, Euwe, Alekhine... The Philippine chess theoretician, Gloria Sukhu, also came to visit us for a couple of days, and the endlessly kind Yasser Seirawan showed his joy at the fact that Fischer was back in action, dressed sportily with a bag over his shoulder, he took walks along the paths of the island.[29] His older countryman took him in with uncommon friendliness and spent a couple of hours talking to him on several occasions. Bobby would later repeat the resulting anecdote many times. Attempting to establish the background of his partner in conversation, our hero asked his younger colleague what his faith was. Clever Seirawan answered that he was "halfway" Moslem and "halfway" Jewish. Bobby always smiled beneficently when he remembered this creative answer, especially

---

[29] Yasser Seirawan, born in Damascus, an American grandmaster, was thirty-two at the time.

the fact that his guest did not specify where the demarcation line was on his body for these two great monotheistic religions.

As the start of the duel grew near and work intensified on the preparations and the reconstruction of the hall in the Maestral Hotel, where the match was to be played, our "inspections" took place more and more often. The small auditorium for just a couple of hundred viewers, a glass wall framed by a concrete wall between the auditorium and the players, a thousand lux of lighting above the table without reflecting or shining in the eyes of the players, exceptional sound insulation and temperature control. The players were to come to the battleground through a special entrance. In the playing area there were two rooms for reflection and rest, each of them furnished with an armchair and a refrigerator with specially chosen food and beverages.

Bobby and I were to walk to the Maestral Hotel, using the opportunity to get some exercise and relax. The ten minute walk along the seaside through a lovely pine forest was a true satisfaction. My protégé was quite happy with the general playing conditions. He insisted especially on the lighting and got exactly what he wanted, the air conditioning was set especially so that his tailored suits would be noticeable, and a lot of work had to be done on the armchairs they were to sit in while playing. However, once again a doubtful voice echoed from the dark. At the end of one evening, when he had finished working with Eugene, Bobby told me in person, or rather made a request of me. "I want you to check somehow, and to be completely sure, that in Boris Spassky's break room there is no place or possibility for someone to hide, someone who could help him in the analysis or give him advice during the game. You know," he went on, "the Russians would happily find some sort of dwarf, a midget analyst they could stick in there." Even he himself, realizing how absurd this request was, he laughed out loud, but he did not retract the request. Of course there was no such possibility, that any kind of message or idea arrive at the match hall, but anyway I did what was requested of me.

With some slight changes to the room, everything there for privacy during game play was so transparent and visible that no one and nothing could be hidden. A couple of days later, around midnight, I took Bobby to see this for himself. He was satisfied (again a smile, to show that he was aware he was overdoing it, but he was actually being quite serious), but he once again asked that I check Boris's break room before every game. Even though in my plan, besides all the checks that had been done including control of the special forces of the Montenegrin police with their specially trained dogs for detecting explosive devices, it was already foreseen that I keep everything under constant control with my closest team, especially the entire hotel complex. I then redoubled our efforts, knowing ahead of time to what kind of unbelievable details would come into play. Another challenge appeared in those days. On one of the last visits to the hall before the very start of the chess duel, when I had already concluded that everything was all right, Bobby cast a glance at the chess set (it was perfect), the armchairs (finally good), the lighting (there was no reflection), the temperature in the hall was set (and correct, the jackets would not come off). Then Fischer also looked at the little flags on the table above the names of the participants. While everything with Boris's French one was all right, he almost screamed in horror and surprise when he saw the American flag.

And indeed, as if someone had wanted to play a bad joke, perhaps inspired by the thought that, in line with Bobby's statements, a caricature of the symbol of the country from which the champion hailed might satisfy his esthetic criteria. Something like that would be in accord with the powerful expressions of disdain and hatred for the government of the country of his origins. The little flag on the small table flagstaff undoubtedly looked catastrophic. The uneven placement of the stars and their disproportions, the curving red-white stripes and the poor-quality material it was made from – it all left a really bad impression. I immediately called the interior designer and other members of the team who worked on the hall so that we could react quickly to this problem. We were told by the woman who was in charge of the stage design that the flag was only there temporarily, as a model, while a new one, the real one, was still being worked on and would be placed the next day. "But who can stop the doubt once it appears?"[30] a famous writer once asked. Bobby was quite angry and insulted.

Accompanied by the whisper of the sea and the sound of our footsteps, we walked "home" along the pebbles, Bobby explained something I already knew and had heard from him. "You know that I really love my country, though it never returned that love to me. I hate 'only' those who have turned it into what it is today. The bankers, usurers, Zionists, the lying impotent politicians who send my countrymen to die all over the world for the sake of 'exporting democracy', behind which the personal, selfish interests are hidden of those who actually rule from the shadows, from behind the curtains. They are the greatest enemy of America and Americans. The media control their minds, fill them with false information and create a consciousness containing general stupidity and lack of interest."

Based on a multitude of previous experiences, I knew that this would not pass easily or lightly. That I was right was confirmed by the fact that the satisfactory American flag Bobby finally chose was the fifth variation of the solutions offered. Made of silk, the symbol of the greatest empire of the twentieth century, which gave the world so many achievements in everything called civilization, among other things the greatest chess player of all times, so that it would remain so for all times. If we were to imagine that all of civilization vanished, and that visitors from another galaxy came and accidentally found an encyclopedia of important people in the history of the small blue planet of the solar system, they would surely also find the name – Bobby Fischer, chess player, USA. Perhaps they would understand that, perhaps not, but it is important to me that we understand it while we still exist.

And now a cliché, and those are oft repeated truths – time passed quickly. Chess, enjoying the swimming, the sun, nice tasty food (we often visited the excellent Chinese restaurant in Budva), contacts and visits, enormous effort in all segments of the

---

[30] Meša Selimović, *Death and the Dervish*

organization, and above all the spirit and breath of exceptionalness, history in the making.

The day before September 1, the first long awaited press conference, a calm sunny morning. A gentle hint of autumn in the air, a few moments of fresh breeze in the afternoon heat, Bobby still asleep while I was working downstairs, looking through the mail, summarizing the press clippings for the start of the daily schedule, when suddenly I heard something like the sound of a boat motor. I was accustomed to those two-stroke engines, because a lot of boats traveled beneath our walls, but this approaching sound was somehow different, faster, sharper... more dangerous! I went out into the yard, climbed up on the terrace, the lookout, at the top of the steep crags where I usually sat on my break, and in the distance I saw something headed right at me, at the island, from the open sea, a form which quickly took its final shape, a helicopter. I knew immediately it was not "one of ours",[31] and I immediately gave the alarm signal. I ran down the steps, "tossed" a bathrobe and slippers on Bobby, and then took him, groggy and confused, to another suite several doors down. This backup, defensive "position" had been predetermined, so that my protégé was in a different place and safe within less than a minute.

The sound of the propellers got louder and louder, the steel dragonfly with unknown plans and intentions grew closer. Within seconds villa 118 became a fortress. Thirty-odd armed men stood ready to go into action. Even the energetic Mr. Vasiljević grabbed his pistol and pointed it toward the sky.

The drama reached its climax when the helicopter hovered above the house at a height of about thirty feet. The flying machine had no markings whatsoever. The bushes and trees were bending down because of the artificial tornado above our heads, a heartbeat, a second passed, a heartbeat, another second passed... An attack, an attempted kidnapping, a final warning that the match should not take place, overly ambitious journalists, it was not important. At the moment when I was about to fire, because it

---

[31] It was easy for me to recognize the helicopters of the Yugoslav army and Serbian or Montenegrin police.

was close and we would surely have shot it down, the pilot swung to the right toward the southeast, toward Petrovac, Bar, Ulcinje, and quickly vanished behind a nearby peninsula. Who it was and what they wanted, we never found out. There were a lot of possible answers, but we did not look for them, because all is well that ends well, and the upcoming days would bring question after question, and there was simply no time to look back at passed events.

I went to get Fischer who was visibly upset, having been guarded by some of our colleagues.

"Nesh, where were you!?" he shouted, "and what the hell is going on?"

"An exercise, Bobby, an exercise. We had to practice saving you if there was a surprise attack like this from the air. I'm sorry I couldn't prepare you for it because then it wouldn't have been so realistic."

"Well, how did it go?" he asked.

"Excellent, everything functioned perfectly. You are completely safe," I said.

The grandmaster in his pajamas, bathrobe and slippers congratulated me on my team's readiness and slowly walked back to his room to go back to sleep. Our team all had drink out of relief, and the self-confident, defined collective spirit now grew even stronger.

And thus we come to the beginning of the spectacle, to the last day of August. Since we knew that everything was completely ready in terms of organization, there was no special tension. We spent a nice day and lovely evening in which the holiday, celebratory spirit hung in the air. After supper, a merry, laughing conversation: Mr. Vasiljević, Mr. Kubat, Mr. Torre, and I. The sweetness of success, we had reached the beginning, the satisfaction of victory over many hurdles and difficulties, the feeling of spite, alone "against" the rest, and the completeness of the now real hope in a good and successful future. It was if the harmony of energy and excitement had turned the island into a ship in safe harbor, after a long voyage, joyfully waiting the next day's disembarking of the crew who deserved a good time and some fun after a lot hard work and investment.

When they all left, Bobby and I carefully prepared every detail needed for the big day ahead of us. With the knowledge that the backdrop on the stage for the next day's performance would be green, we chose a suit, shirt and tie. The champion cleaned and shined his new shoes and placed his socks on his suit. Then we prepared a new leather briefcase and placed all the necessary papers and documents in it. When we had finished everything, a glance at the clock told me that there were just a few hours until the agreed wake up time. I suggested that he rest a while, because we were going to have a long, intensive, but by all means exceptional day. After twenty years, we counted the time, the undefeated world champion was returning. The dreams of millions of chess fans would come true, the grandmaster who had pushed back all the borders, the *enfant terrible* of the ancient game was back, ready for a new start and for the end of the first end which looked like death to the world and the world of death.

The next day everything was to be born again. He offered me his hand, the first time since we met. I took it and squeezed it.

"Nesh, you know..." he hesitated.

"I know, I know, Bobby," I interrupted his sentence midway.

"Good night," he said.

"Good night, Champ," I responded.

His steps on the staircase, the sound of his door closing.

The smell of the cypress trees. The whisper of the sea. Crickets chirping. Around the light in the yard a million different insects, large, small, transparent, colorful, the harmless ones and those which can sting when they want.

Every light in the darkness can be seen from afar.

Good night, Bobby.

Good night, Champion.

Good night, lonely traveler.

CHAPTER 7.

SEPTEMBER FIRST

"The night is cold before the great event..." says a line woven into a song of the legend of the Yugoslav rock scene at the beginning of the nineties, the leader of Zagreb's band Azra, Branimir Džoni Stulić. And indeed, after a short sleep I was awakened by the cool morning of a day being born with the first rays of the sun peering from behind the mountains, shining on a sea of memories. History, tainted with nostalgia, after twenty years in a time which could now be felt beneath my hands took on an entirely new dimension. Was it going to be a hint of future days of glory, or the epilogue of a story about life and chess? The years to come would give us an answer to that dilemma, but the dawn of September 1, 1992 awakened hope, confirming the importance of that magical moment.

After two decades of silence, isolation, self-isolation, anger, hiding, flight from others and from himself, secrets and darkness, truth and lies, Robert James Fischer was to officially show the world his face, grown old in the meantime, at the first press conference. From the distant platforms of North and South America, from Moscow's Sheremetjevo airport, from harbors in Spain and the Philippines, from the Bronx, Portorož, from the streets of Reykjavik and Pasadena, all the steps of the chess king led toward the Maestral Hotel, the place where the big comeback was to take place, and where the forthcoming match would be staged.

It was as if all clocks had stopped for a moment, the war surroundings quieted, and that everything and everyone had turned toward the greatest of possible performances which could happen in those times. The frame for the picture was interesting at the very least, made by the skillful hands of an anonymous master, not of Bobby's favorite wood but of shiny gold. Later analysis, time is the best judge, would show whether that precious metal was real or fake.

That morning I did not have to wake up my protégé. Movement upstairs, footsteps, doors opening and closing, the sound of water in the bathroom, all said that Bobby wanted to be ready and on time on this special day. According to our internal agreement, no one could enter villa 118 until Fischer was completely ready for his public appearance. Thus all forms of exaltation, pressure, confusion and needless hurry remained outside the door.

His suit was already prepared. New, grey, and single-breasted, it matched well with an ocher colored shirt and a discretely colorful tie. Happy, he dressed slowly and took special care of his hair and beard. He stood for a long time in front of the mirror with brushes and combs preparing for his "performance". When ready, obviously satisfied with himself, he came downstairs. Then the small inner circle also gathered. A special excitement fluttered in the air, but there was no stage fright. Everyone had breakfast, accompanied by a merry conversation where Mr. Vasiljević played a leading role with his remarks and loud laughter.

The security team was waiting in front of the villa, and two new Mercedes were parked just in front of the entrance to the fortress of the resort. Information came to us that the hall at the Maestral Hotel had been full of journalists from early in the morning. The interest and accreditation had been confirmed for more than two hundred journalists from all over the world. It had been announced earlier that Fischer wanted the questions sent to him in written form before the beginning so that he could pick the ones he wanted to answer. They had to be sent to the press center by 9 that morning. On paper, the curiosity expressed by the fourth estate was really fascinating in terms of its volume.

As noon approached, tension began to appear and increase after all, even though Bobby and Eugene were drinking orange juice at the chess board and analyzing chess problems. The time came for departure. A large group headed off down the winding, steep, stone paths and passages, but the main hero suddenly stopped, as if he had forgotten something, and said, "Nesh, let's go back to the villa for a minute." I was sure that we had taken everything we needed, but I quickly went through all the options in my head.

As soon as we entered the ground floor, Bobby interrupted my thoughts with his directness, "I have to tell you this after all. No one knows this yet," like a secret entrusted to a best friend so that there would be no pangs of conscience later, "When they ask me questions about the threats from the U.S., I'm going to...?!" The creation was all ready. A couple of sentences. A smile on his face. He knew what to do. He would do what he knew how to do.

"OK, now let's go!" he said.

In the car, Fischer, Vasiljević, the driver and myself. The ride would not last long, and Jezda filled it with images, expressed with eloquence and charm.

And then things really sped up. The car stopped in front of the Maestral. We got out. A large crowd. A multitude. I checked the people's faces. I kept an eye on Bobby. Sima and Buca went ahead of us, blazing a path for us with their physical presence, moving the careless out of the way.

I was just behind my ward on the left side. He was used to having me there whenever there was a crowd. On that side, I had a clear perspective of the crowd. If he wanted to tell me something, he just tilted his head in that direction, if I needed to tell him something, he already knew that the voice in his left ear must be heeded. Beads of sweat on his face. Bright lights. People talking loudly. He was a bit nervous. I know him. I can read the signs.

It would be all right after all. Like the wagons in a giant rollercoaster, or the *Eurostar* before entering the Chunnel, we stop and then the whole group seems to rock back to rush forward, and there we are. We go inside. Exactly fifteen minutes after 12 noon.

Flashes go off. Cameras, noise, applause. Sixty feet to the podium, to the table where he will sit. Walking fast, certain, straight into a new beginning, a new day, an old dream.

There he was awaited by the unforgettable jewel of Serbian journalism, Mr. Nebojša Đukelić (unfortunately he is no longer among the living), the creator of popular television programs, an influential mover and shaker on the Belgrade cultural scene, and the anchor man for this and all the other press conferences during the match. There was a moment of quiet. From left to right, sitting at the long table with a banner saying JUGOSKANDIC, were: Nebojša, Bobby, Jezdimir, Boris Spassky (in a white short-sleeved shirt with a red tie), and his wife Marina who was serving as his personal translator. The anchor introduced Bobby Fischer as the chess world champion, because on the panel with the match logo in the background it said exactly that, and this caused great enthusiasm by those in the audience who loved and respected the American grandmaster.

From the many questions he had made notes on, he was to choose, of course not by accident, the one from the reporter for the *New York Times* for the start. Only a careful listener actually heard that Bobby called the title of the famous newspaper from his homeland the "Jew York Times".

Why hadn't he played all these years? Because no one wanted to play against him, because when Karpov refused to do so in 1975 and got the FIDE title of the world champion, he had since been excommunicated from the family whose motto is *gens una sumus*.

Had his chess game improved? The second question.

"We'll see," Bobby answered.

When asked to comment on the war in the territory of the former Yugoslavia, Fischer remained silent. He did not want to talk about it.

Would he play against Kasparov? With the index finger of his left hand he pointed to the panel behind his back that said he was still the world champion. "Can you read what it says?" he asked the audience.

Then the fourth question, an opportunity for Fischer to make a point and carry out his secret plan. Is the position of the USA related to his participation at this match a hindrance to the upcoming event? A brief dramatic pause. A bit clumsily and awkwardly he took the Treasury Department document from his bag. He raised it high and then leaned over toward the microphone. He read part of the piece of paper in his hand then slowly lowered this legal act from the greatest power in the world and then to everyone's surprise he spit on it, with the words, "This is my reply to their order not to defend my title here!"

Dead silence. Then applause. Boasting. Bitterness.

To some this gesture was an act of pride because, in spite of everything, the policies of the USA in an important part of the world, where those policies were and are considered to be unjust, interventionist, and imperial – and this act reflected the spite of the oppressed, the repressed and the weak. The rebellion that gave strength to such people was now materialized in that piece of wet paper. The resistance of the weak? The only way to make a point? Courage or hopelessness? Even from this distance in time one can still discuss it. However, that which remains, the unfixable damage, was the directness, the banality of such an act. If I had only had a little more time before we departed, at the moment when he told me in private about his intention, I certainly would have asked him not to do something like that. No matter how angry, resigned, mad from suffering, tired of fighting with windmills and wild beasts, he gave his opponents the chance to judge all the good and positive things in him through the prism of that action. Because Fischer's comeback had a lot of meanings, it offered a variety of possibilities and woke new hope in chess which, in the time to come, would be remembered by a single gesture, a single movement, a desperate act remaining for the weak. Nebojša Đukelić, a polite man, would later joke that the well positioned document from the American government fortunately saved him from being "showered" by the anger of our guest. His strength, greatness and spite – my dear Bobby could have demonstrated them in a much more dignified way, for example in a future match with Kasparov in which he would, most likely, win. His directness like this was obvious, the message was clear, but it was undiplomatic. Because "do not answer a fool according

The Greatest Secret of Bobby Fischer

to his folly or you yourself will be just like him, answer a fool according to his folly or he will be wise in his own eyes."[32] Even if Robert Fischer was right in his own hermetic world, and wet himself from all those who had spit on him, I would have been happier then, and would be happier today, if he had come out of that moment more elegantly, with more dignity and diplomacy. I am saying that because of him, because of history, because that was the image, unfortunately, that marked his comeback.

After this, he went on rocking gently in his chair and let Spassky answer questions directly. The press conference lasted about an hour. From the organizers' point of view, it served its purpose. The recordings of Bobby Fischer entering the hall were shown around the world. Even CNN, not really Fischer friendly, set aside ten seconds of prime time coverage for this news. Everything that had come out of Yugoslavia (Serbia and Montenegro) in the preceding months had been painted in dark colors by the media. Justifiably or not, true or not, the world had an image of a small Balkan nation which was not allowing any one else in its surroundings peace and quiet, and which was only proud of war drums and threats. Now, because of the magnitude of the event, those same media were "forced" to broadcast the information, images and sounds of a sports event that was impossible to ignore. In ten seconds there is not much room for political commentary. The goal was achieved. A grain of sand in the endless gray desert of the media blockade. A colorful, shining grain, one that can be seen, one that gets found.

The return to Sveti Stefan, relaxation after a job well done, as the entire team around Fischer and the organizers of the match interpreted the introductory press conference. An hour or two of relaxed conversation in the garden of villa 118, comments, perspectives and comparisons. Bobby was in a really good mood after his clearly stated opinions, obviously enjoying the "power" which certainly did come from inside of him, rather as a reflection of the circumstances seen through his personhood and the moment, and the certainty from which the unambiguous message

---

[32] Proverbs 26:4-5.

was sent to the whole world, especially to the administration of the USA.[33]

The afternoon was absorbing the day which was demanding much more effort and offering many new challenges. The opening gala for the match was still ahead, so we had a quick lunch, and almost everyone went to rest up and prepare for the evening which seemed to be very promising.

For my team and myself, of course, there was no time to rest. The conception of the entire ceremony meant that there would be a lot of guests with invitations but, as we would soon see, also a lot of people who invited themselves, a multitude of new faces, stand-ins and artists, and therefore possibly unexpected challenges. The fairytale island full of paths, terraces, extensions, lookouts and passages was indeed a lovely stage full of possibilities for the creativity and imagination of the directors of the event, but for us it presented a multitude of demands. Therefore, the whole island was once again inspected and checked, and the guest list was also double checked.

The hotel staff, especially the exceptional cooks and bakers, had been working forty-eight hours almost non-stop. Over the preceding days, Mr. Vasiljević had told us privately that the investment in the offering of specialties and delicatessen foods would exceed several hundred thousand dollars.[34] Every terrace, the area around the small but exotic swimming pool, and every other romantic Renaissance corner of the hotel would be decorated with tables covered with all possible specialties from the sea, the air and the forest. Domestic fruit and vegetables, chosen according to Fischer's wishes, but also exotic ones we joked about that no one present would know their names or places of origin. Collectable wines, again the best, Mediterranean and Montenegrin, along with everything else the god Bacchus would want to quench his thirst.

One might hear, from then or now, a voice objecting to the

---

[33] France, for example, did not consider this sports event as a violation of the UN sanctions on Yugoslavia.

[34] According to the words of the main organizer, the entire celebration with the opening ceremony cost 700,000 dollars.

opulence, or even the arrogance of such gastronomical and other luxuries in a country where, at the end of the last century, inflation was rampaging, driving the standard of living of most of the citizens into the abyss of poverty. Certainly a justification for them could be that almost two decades later, when the concept and word "democracy" is the mantra of everything and everyone in this transitional part of the world, and almost everywhere else, it did not all remain that way. The single constant is what is on the tables. Only the host and guests are named differently and keep changing. However, not always and not completely.

Thus, in every possible way the remarkable hotel staff absolutely met the highest expectations, proving their skill and turning their efforts into a masterpiece for all the senses. The epicenter of the celebration was the central terrace of the restaurant which offered a lovely view of Budva, the tourist capital of Montenegro. The main actors in the spectacle would sit at special tables, rare antiques, and expensive golden cutlery, special not just because of the precious metal but also because of the date of its production, on this occasion would bedeck the hands which were to produce equal value as they moved the wooden figures about the board. The concept of the entire ceremony of the gala opening proposed that at 9 p.m. we all leave the island, and that the guests gather on the wide plateau before the stone isthmus and breakwater that connected Sveti Stefan with the mainland.

It was a lovely, mild September evening in which everything shined and twinkled heavenward. Along the ramparts, an endless gauntlet of young men and women holding torches, dressed in traditional Montenegrin folk attire. A procession of guests and celebrities. Leading them, of course, was the chess legend in whose honor the entire event had been orchestrated. A few steps behind us, the president of the presidency of Montenegro, Mr. Momir Bulatović, Mr. Milo Đukanović, Prince Tomislav and Linda Karađorđević, representatives of the federal institutions, many ministers, the high command of the Yugoslav army, and many famous personalities from the worlds of business, art and entertainment. Sveti Stefan that special evening was to host several hundred selected guests who were now slowly entering the walls of the old city.

The absence of the desired and invited guests from the outside world was hardly noticed because the atmosphere itself was enough – filled with troubadours, masked people, jugglers, court jesters, fire-eaters, in addition to the explosion of colors, the fragrance of the ocean and the cypress trees, the sounds of the mandolin, lute, harp – every thought and all the senses were engrossed in this moment which was filled with beauty, harmony and importance.

On the central terrace, in parade uniforms, the large orchestra of the Yugoslav army played evergreen standards, accompanied by opera singers. Alternating with passages of Nabucco, the Barber of Seville, Carmen and other classic gems. Proper and measured, suitable to the time and place.

Bobby was in an excellent mood the whole time, talkative, open to conversation with anyone I allowed near him. Obviously satisfied and carefree, he was especially enjoying Zita's company, but also that of his chess colleague and opponent, Boris Spassky.

Journalists had not been invited to the gala opening of the match, with the exception of the TV crew of Mr. Vasiljević's station and one official photographer.[35] Exceptions prove the rule or disprove it.

I was watching the crowd of faces that inched toward the central table and noticed several famous representatives of the fourth estate. I knew that some of them, like the eternal legend, now deceased Mr. Radojčić,[36] were here as masters of the journalist pen to enjoy the repetition of history, because they had been in Reykjavik twenty years before, but we had to watch out for those who were looking to advance their careers without scruples. Here, throughout Fischer's stay in Yugoslavia, but especially that evening, there was a "tandem" who stood out, the then famous editor of an important Serbian newspaper, magazine and TV

---

[35] Visitors were allowed to take photographs.
[36] Miroslav Radojčić, the doyen of Serbian journalism, passed away in Belgrade in the year 2000.

station, and his better half, likewise a famous TV and media personality. To the tune of "Green, Green Grass of Home" they were still at a distance, at the table with seafood specialties and wine. By "The Saints Come Marching In" and a gentle breeze from the open sea, they sailed to the central stage of the event, and their final approach came with champagne and the aria of the toreador from Bizet's masterpiece. Perhaps they saw the red cape in front of Bobby's face when I noticed the turquoise dress, more of a slip really, on the figure of the famous media star. From behind her tanned, thin torso which was harmoniously accompanied by her shapely legs, peered the face of her rather short escort. In lady-like fashion, tossing her half empty wine glass from side to side, she self-confidently asked me to set up a time for her to interview Bobby. The solid foundation of her self-confidence was built on the direct recommendation she had from the Yugoslav premier, Mr. Milan Panic.

In certain other and different situations, support from such a high place would surely carry its weight and ultimately have a positive effect. But that night it just made me smile and it caused the same reaction among my colleagues who were stationed around the head table that night. In truth, referring to the federal premier at that moment carried the weight of a grain of pollen. It was not difficult to tell the charming lady "no", because in the political and all other senses in the territory of Serbia and Montenegro at that time, there were only two addresses, two voices and two recommendations for which my answer could and would be different. One was in Serbia, in Belgrade, and its owner was now deceased Slobodan Milošević, and the other was and still is in Podgorica, and the man's name is Milo Đukanović. In present times the first is no longer alive and is important almost to no one, the second, to this very day, carried by historical skillfulness and wisdom, is still full of authority and functions in a relevant sense. When I made it clear that her planned first whole interview with Fischer was not going to happen, she persistently demanded that I respect her ultimatum, her wish. She leaned gently toward me and began a detailed description of her erotic capabilities and attributes which just might be at my disposal if I granted her wish.

The Greatest Secret of Bobby Fischer

She said it quietly, but loud enough that my colleagues heard her, and the smiles on our faces grew wider and lasted longer. All the while, her escort, the media mogul, participated in the negotiations by gently pushing his darling toward me. Of course, the interview never took place, her moment of fame was lost forever, at least in this case, but my smile disappeared before the crude simplicity of people who are ready to do anything (or is it nothing?) for an ends that does not choose the means, unless means are not the ends themselves.

When the gorgeous fireworks split the sky with bright colors to the sound of traditional Montenegrin folk songs, we knew that this exciting evening was drawing to a close. The guests would stay on the island deep into the night, while I escorted my protégé to his quarters at a half an hour after midnight.

As we headed "home" we passed through the ranks of guests who said good night to the guest of honor with applause. Nodding his head and waving, already a bit tired, Bobby politely returned their warmth. Then I noticed just ahead of us the well-known face of Mr. Cadik Danon, now unfortunately deceased, who was at the time the head rabbi of Yugoslavia. That wonderful man who, with his goodness, his intellectual and spiritual edification, left a deep trace on his time and the time to come, had honored all of us on the island that night with his presence, as well as honoring the entire organization of the match. Since I knew Fischer's anti-Semitic opinions quite well, for a second my adrenalin shot up.

Of course I knew that the respected rabbi was with us that evening, but my intuition told me that Fischer's reaction, at least at first, would be kind and polite. As if the rabbi was intentionally being discrete, or perhaps because it is sometimes hard to see the most obvious things, I had seen him only once during that evening in the mass of people. I nodded my head in greeting to our respected guest, and then a second or two passed, one step and then another, and we passed by him. After ten steps or so I whispered to Bobby that the head of the Jewish religious community in our country was here. Fischer stopped, smiled, and asked, "What? Where? Here?" and turned around. He was still smiling as he walked on. He mumbled something to himself, to the rhythm of his thoughts.

At villa 118, the noise and racket which still echoed all over Sveti Stefan could not be heard. My protégé went off to rest and prepare for the next day's contest between two old rivals, the first game of the "revenge match of the twentieth century." The guests left the island. Slowly, satisfied, full of joy, with the feeling that they had participated in something special. To be honest, some people (mostly female) remained.

Wherever there is money, there is love as well. If nothing else, then the quick kind of love, till morning, which might finance a CD, a film, or some other artistic project. However, of all the things that happened back then, of everything I remember in detail till this moment, the only thing I seem to have "forgotten" by some miracle were the combinations and room numbers where some of the great Yugoslav musicians and actors slept that night.

I sat in a comfortable armchair on the lookout of villa 118. Peace again.

Crickets and the sea. Nowhere like in Montenegro, and I have been all over the world. The guards at the door let the waiter on duty approach me.

"I beg your pardon," said good old Risto Pastrović, legend of hotel catering on this part of the coast, "what would you like to eat and drink, Mr. Stanković?"; I saw the familiar face and his kind smile under his moustache.

"We have anything in the world you would like," he said in his waiter's voice.

I glanced at him. "Everything in the world" did not interest me that evening. Then I remembered that I had not even thought of food for the last forty-eight hours.

"A sandwich, Risto, a sandwich. Prosciutto from Njeguš, a bit of cheese from Pljevlja and three olives between two slices of homemade bread."

I had already gotten everything my body and spirit needed by myself, still not completely aware just how much of that "food" was to come in the upcoming months.

The day, September 1. Night.

The Greatest Secret of Bobby Fischer

CHAPTER 8.

THINKING ABOUT THE UNTHINKABLE

We have established, therefore, that two basic, uncompromising and unchanging beliefs were the foundation of everything that Bobby Fischer did and lived for, and for which he will be remembered in the days ahead. First, already mentioned, was the all-encompassing edification of chess, the game, the skills, and the art, to the level of being all-encompassing, its unbelievable permeation into the being, into the soul and the spirit of a man. The only reality, the life and tragedy of the main protagonist of this story, took place on 64 black-and-white squares. He was born and died there, and between the darkness and light he irreversibly connected existence with his endless talent for this facet of human activity.

Yet, walking the marvelous flowering fields which are lit by the bright light of the geniality of the "undefeated champion of the world", with all respect and amazement, as we merrily sing a hymn in his honor for all time, to the best among the best, suddenly we come to the very gates of hell. What are they doing here? Do they have to be in this story and in this life? And before we answer that question we can still stop here and avoid all the traps which the demons of lies and hate have prepared for us. What have we been offered and what will we get if we stop here? Ultimate simplicity. Unbearable, but easily acceptable lightness of being, simplification and one-dimensionality. We will escape without consequences, but we will never find out what really happened, where we are headed, and above all we will never have an answer to the question, "Who, really, is Bobby Fischer?"

The Greatest Secret of Bobby Fischer

If you wish to leave us here, then you probably think: Robert James Fischer was a wunderkind who, as Mikhail Botvinnik said long ago, "should be watched out for"; he was undeniably a genius at chess, crowned with many tournament titles, the zenith occurring in Reykjavik in 1972 as he captured the throne of the world champion, but he was also a complete lunatic. He was paranoid, anti-Semitic, a despiser of America and an oddball who died as he lived, alone, outcast, and infamous, which was just what he deserved. There is no understanding for the unforgivable, nor is there a need to explain the inexplicable.

The alternative is for us to choose the more difficult path, to call upon the guardian angels and go forth, not afraid to face the oncoming dangers as we hear the screams of demons from the darkness. Many worthwhile challenges await us, without a single wish for even a moment to justify anyone or anything, so we can move bravely ahead to the final goal, to the reward that waits – the truth.

The second postulate hinted at, as hard as marble, which Bobby's personality depended upon, was his unswerving belief (equally as strong as his love of chess) in the global conspiracy, the invisible hand that directs every country, nation and individual, creating a world politics and sketching out the history of man on the canvas of time, focusing carefully on the hero of this story. The secret hidden powers, a world government of absolute planetary power, grasping the fate of everyone and everything in its iron hand, the lords of all the media and of the economy. The presidents of countries and governments are insignificant puppets on strings, the effective transmission for hidden desires and powers. The signs and indications are certainly public and are felt quite well, but in Bobby's understanding the creation is a conspiracy that people do not recognize exclusively for two reasons. The first is that they cannot reach the truth and understand the mainstream of the present and past with their intellectual abilities, while the second is that they voluntarily participate in the big game, in the roles of "useful idiots" who, for the sake of earthly "power", wealth and counterfeit social standing while they submissively serve their masters. The demons scream and the phantoms dance. Through clenched teeth he says, "Damn them, they're always here to torture and hurt me. They are not just anybody, but all and everything, nowhere and everywhere, visible and invisible, but always evil and filthy." And it should be said: Robert Fischer never, ever once pronounced the proper nouns "Jew" and "Jews" without the preceding adjective "dirty". A forceful and unchecked belief that the members of this nation and religion are guilty for everything bad under the heavens, including the dark clouds that loomed over his life and career.

Every conversation not about chess was an occasion to talk about world politics, shifts in society, culture and sports, seen through the prism of the above-mentioned way of thinking. In the life of this "prisoner of his own beliefs", every action away from the chess board took place by these principles, as the sine qua non, without measure or boundaries. Where did all that come from? How and when did such a painful weltanschauung settle into his heart, mind and soul? The lobby of the Intercontinental Hotel in Belgrade had been empty for a long while. The lights dimmed, the quiet pervasive, the receptionist at the desk was napping, and after supper and a long walk and hours of talk, the chess player had fallen asleep. I gazed into his face and wondered (though I really already knew) what this man would do if he could dream my thoughts.

Sunk deeply into the comfortable armchair, his arms crossed over his chest, he was sailing peacefully on a sea with no coastlines, without a tremor, breathing steadily. And while he was asleep, I played games: in my mind I put a Hassidic hat on his head, I drew in the long curls of hair over his red beard, those of the most Orthodox of Moses' faith. Mea Shearim, Amsterdam, Manhattan, Warsaw. I was pleased by the idea that, without the dark silt of the past and the hatred, an American was sitting across from me, conscious of his Jewish background, with endless talent for chess and with his baggage filled with titles and awards. A complete, harmonized personality who recognized and knew his roots, and was proud of them. My sleeping, far away protégé would certainly be so much happier that way, and the world, no matter what difference it made, would be more satisfied with him. As if the fences would come down if the hatred and anger were to disappear somehow, if the aggression were exchanged for calm, and the everlasting misunderstandings with peace. I caught myself a thousand times: instead of greeting him with my customary "hello", I wanted to greet him with the Hebrew "Shalom", just as I greet my Moslem friends with "Salaam". I would like to tell him that, as an Orthodox Serb for whom the history of religion is of essential intellectual interest, I adore the Psalms of David, the entire Old Testament which I have read a hundred times, the Talmud which I quote often in a variety of circumstances, especially the Jewish mystics, Isaac Luria for example, and the mind of the great rabbi Moshe Maimonides. My words would be accompanied by a ballad of the Sephardic Jews who, to the guitar and in the Ladino language, would bring in the breath of Spain, the scent of Sarajevo, magically transforming into the murmur of the children who played next to the old synagogue in Belgrade's Dorćol quarter, mixing their mother tongue Hebrew with the local Serbian.

But Robert Fischer was never to awaken from that dream, because an eraser cannot undo memory, just as blood is not water. Unfortunately, little Bobby never drank his fill of those waters, nor did he eat all the food from that table covered with marvelous and fragrant dishes. The misunderstanding began very early on. His childhood traced a path which grew into a road. His mother's aggressiveness and strength, the self-sufficiency of her personality which she expressed so dramatically but which he was ashamed of, and the essential lack of care for his boyhood needs, together with the vacuum left by his father's departure – it all left a lasting mark on his fragile psyche. His distant sister, his rare friends with "a limited shelf-life", his loneliness and the icy cold.

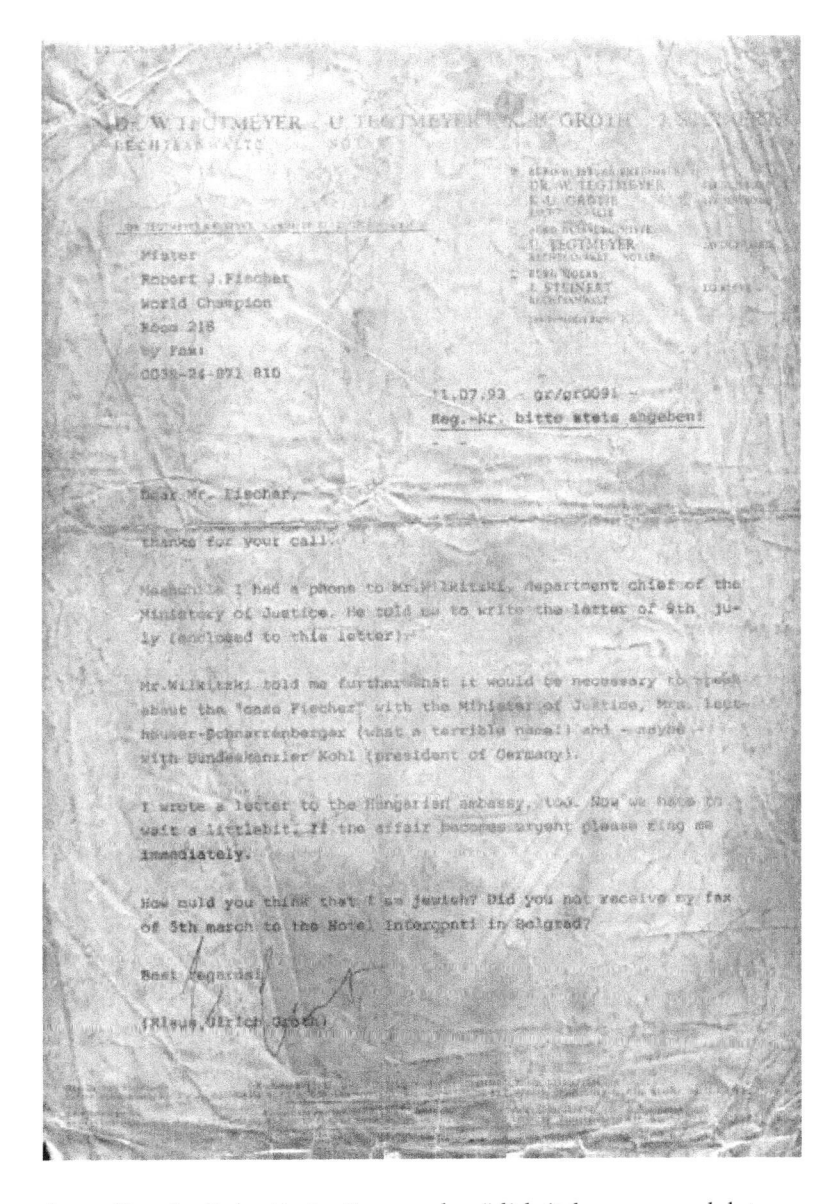

According to Robert's testimony, he "didn't have a model to emulate and grow up by." This was related to his everyday life, but also to chess. He was to tell me hundreds of times that he never had a teacher for the game.

Certainly, we can now all say in unison: millions of children all over the world have grown up in similar circumstances, but they did not become people full of hatred and anger, of destructive feelings which are focused on a single nation and a single religion. However, there is one more extenuating factor here. His enormous, breath-taking talent for chess. The absence of a direct model certainly contributed to the fact that he was often lost in everyday matters and that he often accepted various influences from the surroundings uncritically. Yet, I do not mean just the period of his childhood and youth.

Quite often I saw him in situations where he would try for an hour or for a day to be someone else, unsuccessfully of course. BUT THE HATRED, WHICH WAS ACTUALLY A HUGE, PAINFUL SHOWDOWN WITH HIMSELF, HAD ALWAYS BEEN THERE.

As far as his past memories could reach, he faced trauma, shame, fear, pain, rejection and misunderstanding. Explanation was necessary, and on one hand it was easy to find, yet on the other it was hard and far away. It did not come from the side of someone who could help, because there was no help to be found, but it actually erupted like a volcano from the interior of Robert's being. My father left while I was still little – whose fault is that? My mother did not love me, she was most important to herself – whose fault is that? My sister is far away and I am growing up alone – whose fault is that? No help from anywhere in developing my chess skills – whose fault is that? It is difficult to live in my line of work, and I have given everything to chess – someone must be at fault for that? I am the best player on the planet, I became the world champion and still there are no proper game conditions nor is there any respect. Alone I defeated the damned communists, I triumphed over Spassky in the Cold War era and showed my beloved country as an empire of intellect, and not just of baseball, football and basketball, raising its colors above the region of the Warsaw Pact, and I was never invited to the White House – someone must pay for that.

The Greatest Secret of Bobby Fischer

It was important to "them" to greet the Soviet gymnast Olga Korbut with pomp – what is that all about? They arrested me in Pasadena. Me, the world champion?! They exposed me to humiliation and torture – who was behind that? Those who pray falsely to God, the Worldwide Church of God, got their hands in my pockets. I must have been out of my mind! A question without an answer, at least not a real one or a self-accepting one. Early youth, parents, surroundings, our beginnings, none of us can choose those things. However, as the years pass with the process of maturing, we are forced to grow up, and above all we need to, we must turn back and chop through the undergrowth with a machete in our hands to our earliest memory, to our first conscious sight and sound. When we do that, when the primeval forest of emotions in our early growing pains (and is there a human being without them, no matter how great was our comfort and protection as we set off into life?) is cleared out and our cognition is passable, only when the light shines on that residual dark place, only then can we move on, heading off into the days ahead.

Robert did not have the strength to do that. It is clear that for most of his life, a guilty party could easily be found for his slips and mistakes. He is looking at all of us, including the persona I am writing about, always and unmistakably directly in the eyes from the mirror. That person is ourselves, that was Bobby to himself. However, the nature of humanity is not to admit our failures, arrogance or our own responsibility. The error is always in someone else. That other world – those are evil people, but so are those countries, skies, animals and plants.

Certainly they would not be that way if someone had not taught them to be so. Buried deep in his own being, Bobby came to an answer by means of an derived principle: THEY are to blame. Without them, world governments would be different, the creators of war and peace would be more humane, chess would be more honorable, and Bobby Fischer would be the legitimate world champion. He had the constant, strong and indelible feeling that he was being cruelly punished because he was different, more talented and on a higher plane of chess than all the others. And thus he was helpless, the tragic character is weeping in the valley, as the loser in spite of all his victories.

Therefore, for this book it would be easiest just to say that Robert Fischer was mentally ill. There was certainly a lot of paranoia, fear, irrationality, and hatred in him. Unfortunately, he truly believed what he said in a completely self-aware, sober and unwavering fashion. Thus he should not be hidden behind mental problems or madness. May he walk in his own glory and in his own shame for all time, just as he did when he walked the earth.

During the match, I often heard stories describing Bobby's anti-Semitism, saying that one could find a picture of Adolph Hitler above his bed along with other photographs of the leaders of the German nation during the Third Reich and the Second World War. The gossip spread that he was also a collector of Nazi symbols. This was not true, even though he did sometimes say that "The Fuehrer (sic) was actually not so bad". The Austrian corporal, unsuccessful amateur painter, political dark horse, who was elected by plebiscite as the president of the country which is today the leader of the European Union, was certainly not Fischer's favorite historical figure. "Not because he was at fault in his battle against world evil," the chess master would say, "but because, no matter how paradoxical that may sound, he himself was a dirty Jew by background." That is why we will not find Bobby glorifying Nazism, or a demonic connection with the failed, bloody empire, because in his overwhelming hatred toward everything Jewish, he embraced an equally powerful anti-communism that he was proud of. He said, "Communism is the same as Bolshevism, which is just another name for Judaism."

When he came to Montenegro, he did not bring any sort of special literature about chess or any quasi-historical books, with one exception: Count Cherep-Spiridovich's *The Secret World Government*, a reprint of a text published in New York in 1926.[37] From our numerous discussions I clearly understood that he had read all the essential works on conspiracy theories and the

---

[37] Count Arthur Cherep-Spiridovich (Maj.-Gen.), *The Secret World Government or "The hidden hand"*. The Anti-Bolshevist Publishing Association, New York, 1926.

hardback hatred pamphlets, but even that knowledge was not of significance in a quasi-factual sense. All of this led to the unambiguous final conclusion that his escape from reality into the darkness of evil was above all a personal drive, an internal re-examination, self-destruction, a painful, vain search which led him into the jaws of conflict with his own self, with everyone and everything around him, and ultimately, into a self-imposed isolation from which he never returned, in spite of the "revenge match of the twentieth century."

Naturally, no one in Fischer's surroundings accepted ideas like these. Having studied the history of religion, sociology and political science, among other things, I had heard a lot of varied conspiracy theories about which, this must be said and repeated, a lot was written in that period in the Serbian media, in order to explain the ongoing historical vortex of the time. Hence, it was easy for me to be an adequate partner in conversation on that topic with my guest. By the very nature of my job and the responsibilities I bore, I could not and dared not, even in the broadest sense, contradict Robert, because that would mean the instantaneous end of everything in which so much effort and money had been invested.

Balancing words and situations became my life work. It certainly was not simple, but my motives were strong and the bar was set fairly high. I did not have the right to make the wrong move, especially in the days and months when his "dependency" on my presence was so obvious that he would not even leave his apartment unless I opened the door for him.

But a catastrophe certainly could have happened. Once I was sitting at my desk in my room waiting for Bobby to appear at the open door so that we could set off into the new day. Over light conversation with my colleagues I was sorting out a pile of personal documents, letters, messages and papers which were beginning to threaten the very order of my living space. Just when I got to my personal documents and passes, I received an emergency call to go down to the hotel lobby.

I returned after a few minutes and saw Bobby sitting at my desk, holding an ID card in his hand. On it was my name and surname, above which there were a stylized Star of David and the Serbian coat of arms. To Fischer's eyes this must have meant a direct confirmation from hell, signed by Satan himself, that his apprentice, i.e. I, had been caught in the act. I was completely calm, collected and ready for his reaction.

But there was none. Nothing at all.

"Hi, Nesh, shall we go?"

"Hi, Bobby, yes let's go."

He gently put the card down on the desk. I glanced at Dane and Voja whose faces had gone pale, but then I saw Bobby jump up out of his chair with visible relief, and then he caught stride with me. He never mentioned it again, never asked me about it. A hollow spot in the firmness of his beliefs. Pragmatics. Momentary usefulness as opposed to eternal doubt. Did he forget about it, or did he remember it when we finally said good-bye? Perhaps the fact that I had a piece of paper written in Arabic at that moment on my desk (I often used short breaks to practice my knowledge of Farsi, the language of Iran) forced him to decide not to solve the puzzle.

Repeated truth. Exceptions prove the rule. Before Bobby Fischer met the Polgárs the first time, I felt the need to turn his attention to their background, so that the acridness of his anti-Semitism would not ruin the experience of meeting them. "Are you sure?" he asked me a dozen times, and then would drawl every time, "Nooooo..." as if at just that moment it was not "useful" for the Polgárs to be what they are. When I asked him that same evening whether he had noticed the Star of David necklace around Zsuzsa's neck, he awkwardly lied that he had not.

I was always interested in just how far he would go? How deep are the wounds on his body, the pit in his soul, the bitterness in his heart, the readiness to make evil real? I remember a moment – we were sitting in the Duna-Intercontinental in Budapest.

"Bobby," I said, "we've spent so much time analyzing world political and historical events, you battle so courageously for justice in chess, blaming the secret world government and the Jews for everything bad that's happened since the beginning of the world, but now, please tell me, could you ever kill someone?"

The Greatest Secret of Bobby Fischer

He jumped up from his chair, "What do you mean could I kill someone?"

At a time when the Balkans were already rattling from the gunfire, houses were being set on fire, knives were cutting into the throats of men who had been brothers until recently, this question could have been hypothetical, but also very real. Just a few hundred miles to the south, some people were killing other people just because they had different names or surnames, crossed themselves with three or with four fingers, or prostrated themselves before their one and only God. Thus my question was not just rhetorical, or without a particular kind of sarcasm, "Robert Fischer, if you truly hate them that much, how far would you be willing to go? Could you kill someone? Let's say that you start from the first, one, the only Jew whom you truly despised the most, even if it were me?"

"But you..." he squeaked, "you're not a Jew!"

I am a Serb, and he knew that very well.

"You're not a Jew," he repeated and waved a finger at me as if at a naughty child who had scared a close relative for a moment with a dirty joke.

"But if I were to kill, what do you mean? I'm not a killer," he added in a falsetto, "I'm just talking explaining. Never! Never! No! No! Never!"

In that second, in the vortex of war in the territory of the former Yugoslavia, some had lost sons, a sniper's bullet had pierced others' skulls, mothers were raped in front of their children by hordes of evil men, as the scream of mortar rounds covered up the sound of the innocents wailing and weeping. So, not far from where we were sitting, hatred was being incarnated with knives, bullets, grenades, there was screaming, wailing, blood and death. And all of that began with words of hatred. However...

Bobby Fischer could not kill anyone.

If strong language does not also kill.[38]

---

[38] "Too strong a word killed me", Brana Miljković, Serbian poet.

"I'm not a murderer," as if it is still echoing around the hotel lobby, and praise be to the angels that we did not reach the seventh circle of hell.

I still feel his faraway profound look of surprise at the directness of my question, which seemed to leave him naked before so many eyes, along with my question, "Why not take a step back to the absence of hate, another step to indifference, then another to liking, and then just a short step toward loving your neighbors," I thought to myself, but I did not say it.

But he could go no further, he could not go back, at least not at that age, and not if you are Bobby Fischer. All of it could be changed, except for those two essential postulates, those two legs on which this ambivalent man stood and used to walk, they would never change for any reason till his dying day.

I loved Bobby in spite of it all, because time brings people together, loved him like a weird uncle that the whole family was ashamed of, who suddenly returned to his birthplace after decades of roaming the earth, with no savings, but with stories and lessons for everyone. Like a neighbor who was sent off to war where he lost his legs and his memory to a landmine, so that everyone in the neighborhood now pities him and buys him drinks, always listening to the repeated stories about the blood-soaked front lines. Like a famous rock star steeped in alcohol and cocaine, to whose beautiful ballad you first kissed the love of your life, or like the genius who has just finished a lovely landscape with watercolors on the sidewalk at the moment when it starts raining.

How can you explain the things sifting through your fingers, the things that crawl upon stones, sail the open sea or fly across the heavens.

What is left behind? The trace of a man in time.

The impression of the soul in stone.

Dust hidden in ashes.

A grave in Iceland.

CHAPTER 9.

LIKE IT ONCE WAS, LIKE IT NEVER WAS

Now, almost five years after Robert James Fischer passed away, if we were to analyze the books, newspaper articles, films and documentaries, all of which have certainly influenced and created the all-encompassing collective memory of a large part of humankind, we would easily notice that the "revenge match of the twentieth century" was held in 1992 on Sveti Stefan (Montenegro) and in Belgrade (Serbia), thus in the former Federal Republic of Yugoslavia, a country which no longer exists. The match has been wiped from that memory almost completely. In the most detailed reviews of the life of the greatest chess player of all time, the match appears in a sentence or two, just to keep the story moving or as a hint of viability so that nothing is left out. If Fischer were alive today, perhaps he would see conspiracy at work in this, the directors of reality who, led by their desires, cut the tape of history and then splice it so that it fits into and serves their goals.

That is why it should be said that Robert Fischer's return to the public scene and his emergence from the sea of oblivion after twenty years of drowning in the murky waters of everyday life was a bright spot; being in his prime (his fifties, when it is not too late for a new beginning when one has the strength of "new blood from old wounds"), it offered him a real chance to turn his life toward brighter horizons or, no matter how cliché that might sound, toward happiness. The main hero of this story would often tell me during the time we spent together that the period when he came to Yugoslavia till he broke up with Zita Rajcsányi and the departure of Jezdimir Vasiljević from the country was doubtlessly the nicest and most fulfilling part of his life journey, now seen in its entirety.

The Greatest Secret of Bobby Fischer

The glowing moment of the new dawn was the idea of love, hope in harmony, an opportunity to collect what had been scattered, to gather emotions, to polish things up, to return what was lost (pride and fame), to confirm the achieved (greatness in chess and values), and to dock in the calm port of tranquility leading to old age. But fate, the confluence of circumstances, or higher powers – all have their own internal logic as well. Their rhythm and order, often hidden to us at the moment when they are important, or are far away when we need them close by, indecipherable and unclear (or at least it seems so in retrospect) when they should be clearly transparent.

Take my word for it, just the blink of an eye, a single flap of a butterfly's wing separated Robert James Fischer from the gates of that other, different world. But... believers would say in line with the Psalms of David, "If the Lord does not build the house, the work of the builders is useless; if the Lord does not protect the city, it does no good for the sentries to stand guard."[39] We all know that a little quickly becomes a lot, becomes difficult, becomes bitter and leads to an unavoidable end, tragic and cold. Especially if you are talented, rewarded with cognition and worthiness. Our hero was certainly in the game, in skill, in scholarship and in art – in chess.

In his private life that hope appeared but was extinguished exclusively through Bobby's fault, it disappeared in those 365 days of renewed "fame". In a sporting, chess playing sense, the match against Boris Spassky in this revenge variation of the match played now long ago, brought everything he had always wanted to the uncrowned champion of the world in terms of demands and egocentricity. If that grandiosity and perfectionism were related to chess as a whole, to chess players as objects of respect, then beyond all doubt and game play, its leading protagonists back in 1992 got from the organizers a quality that had been unreachable until then. It is difficult to compare times, although constants surely exist, but the prize of five million dollars reaffirmed the exceptional character of the match in a world where everything is

---

[39] Psalms 127:1.

measured by the material. We should remember that Boris Spassky earned 1,400 dollars when he won the world chess crown. The prize won at the FIDE title match in Reykjavik was 250,000 dollars.

Years had passed, material things were not adequate for comparison, but both in 1972 and in 1992, and even today, five million dollars is still five million dollars. We know, offers were made even earlier.

Philippine president Markos had reportedly offered four and a half million. Spain had offered four million. But that was not enough for Fischer, or perhaps the time was not ripe. And then from Serbia, from Yugoslavia, a number which fit into the rhythm and moment in life for the one it was intended for. The high quality, sincere concern of everyone (Fischer had always been popular and loved in this country), the security team that made him confident and gave him a real sense of safety (so important to him in particular), feeding his ego and giving him a feeling of power, then all the technical demands (lighting, cameras, chairs) so that no complaint could be made, all the way down to the opulence and greatest possible luxury (clothing, room, board, the most expensive automobiles) – all for a man who had been rejected until shortly before, who had worried about his future. Even the large stage at the Sava Centar Congress Hall, with a capacity of 4,000, was separated from the audience by an enormous glass wall, so that no sound, no voice, no accidental noise could reach the players from the darkness.

And all of that in Serbia, at war, in the capital city of the "usual Balkan suspect".

Is that why, perhaps, this moment is being shoved into the dungeons of oblivion though it was so important to Fischer's life and the history of chess? Is it bothersome? Would the discomfort caused by not recognizing one's own stature be less if we say that others also did not know it, acknowledge and appreciate it, in spite of his "faults"? "No, and again no," the voice of his opponents will say, "all of that could be true, but Fischer was a renegade who didn't obey the laws of his country, and brutally and crudely mocked them."

No one in their right mind would not oppose him. His explicit anti-Semitism, and ultimately utter and open hatred, to the point of madness, toward the American administration. Toward his own roots without justification, a cruel showdown with himself which took on these terrible forms in its appearance, expression and public manifestation.

But at the press conference on September 1, to the question of whether he expected the support of his countrymen, the Americans, Fischer replied, "From the government of the USA, no, but from the American people, yes." In conversations, when publicly expressing his thoughts and feelings, the chess champion always used that differentiation. The ruling oligarchy vs. the people. This was applied not just to the USA, but to Yugoslavia at the time, and to all other countries and governments in the world.

It seemed, like in his relationship with his mother, Bobby always wanted the love and attention of his homeland which he actually wanted to serve. Once, there on Sveti Stefan, in a break between the second and third game, between two draws, as we sat on the ground floor of our stone home, he told me a story from long before.

"The Russians, you know Nesh, always had the direct and unreserved support of the KGB. They accompanied them to tournaments, guarded them and helped them set up matches to help take care of Soviet prestige, and the KGB supplied the players with important information. I never had anything like that." Then he went on, "I remember one exceptional occasion after a tournament in New York when two men asked to talk to me. They came up to me and said they were from the CIA. And besides that's how they looked," Bobby said excitedly, while I tried to imagine what he might think intelligence agents should look like, "but I asked them to show me their IDs. They did. Then they told me they were quite interested in working with me. Their curiosity was focused on the possible application of chess theory and logic to fighting modern wars. I agreed to it, and they gave me a solemn promise that they would call me soon." For a moment, a thrill could be seen on Bobby's face. "But they never got back to me," disappointment then, just a glimpse as he said that.

From this story and others, Bobby's wish can be recognized to be "a soldier of his country", playing against the Soviets in the first place but against others as well, to the honor of his background and his nation. That great unrequited love, that unreturned passion gave birth to the equivalent of hatred. I hate you, mother, I hate you, my country. I remain alone.

And then after many years, little Serbia and even smaller Montenegro showed up, certainly not as a new mother because the real one cannot be replaced, but rather like a good fairy, at the beginning, and at the end more like a stepmother or evil witch. Accordingly, this was a perfect chance for Fischer to express his anger and rebellion. He did so during the whole match, focusing his negative emotions primarily on the government of his own country.

During the time we spent together every day, we always had a pile of newspapers from all over the world. In the moments when Bobby was relaxing from a game and from chess analysis, the practice was that we would sit across from each other, each with a magazine or newspaper in his hands, paging through them and reading interesting articles. If one of us would notice something especially important, he would read it out loud, and then the contents would be analyzed and talked about for a long while. One of the passions of my protégé was the careful analysis of texts and pictures.

Sitting in lounge chairs on the beach at Sveti Stefan once, on a day off from play, he came to a large photograph of Bill Clinton. At almost the same moment, I praised a moment immortalized on film, published in an important American political magazine that I was holding. Before me, in a black and white photo, was also the American president, relaxed, barefoot in summer pants rolled up above his ankles, accompanied by Al Gore, walking leisurely on a sandy beach. Smiling, handsome men in their best years. A beautiful image of optimism in which I recognized a clear reference to a much older photo where, in almost identical form, stance, movement and surroundings, one could see the Kennedy brothers. I recognized, for myself and in myself, this as exceptional political marketing, the connecting of two times which also connected the two American leaders, Clinton and Gore, with the charisma of the famous brothers at the height of their popularity. The skillful author perhaps wanted to thus note the similarity of positions and opinions, perhaps also with the private relationship of the two leading men in the dominating world power. However, in that black and white impression, for a second it seemed to me that I could also see something ominous because of the tragic end of their predecessors. I related this to Bobby, more as an association and artistic impression in order to provoke him to make a comment.

He cast a quick, sidewise glance at the publication in my hands and then returned his focus on his own. Two or three quick page flips, he was looking ahead, looking left.

"Nesh, do you see how quickly Clinton has gone grey. In your photograph, he looks much younger," he said.

I nodded. It really was like that.

"What does his white, thick, wavy hair remind you of?"

I knew this look, this facial expression. He had an answer ready. It was my move. I had to make it.

"With that smile on his face, framed in white, he looks like a lamb," I said.

"Great, great, great, that was what I thought, too. A lamb," Bobby went on, "can be either innocent or sacrificial, right?" he looked at me again. "You know those religious things. What would you say, innocent or maybe...?"

The game could not be interrupted. It must be controlled, and so I said, "We know that there are no innocents in politics, it's a cruel game, the mastery of the possible which demands perspicacity, decisiveness and most certainly cleverness. But Bobby, you shouldn't take this analogy to the Kennedy brothers too seriously, in a fatalistic sense. Here I really do see just beautiful photograph with a certain dose of intimacy."

The Greatest Secret of Bobby Fischer

"Nesh, Nesh, you can do better than that," said Bobby smiling. "You know *they* often send omens ahead of time through symbolism. They want to see if 'out there' someone is able to 'read' and 'see' it." Bobby was definitely "asking me to dance".

"All right," we will take it to the end, "I don't believe that one of them will be killed. But something might happen before their term is up.

"Concretely," Bobby said, "will someone kill them, or will they be publicly shamed? A or B?" It was not easy for me to constantly play with these political and historical prognoses, but I said, "B, Bobby, B."

"Excellent, that's what I thought, too," Fischer replied.

We went on looking through the papers, with no further commentary. Swimming. The marvelous chilly autumn sea, the turquoise water. Refreshment.

Much later, this story was to have its epilogue.[40]

Headlines in all the printed media all over the world. Large ones.

In bold. Highlighted.

I knocked on his door. I woke him up.

"What happened, Nesh?" he asked. "Did something happen?" he went on groggily.

"Nothing special, Bobby. B, B finally happened." I pulled the curtains back, let the sunlight into the room, dropped a pile of printed matter on the table and showed it to him. The Lewinsky Affair.

He asked me to translate the Serbian press. He read the rest on his own.

As I closed the door behind me, I heard him roaring in laughter.

It was time for lunch. Refreshed, dressed up, smiling, he offered me a piece of paper that said: Circle one. Monika Lewinsky is: A – A Serb, B - Chinese, C - An American of ... background. Now I nodded my head with a laugh, and jokingly waved my finger at

---

[40] This is the only event described in the book outside of the period of our continuous work from July, 1992 to September, 1993, which happened during one of our two other meetings later on.

him like a friend who has gone too far in a game and needs to settle down.

Europeans easily recognize Americans. Already from first impressions and when we made acquaintance, Bobby Fischer was a real American. He was completely rooted in the culture and time from which he came. In his conceptual world, the music, media, especially the radio and TV, and popular facts were completely dedicated to his country of origin. That was also a fact about chess. When asked what he thought about American chess of the time, Bobby answered, "There are a lot of talented players who need to be worked with."

More than once during his career, when asked about the best players of all time, he would offer his ranking list of exceptional players. On that list were Morphy, Steinitz, Alekhine, Najdorf, Tal, Capablanca, etc. For days and nights I observed my protégé as he analyzed and played, preparing himself for the match, or enjoying what he loved most. I can testify to the fact that for every one mention of any player of the past or present, ten mentions would be made of Samuel Sammy Reshevsky. This American of Polish background was certainly a great and important name in chess. However, it is certain that in the past there were more brilliant and, one might say, better. Regardless of that, Reshevsky, who was significant to Fischer because of his career early begun and his impressive childhood talent (which he showed already at the age of four), on this occasion served as a good, old genie from the bottle who appeared at the moment when Bobby needed him most. Because under the flag that so proudly stood on the moon, Bobby was not alone. Sammy was there, too. So, Robert James Fischer's anger was always exclusively aimed at the administration of the USA and not at his countrymen. That certainly is not, nor should it or can it be, any sort of justification for anything, but it is a small but significant addition to Fischer's biography.[41]

---

[41] Fischer obviously put the principle of democracy in the background, that the people elect the government and the president. It is an old and often used cliché that "a nation has the kind of government they deserve."

It is, thus, no wonder that the Fischer-Spassky match in 1992 has been shoved into the outer reaches of memory consequent to all the circumstances and factors, and also for political reasons. Many of the western media and reporters, although they were completely safe in the territory of Yugoslavia at the time, were actually not very happily received guests. While on the other hand stands the fact that they themselves, by dimming the picture a bit, actually did not want to see things the way they really were. The future will show that this, in spite of everything, will be a part of the same story in the end.

Ultimately, not as the least important, we must wonder about the value of the match in terms of chess. Can its importance be minimized and its content disqualified in terms of its value? It would be easiest to avoid responsibility and reach for the phrase "we'll leave that to the chess players, analysts and theoreticians." However, the beauty of a true testimony lies in the fact that it is sufficient in itself and speaks of itself, not asking for confirmation, other perspectives, because it is direct, experience-related and unswerving.

It is so in this segment as well, because Fischer's return, certainly an exceptional event, beyond all doubt demanded to take form and content above and at the chess board. After all, it was all about a specific, physical duel of the black-and-white armies of two legendary "commanders". And that is the place where time cannot hide the facts, nor does it have reason to.

Excitement electrified the air on the morning of the first game of the match which was to repeat history. The procedure of taking the path from Sveti Stefan to the Maestral for the first part of the duel of the two old opponents remained the same as the first scene prepared and carried out for the September 1 press conference. Waking up, breakfast, personal preparation lasting forty-odd minutes. The drive to the hotel, named after a gentle warm wind that stirs the blueness of the sea. We enter through the back door, directly into the game hall. That day, and afterward, there were about twenty people from the organization and management of the match in the room when we arrived. They all had to go sit in the audience very soon after. First I would inspect Bobby's rest and reflection room, checking that everything necessary was there, then I would discretely give Boris Spassky's room a once over. When I would nod secretively to my protégé that there were no "subtenants", we would head to the hall for the photographers' five minutes, as approved and agreed to in the schedule, and that was how long it would last. Then I would return to my privileged place (I was the only one who had a place inside the playing area), diagonal to Bobby, hidden from the public. After the start of the first game, before he was to touch the figure, he gazed off into the distance with a facial expression that already hinted at the journey of the champion's soul into the black-and-white land of battle, creativity and talent.

The first part of the match foresaw play up to five victories in the sessions that were played in an agreed rhythm and schedule on the Montenegrin seaside. I remember it clearly. After the end of the first contest, great excitement, exhilaration among the visiting grandmasters, chess journalists, guests, and among them were those who had come from as far away as Chile and Australia to see the return of their favorite. Everyone in harmony, in unison, smiles on their faces, some in disbelief with affirmative nods of the head, as if to confirm what they had seen, and the next day there were headlines in the papers, comments in the media. Fischer was back in grand style. The first game of his return lasted for six hours. Up until the thirteenth move it was a replication of the tenth game played twenty years before in Reykjavik. But then Fischer, instead of the Icelandic b4, moved f1. A move which caused a lot of excitement – a theoretical novelty, a4. The seventeenth move of the Spanish game. Grandmaster Gligorić commented on it and characterized it as "a strong initiative of white along the A vertical." All together, fifty artistic moves to be remembered. At the brief press conference after it was over, Bobby and Boris emphasized the advantage white gained in the opening. Boris added, "The victor had a brilliant idea, and the result – my defeat." A great victory, in Fischer style. It seemed like there had been no break, and indeed there had not been, he was the same, if not better, he had just been in a dark hidden place, frozen out of time, on the margins of reality.

The Greatest Secret of Bobby Fischer

Of course the questions and doubts were justified, at least among the chess playing element of humanity who were liable to skepticism often expressed in *freudenschade*, as people who nurture that spiritual illness like hypochondriacs who fret about their non-existent heart defects. Such people were saying: Bobby is too old to seriously play chess (and in doing so, it was as if they had forgotten Botvinnik who lost his title to Tal when he was forty-nine, only to win it back when he was fifty), or that he had not kept up with the chess world, or that he could not be in shape after all those years. As if with a giant eraser, on September 2 all doubts were removed, ill-wishing smiles were wiped off of faces, and in that last defense were those who secretly admired him and publicly hated him, or even those who publicly admired him but secretly hated him.

With his physical and mental strength that he would demonstrate over those months, if the flow of destiny would have permitted something like that, his career could go on for a long time, or at least until the world got a proper heir to the throne, a head worthy of the champion's crown. Later, at a press conference, Boris Spassky formulated it in words, in a gentlemanly way, "The world of chess needs a king and that can only be Bobby Fischer."

No less important for us to understand the reality of the situation, let us imagine for example that Tiger Woods did not play a single tournament. All right, an occasional recreational golf game on the weekend with friends. He keeps up with specialized magazines about "elegance on the green" and talks from time to time with his friends about the good old days. Then, after two decades, he goes to play a tournament. The first stroke, a brilliant swing, high elevation, the perfect arc of the ball despite the wind, the gasp of the public, straight into the far way target, a hole in the green. Worthy of praise, there would certainly be applause.

Anyone or anything else. A great writer, for twenty long hot summers and the same number of cold winters not picking up pen, and then the perfect sentence, a harmony of words that reaches into the depths of your soul; a painter without a brush or canvas, twenty times 365 days, and then a masterpiece, inspired by longing, bringing joy to be viewed by millions of people. All the

The Greatest Secret of Bobby Fischer

senses are satisfied, the angels rejoice, and *people* are enlightened when the special return. It ought to give us all the hope that was confirmed at that moment, that there is a second chance, that a man can be born again into one more life, just as the sun is reborn, and that doors can be opened again even though they have long been locked. So it was that the grandmaster returned in magnificent style. Certainly the quality of the play shown was not equal, but then all agreed that the first and eleventh games of the first part of the match were legendary.

The second game after quite a bustle in the Samish variant, the King's Indian defense brought a correct draw.

FISCHER - SPASSKY (m/1)

1. e4 e5 2. ♘f3 ♘c6 3. ♗b5 a6 4. ♗a4 ♘f6 5. 0-0 ♗e7 6. ♖e1 b5 7. ♗b3 d6 8. c3 0-0 9. h3 ♗b8 10. d4 ♘bd7 11. ♘bd2 ♗b7 12. ♗c2 ♖e8 13. ♘f1 ♗f8 14. ♘g3 g6 15. ♗g5 h6 16. ♗d2 ♗g7 17. a4 [17. ♕c1 – 10/362] c5 18. d5 c4 19. b4 N ♘h7 [19... cb3 20. ♗b3 ♘c5 21. c4! (21. ♗c2 ♘fd7) bc4 22. ♗c4 ♖f8 23. ♖b1 ♘fd7 24. ♕c2!»] 20. ♗e3 h5 21. ♕d2 ♖f8 [21... ♘ df6!?] 22. ♖a3± ♘df6 [22... h4?! 23. ♘f1 f5 24. cf5 gf5 25. ♘g5 ♘g5 26. ♗g5 ♗f6 27. ♗h6 ♗g7 28. ♗g7 ♔g7 29. ab5 ab5 30. ♖a8 ♗a8 31. ♖a1±] 23. ♖ea1 ♕d7 24. ♖ 1a2 ♖fc8 25. ♕c1 ♗f8 26. ♕a1 ♕e8 27. ♘ f1 ♗e7 28. ♘1d2 ♔g7 29. ♘b1 [△ 30. ab5 ab5 31. ♖a8 ♖a8 32. ♖a8 ♕a8 33. ♕a8 ♗a8 34. ♘a3] ♘e4 30. ♗e4 f5 31. ♗c2 ♗d5 32. ab5 ab5 33. ♖a7 ♔f6 34. ♘bd2 ♖a7 35. ♖a7 ♖a8
(diagram)
36. g4! hg4 37. hg4 ♖a7? [37... f4 38. ♖a8 ♕a8 39. ♕a8 ♗a8 40. ♗b6±] 38. ♕a7 f4 39. ♗f4! ef4

40. ♘h4!! ♗f7 [40... ♘f8 41. ♕d4 ♔e6 42. ♘g6 ♘g6 43. ♗f5+–] 41. ♕d4+– ♔e6 [41... ♔q5 42. ♕g7 ♕g8 (42... ♕h4 43. ♕h6 ♔g4 44. f3 ♔g3 45. ♕h2#) 43. ♘hf3 ♔g4 44. ♕h6 △ ♘h2#] 42. ♘f5! ♗f8 43. ♕f4 ♔d7 44. ♘d4 ♕e1 45. ♔g2 ♘d5 46. ♗e4 ♗e4 47. ♘e4 ♗e7 48. ♘b5 ♘f8 49. ♘bd6 ♘e6 50. ♕e5
1 : 0

Brilliance after twenty years of absence from the chess scene, the first game of
the "Revenge Match of the Twentieth Century" resulting in Fischer's victory.

After the opening move by white, five minutes passed before Fischer's answer. Boris had the advantage all the way up to a mistake in the thirtieth move when he got into trouble. Could Bobby do even more after that? After the analysis that evening with Gligorić and Torre, the conclusion confirmed the champion's words after the game, "It was a good game." The satisfaction of dividing the points, perhaps either one of them could have won, but...

Fischer's longtime friend Miguel Quinteros called from Argentina; an influential man, not only in the world of chess, in the land of the tango. Because of his obligations, he was to join us only much later in Belgrade. That night he announced that all of Latin America was caught up in the fever called "return of the legend". The great Miguel Najdorf also sent greetings and congratulations from the other side of the world. Similar news about the great interest in the match arrived from Russia, Spain, Great Britain, Iceland... Everything else that had been happening in the world of chess was completely shoved into the background: Kasparov attempted to parry, seeking sponsors for his planned match. The challengers, Short or Timman. All of that now paled in the light of the news from Sveti Stefan. But then there was a little unrest, to make things more interesting.

In the daily papers those days, several times we came across articles on the match with a catchphrase related to the events of the day, and it said "the so-called world championship". After that second game, Bobby asked us to intervene immediately so that every possible indiscretion could be punished by removal of the credentials of the journalists who used that phrase.

It seemed that the third game in the series, which likewise ended in a division of points, also produced satisfaction with such a result. Spassky was playing black, but that evening Eugene told me quietly as we talked in the yard of the villa that, to his thinking, the Russian-French grandmaster was actually closer to victory. And then, Spassky showed his real quality. Here I finally met Bobby also when he lost at the chess board. From the retrospective of looking back on the tragic destiny of this man, it is easy to understand that these losses were less painful than those he faced in life.

Through the chess related and biographical literature, stories and narratives, but especially through newspaper articles, the claim was asserted that one of the key reasons for Bobby's oddness, his disrespect of chess and life etiquette and norms, was actually his overwhelming fear of loss in the game that was his life. They said, "He cried after games where he didn't manage to win." I hope we can agree that there is nothing wrong with a man's tears. We remember the knights of literature or reality, the heroes who did not cry, because courage is an attitude but also an emotion. In order to, at the extreme, give one's life for someone or something, it must be loved passionately, and that is the ultimate of sensitivity of the soul and the ecstasy of the spirit. Thus, the Bobby Fischer whom I knew, and I met him in his very best years, would never have moistened his face with rain from heaven of the soul running down its face.

Bobby's remarkable egocentricity was not familiar with such emotion, not even in himself or for himself. Feelings were a flash, a thing of the moment or circumstance. Whatever brought them out, they were as fleet as a deer, as steady as the wind, and they lasted as long as the moment that separates silence from sound. Even though he deeply felt and recognized his own pain, to him it was like a nagging tightness in his chess, it took expression in a dull stare on his face, and to his ear it echoed like the unpleasant sound of metal balls slamming into one another. Thus, there were no tears even in the midst of life's hopelessness and suffering, because for him they had a specific frequency, vibration and color.

He experienced defeat at the board as a mistaken momentary rhythm in the symphony of his exceptionalness, a bad day which "would never happen again." His self-confidence at chess was stabile and immovable. After a defeat, he would offer his hand to Spassky and, putting on his famous leather visor, he would gracefully head for the car with a grimace on his face that looked like a forced smile. Although he lived chess, the internal winds of his thought blew in from the direction of the most hidden corners of his soul, and as such had an influence on him as an individual playing chess.

After the first brilliant victory and two ferocious draws, the first defeat came. The Queen's Gambit, which equalized the match at 1:1, actually had no great effect on Bobby's mood. Those days in an interview with the Spanish paper *El Pais*, Kasparov piped up, emphasizing that the renewed measuring of time in chess should be turned back to the Fischer-Kasparov match. After that, Garry would be willing to play Fischer, under the condition that "Fischer's talent at chess be more important to the public than his neo-Nazi leanings."

Then, the second defeat in a row came. Watching from the sidelines, it seemed that a crisis was on the horizon. For a moment, the journalists seem to forget the brilliance of the game's opening in the light of Bobby's loss with white. Spassky was inspired and enthused.

After this came Fischer's demand – a glass wall between him and the public. But, somehow from the very beginning Bobby had said a couple of times, though not in the form of an ultimatum, that they ought to undertake this task of separating him from the observers present. On September 10, the organizer fulfilled the champion's wish. And as the chess duel intensified, after all the long, turbulent days of his arrival in Yugoslavia, his preparations for the match, in the background the other events sailed into calmer waters. Everyone present—the observers, journalists, guests and the large number of people in the organization and accompanying services—got their own comfortable place in carefully built tower of blocks. Even so, the torch for the conflagration of future events was already prepared, even though it was far away, still invisible at that point.

As if in a film, the director was using a wide-screen shot, the storyline was successfully carrying the story, but as usual, the essence was in the details, in the news between the lines, the truth in hints. Back on August 16, almost unnoticed, a short piece in the printed media: "The contract between the government of Montenegro and *Jugoskandic* owned by Jezdimir Vasiljević will be suspended until the UN sanctions on Yugoslavia are removed. Its reactivation will occur three days after they are suspended." The news passed almost unnoticed, it seemed benign, and it did not indicate misfortune in the perspective of that time.

That a pebble thrown into a quiet lake will cause a movement in the water which will sooner or later be called a wave was to be proven by the enigmatic story of the television rights for the match. This segment of the financial element remained contractually unclear and unfinished between Bobby Fischer and Jezdimir Vasiljević. Of course, the very organization and occurrence of this spectacular event achieved its primary goal in the interest of state since it attracted great attention from the world media, which at least for a moment was distracted from the events of the war and the participation of a "sanctioned" country in them, to the greatest possible event that could happen at that time. But it seemed that this incredible potential was not used to its utmost. Namely, in the organizational and financial circles, the names of the large production companies changed during the negotiations and settlements, as to who would be the possible owner of the rights to the broadcast, recording and commentary on this marvelous chess event. From that multitude, through the filter of expectations and plans, public and private, very early in the chronology the name UFA media became pronounced. Though that part of the negotiation was entirely in the domain of Mr. Vasiljević, Bobby was regularly updated as to its progress. The energetic banker convinced his chess darling from time to time that this part of the puzzle would also fit perfectly into the image that was to be remembered. One day before the opening and beginning of the match, we were informed that the representatives of the above-mentioned German media group were coming to Sveti Stefan to finalize the agreement.

Indeed, the guests were met on the terrace of the villa that we called "main headquarters" among ourselves. Three elegant gentlemen returned our heartfelt greetings, and after a few minutes they went into the sitting room and soon closed the doors. My ward knew about all of this, of course, as he sat thirty feet away at the chess board, living out his one and only life.

The Greatest Secret of Bobby Fischer

After something more than an hour, I got a summons from the negotiation room. The guests had already gone, Jezda gathered together a couple of his closest collaborators, his sleeves rolled up, his shirt unbuttoned, leisurely smoking a pipe. Without a lot of business chatter, direct as always, "They are offering seven million dollars. I'm asking for fifteen, not a penny less. If they don't accept it, the Japanese will," he pronounced with authority, with a voice that I can still hear to this day. "In any case, Fischer will get two million, regardless of the agreed final amount for the owner of the television rights."

Decisive, precise. The rather short, plump, but very lucid and intelligent banker nodded his head at me, "Let's go tell Bobby." Though the gate squeaked and we knocked, Fischer was aroused from his concentration only when I spoke his name. Whenever someone would suddenly interrupt his analysis or training games, and that was "allowed" only in special situations, he always looked like he had just been awakened. It would take a couple of minutes for the connection to reality to be re-established.

He turned with his playing chair slightly to the left, toward us, with the usual smile on his face. He listened, but he did not have many questions. When he talked about business matters, he did so with a different rhythm and speech pattern. Slightly drawling, as if singing, his eyebrows raised, he would turn his wrist as if he was tightening or loosening something. In fact, my dear Bobby was clumsily attempting to act like he understood the business world, the game of numbers printed on greenbacks which existed in real time and space. All of that was far from him, but he had to leave the impression that he understood, that he was absorbing it all, although he really wished it would all be over quickly, without pain to his soul. The real truth is that he was fatigued and tortured by all that in a special way, so he wanted this conversation to be over as soon as possible, like every other conversation about concrete things.

"Two million—okay," said Bobby, his right leg swinging the chair back to the chess board. The television rights to this match, despite the huge interest in them (with certainty we can say that they were somewhere between seven and fifteen million dollars),

The Greatest Secret of Bobby Fischer

were never sold to anyone. It certainly could have been done. Why wasn't it? We shall follow this thread.[42]

One thing is certain: Jezdimir Vasiljević never, not at any cost, wanted to cheat Bobby. Although today in most of this world the concept "business" is quite often equated with the term "fraud", at that time this respectable businessman, seen through the prism of the emotional dimension, certainly had no evil intentions or hidden agendas, at least not concerning the legendary chess player.

Their relationship from the time Fischer arrived in Yugoslavia until Jezdimir's departure from it was one of respect, with the addition that the host and financier showed clear and strong liking for his and our guest. When he would rush into my hotel room, alone or with his entourage, he would first ask, "How is OUR BOY?" In that phrase he clearly showed his background and the tradition he came from and that he felt gentleness and warmth, almost parental directness toward Bobby.

When the demanding American would ask for something, something one might call excessive or exaggerated, Jezdimir would nod and grunt a crude "he's full of it again", give a smile that meant he understood and say, "Give it to him, make sure it gets done..." This care was not based on financial expectation or any other kind, but arose from the interesting personality of the eastern Serbian peasant, a young clarinet player in exile, a worker cutting cane day and night in far away Australia, a stock market whiz, an exile from Israel, and today a resident of Belgrade's central prison. The chess player respected and appreciated his Serbian ally up until the moment when, by force of circumstances, through his own will or someone else's, he left and fled from Belgrade and thus became one more conspirator on Bobby's horizon, in the endless mass of Satanic heads who wanted him to hurt, suffer and die.

An infamous epilogue also awaited the agreed commercialization of the new way of measuring time at the chess

---

[42] The first press conference, the match opening and all the rest was freely recorded by the state-owned television stations of Montenegro and Serbia.

board, materialized in the Fischer clock, the financial extent of which was valued at about twenty million dollars. Yet, the above-mentioned thread will quickly bring us to an answer to that question as well.

So, a pebble had been tossed on the surface of a quiet lake. From whose hand did it fly? There were no waves, or rather they still had not reached the shore. If the match had been held in the winter on majestic nearby Durmitur, we would say that a snowball had set off down the slopes and that an avalanche would soon reach the quiet village at the foot of the mountain.

The sixth game saw a draw. It lasted for seven hours. At move twenty, a pawn down, the Queen's Gambit was used again.

Bobby was close to defeat but he somehow managed to reach the quiet harbor of the draw. From the conversation at the table that evening, it seemed that Fischer enjoyed "saving" this game.

On Sveti Stefan – harmony and peace. Everything well organized. The rivals worked day and night on chess, each with his team and at his own rhythm. In the off hours, my ward preferred to swim, with one rather unsuccessful excursion into tennis, while Boris regularly practiced it. One pleasing fact for everyone was that all the pressures which had come from all sides earlier (political – domestic and foreign, the media) ceased for a while, and a positive atmosphere settled onto everyone and everything. People from all over the world, journalists, photographers and cameramen, guests and observers, numerous collaborators from various professions and jobs, the hotel staff, and the wonderful local folk from the coast and mountains, got to know each other better day after day, so that mutual understanding and trust was achieved as a result of those circumstances. There was harmony in Bobby's relationship with Zita. The champion's young escort, as the journalists usually called her, did not go to the beach with us but she would show up when she wanted to. The couple usually visited and hung out late at night, regardless of the time the games were to be played.

However, in addition to this Bobby was intensively waiting for someone else. One morning, visibly upset, he called me into his room to tell me that I must immediately find a person for whom he had been searching for days. That was the first time I heard the name Miyoko Watai. He was holding a message ready to be faxed:

MIYOKO WATAI
998137223384
FROM: BOBBY FISCHER
FAX: 086/62-223

Dear Miyoko,

I have tried to call you several times, but I keep getting a funny sound and no one answers. Now I will try to send you this # by fax. Please answer me immediately.

Sincerely, Bobby.

Thus, we will introduce another dear person to Fischer into the story, as she was later to visit him twice and stay for a while in Belgrade, and in the future she was to play a really important role.

This newly attained perspective was to be fully expressed in the next three games which the uncrowned chess king won and thus came to a 4:2 lead. The overture to Fischer's well-known winning rhythm was hinted to in the seventh game. Fanfare and timpani resound of the Pyrenees. The Spanish game. Fischer, playing while, forced Spassky to resign at the forty-fourth move. A temporary peak, the eighth trial of strength, the champion's favorite, the King's - Indian Defense.

In the ninth game Spassky, now a bit fatigued, made a crude oversight in the twentieth move and Fischer won as white, waving Spanish colors.

The judge of the match, the thoughtful and friendly Lothar Schmidt, and his aid Nikola Karaklajić did not have much to do. At the board and all around it, everything was in perfect order. There was not a hint of Fischer's well-known whimsicalness. The reason for that surely lay in the fact that he had already gotten everything he wanted.

But Boris was having some small health problems. The doctor's report said he was having kidney troubles. Above all, the amount of nervousness, the early rising, the lack of sleep, and the prescribed tranquilizers. In the *Times* there was praise for Fischer's play at the end of the seventh game, while the Argentine newspapers describe Sveti Stefan as the nicest place in the world to play chess.

One of Bobby's favorite pastimes appeared suddenly, a strangely strong desire to become an art collector, especially of oil on canvas. Namely, on Sveti Stefan, right next to the reception area, when one climbs a few dozen steps and passes by the tiny church on the left side, one reaches an art exhibition gallery. That year, all the exhibitions were taken by famous Serbian and Montenegrin painters. Drawn by the importance of the event, the masters of the brush which expresses the mind, soul and spirit brought their best works to decorate the days and nights on Sveti Stefan. The exhibition openings were especially nice. The guests, connoisseurs and acquaintances, with a glass of the best Montenegrin red wine in their hand, talked into the night which had the fragrance of cypress, sea salt and the perfume of the Serbian-Montenegrin jet-set.

Incidentally, the path we took on our customary evening walks by the sea went inevitably by this place. Once we ran into a real crowd that was attending one of those events, the premiere of the, then well-known but now famous, painter from Belgrade and Paris, Cile Marinković. I had already had the opportunity to meet my charming and genial countryman and his family, so it was not hard for me to recognize him in the crowed small room. My protégé did not like crowds or events like this one, and it seemed to me that he would get angry for my "mistake". But I instinctively waved to Cile and with two quick steps directed Bobby to the artist. Since he had no choice, which was certainly not my intention but a momentary solution, the two of them were introduced. With amazing speed their conversation took on quite a pleasant tone, and Bobby was surprisingly kind. The artist showed his works, his inspiration framed and hanging on the walls. The chess master stood before a couple of the paintings and asked for further explanation of their symbolism and meaning. Since time was running mercilessly, our walk that evening was forgotten. It seemed to me that Bobby was enjoying himself, but I was not certain how well he understood what was being shown and explained to him, because he was searching for parallels to his favorite comic strip in what he was seeing. Whatever the case, "in the good spirit of our people and traditional hospitality" Mr. Marinković decided to give his unexpected visitor the picture of his choice, so that his guest would not leave empty-handed. Bobby took a long time to choose from the paintings being offered, perhaps even too long since a gift was in question. Finally he chose a painting that stood out from the others because of its more noticeable red and black colors. The famous, skilled artist made this gesture from the bottom of his heart, and saw us off satisfied with a smile on his face, regardless of the fact that the other guests were being slightly neglected.

Bobby was happy as he carried the large canvas under his arm and walked quickly toward his villa. Happy at least for the next few hours.

The gentle freshness of the autumn air and the breeze from the mountains lightly caressed the curtains on the windows as Bobby and Eugene sat at the board. After a few hours, since we had encroached deeply on the new day, Fischer went off to rest.

I was sitting in a chair in the garden reading from the light of the windows on the ground floor. The moments while the champion was asleep were the only time I had for myself in those years. I never smoked in front of Fischer, and he never found out that my nightly *Cohiba busto* cigar was my little secret, that with it I gathered my thoughts and feelings. Just when the smoke of my Havana headed skyward in the night, a well known sound came to me, the sound of a 240 pound man coming down the narrow wooden stairs. "Nesh, Nesh," I heard him calling, "where are you?"

I turned the book over on chair, unreadable to specters in the night, I did not extinguish the cigar (praise be to God that Cuba exists), I just left it there and went inside.

"Here I am, Bobby," I said.

"You know," he was waving his arms about, "you shouldn't have let me choose that picture."

The Greatest Secret of Bobby Fischer

I knew what was happening, but I still had to express my surprise.

"I was looking at it before I went to sleep. It's beautiful, but it has too much red and black. It is somehow somber, strange."

"But Bobby," I tried, "you made a great choice. The painting is valuable in every sense, and I'm sure you'll find a place for it in your new home. It certainly doesn't have to be in the bedroom, but it would be a lovely addition, let's say, in your office or library."

My protégé was somehow hanging his head, a little sad, and with a bit of anger he said the thing I was afraid of, "Please, go find the painter and ask him to exchange the painting."

"But it's three in the morning, and it certainly would not be polite to wake up the artist who is sleeping by now, and especially not for that reason. Please, let's wait for the sun to rise."

"You think so?" he asked, his eyes wide open.

"Please, Bobby, we'll take care of it tomorrow. If you're going to have nightmares because of 'a bad choice', we can bring the painting down here to the work room."

He drawled, "Nooo!" and shook his head, I had him right where I wanted him. He did not want to part with it after all. With regret, he said, "All right then."

"Go to bed, Bobby, don't worry, we'll get this fixed."

Now the sound of him going upstairs, the door closed, Bobby had gone to bed. I went back into the yard, my thinking aid was still smoking, and the blue covers of "The Ray of the Microcosm" by the great Petar Petrović Njegoš,[43] was again available for my attention.

The next morning at brunch which we usually had around noon, I confronted my ward with the idea that whimsy can be good for changing one's life rhythm, it could be interesting and cute for those who really love you and wish to understand you, but it could also be bad for your reputation if it is not bound at least by some sort of polite behavior. I was clear, "I am sure that Cile would gladly to do what we want to ask him, but it would be proper in the least and very impolite. It would be nice," I said,

---

[43] Petar II Petrović Njegoš, Montenegrin archbishop and poet.

"when the money arrives for the match, for you to go and buy one of the paintings of this renowned artist. If you saw something last night that you really like, I will go right now and pick it up for you in the wink of an eye."

"But, no not that," he said, "just let it be."

Although Bobby accepted my suggestion, and I must say he always did, I was a little afraid of every further meeting with Cile whom we met often because our paths crossed when he was out, or walking with his family on the beach. As if there was a split second for something shameful in those moments. However, it never happened. But, Bobby did say, "Nesh, please always tell me when there's a new exhibition opening," whimsically, lying back in his lounge chair on the beach.

He was staring at the newspaper in front of him. I put down my own reading materials.

From the corner of his eye he saw the expression on my face and, understanding its meaning, he roared in laughter for some time. We had come to an understanding.

So it was that my dear Bobby suddenly obtained a passion for collecting artistic works which, just imagine, ended at the moment when the money for the match arrived and he could buy them himself. That summer he received as gifts a couple of marvelous, valuable works from world famous Serbian painters and sculptors.

The tenth game saw another draw. The Nimzo-Indian defense ended in a division of points at the sixty-eighth move.

The intensity of events kept us all tied to momentary happenings, not allowing our thoughts, wishes and plans to turn to the future. Still, hope was created at that time in the background of the match, mostly through the creativity and vision of the match director, Janos Kubat, with the support of Mr. Vasiljević, which seemed real, a sketch of upcoming events.

This event with its resounding title "the revenge match of the twentieth century" in that form was only supposed to be a hint of the things to come. Interest in those things was also concretely expressed in the multitude of contacts which regularly followed the individual events. After the duel with Spassky, with whom could the American grandmaster be able to play? Even though the comments of two possible candidates, Anatoly Karpov and Garry Kasparov, about Fischer's return were *a priori* negative, the statements of these two world champions hinted at a certain hope that such a super spectacle might actually take place. Kasparov was especially for the idea, or at least so it seemed. But, the direction the plans and reflections took a turn, it seems. The potential "target" was Kasparov. During the time I spent with Bobby Fischer it was easy for me to feel the hate that filled the aura of his personality, from which came flames of bitterness, resentment and defiance that were aimed at absolutely every Soviet (Russian) chess player of the past and of that time.

On the other hand, the grandmasters being aimed at with such arrows did not spare him either in their rhetoric and written words. Did it all have to be that way? From Bobby Fischer's position it certainly did. He was unable to erase the unwavering essence of his personality from its structure. From another standpoint, it was quite understandable that the grandmasters of the Russian school answered him with cannonades from the most powerful weapons.

And it had always been easier for them because there were more of them. However, even before the announcements of the world media which Garry Kasparov gave after the death of Robert James Fischer in which he offered recognition to his great predecessor for his excellence in chess and the immeasurable contributions he had made to the game of millions in skill, talent, theory and practice, not least of which was the advancement of conditions, technical and material, for all the players in the world, I had a strange dream while I watched the legendary American as he sat in thoughtful silence or focused as he moved one of the wooden figures.

May dear departed Bobby forgive me, may Garry Kasparov forgive me. Just imagine. Apart from everything. In this dream moment, let there be no difference in age, background, political convictions, life experience, memories and future hopes for them, their vanity erased, prestige unimportant, the comments of others non-existent. From this moment – some twenty, twenty-five, or thirty years ago. In some nice place. Perhaps because of the strength of the impression that will not leave me, like an emotional hiccup, let it be the park at Miločer, in the early evening. The sea is foaming, the wind is fragrant, the clouds rush across the sky, and there is no sound, absolute quiet. There are no people, no birds, nothing breathing. Just the two of them at a chess board, Bobby and Garry. But they are not competing, they are playing with the figures on the black-and-white squares. If we could zoom in, I believe in this more than anything, we would see smiles on their faces, and if we turned up the sound we would hear them laughing.

Let us amputate everything except their magnificent love and passion for chess. In that image, I can see no one who looked more like Bobby Fischer than Garry Kasparov. If we erased everything except life on the chess board, I do not see anyone to whom Fischer could say more, or who would better understand him in terms of chess than the grandmaster from Baku, understand at the precise time when their lives overlapped. However, that "great smallest" common denominator would never and will never connect them, except in legend, because opposite to everything else it was too small for reality, for the one-dimensional world that does not recognize dreams. Slowly, one step after another, they will head in different directions as they walk these paths. Bobby into eternity (Plato would say in Socrates apology: "Now it is time to be going. You to live and I to die. But which of us has the happier prospect is unknown to anyone but God"), and Garry beside him, I hope, into a beautiful future. Again, in the early phases of the story on Sveti Stefan, thought was given to upcoming events. Bobby did not directly participate in making those plans. At the first press conference he said that he would think about the future only after the duel with Spassky and some rest. But everything was headed in the direction of new great events. Prize money for the next match was already prepared. The venue – Budapest, the opponent – Judith Polgár. While still far away, two million dollars was enough to capture the interest of the influential family of chess masters. It was necessary also to get Fischer's confirmation for something like that (it seems likely that it could have happened because he had always considered the super-talented Hungarian chess player to be an attractive and worthy opponent), but just in case Boris Spassky was prepared as alternative in the background. However, the very wealthy Dutch financier did not want to hear of it. Fischer or no one. And after that, Garry Kasparov, still too far away, with too much insecurity, with too many maybes, but also... The prize money – fifty million dollars! They would play in four cities. The first idea – Moscow, New York, London and Belgrade, perhaps organized by the *Jugoskandic* chess federation. A nice plan, never carried out, but I believe that it was not impossible had later events not closed the door of fate on such a fantastic possibility.

Where there is beauty in abundance there is also evil which threatens, hard to detect at first and hidden in unexpected places, rejoicing proudly at human vanity which pushes us into excursions too high for us, not caring in our blindness about the signs of the onrushing fall. In the context of the chess match on Sveti Stefan and in Belgrade, it certainly lent a great stimulus and impulse to those who looked more carefully at reality. Could anything bad at all happen to the man who had invested so much money in this spectacle, to the man who brought Bobby Fischer "back to life", which no one had managed to do in the twenty years after Reykjavik? Can it not be understood that the entire event was set up, when one takes into account the fact that the TV rights were not sold, or that the perfection and exploitation of the Fischer Clock was not carried out, as a disposable form which served to break the media and information blockade to the outside world, and to establish belief on the domestic front among the wider public that *Jugoskandic* was there to stay? We would receive answers in the upcoming time.

To be fair, many clients managed to "earn" huge amounts of money before the empire disintegrated, while others certainly lost something or everything. Yet, in those months all that seemed completely clear. "The successful banker" was on the side of the fence which made absolute power possible in Serbian-Montenegrin Yugoslavia. On the other hand, "the hope of the west" was the above-mentioned federal premier, Mr. Milan Panic. With his appearance on the political scene, the American businessman of Serbian origins was supposed to introduce what some hoped were democratic winds and push the sailboat of events in the Balkans toward a quieter harbor. Panic sailed into the vicinity of Sveti Stefan on his luxurious yacht. And while he was enjoying himself on his boat, Vasiljević decided to entertain himself with a little skit. One late afternoon he hired an old fishing-tourist boat and asked a group of people who worked in the match's organization to get on it at 4 o'clock. "The star of the show", the businessman of the year, appeared on time, but his appearance hinted at the forthcoming comedy. He had a dozen or so thick gold necklaces on and hefty rings on each of his fingers. His costume was completed by an interesting Hawaiian shirt with all the colors of the rainbow. He boarded the "ship" and ordered the captain to circle the president's yacht a few times. Merry and inspired, he made fun of the behavior of the federal premier, and joyfully "quoted" him. Thus in an indirect, but somehow up front way, he benignly announced the conflict of the federal and republic institutions which would ultimately lead to the disintegration of the Serbian-Montenegrin federation, when Milošević's armed police forces would capture the building of the federal police in a much later context.

From his very first encounter with Mr. Panic, my ward had insisted that he never wanted to see the premier again and he asked me to make sure that all meetings and contact, even accidental ones, were avoided. The chess master never liked the man's exaggerated gesticulations, his hyper-energy or his quasi-optimism. This would not have been a hard assignment if, on the other hand, the American businessman cum Serbian politician, had not constantly insisted on making contact with Fischer.

This was quite understandable, because Bobby always had his favorite on the Serbian political scene. That was, of course, Slobodan Milošević. It was not a matter of over-glorification because Fischer always had his viewpoint, but even before they met later on during the second part of the match in Belgrade, the chess player was deeply convinced that the president of Serbian was the incarnation of resistance to the new world order, of the rebellion against American hegemony and the unjust structure of all and everything under the heavens. Asking for first-hand information, carefully listening while I translated newspaper articles about Milošević, watching television news programs and listening to his favorite radio, he had already pieced together an image of the personality of the president of his host country. It was enough for the strong positive feelings Bobby had, since he was in a country which was rejected like him, reprimanded and unjustly punished, and yet ready to resist.

Fischer did not return to chess, of course, in order to support someone or something, but the series of coincidences still somehow fit into his ideal. Then the entire story flew high into the blue skies of ecstasy about justice, courage and love of truth, which from this perspective can be briefly written and read as utopia. Many of the native inhabitants of Serbia and Montenegro, among whom I would also be without all this information, believed in quick judgment that in a special way Robert Fischer loved the country and people who had extended him their hospitality.

I will be sad if I dispel someone's illusions – those "emotions", as stable as smoke on the water, lasted only as long as his self-satisfaction needed them and as long as they were practical. That was why Bobby did not want to answer the question about the war in the territories of the former Yugoslavia that was among the first asked at the press conference on September 1. He had no special feelings for the Croats, Moslems (Bosniaks) or the Serbs, nor did he ever express condolences for their sufferings.

He considered the whole thing to be like a video game, the controls of which were being held by someone far away, someone powerful and merciless. The cries in the dark, the screams from the pit, suffering and pain; the Bosnian pain, Croatian pain, Serbian pain, no matter what their causes these were the effects, he saw them in the media but they were not of special interest to him. His memories were important to him: the exceptional textiles from Varaždin, the tasty oriental food of Sarajevo, the tournament long ago on Bled ("how clean is the air there"), swimming on the coast in Montenegro (which is good for one's physical condition and health), grapes from Macedonia, and of course the money of his host. Much later when, taking a lot of risks, I moved us from

The Greatest Secret of Bobby Fischer

Belgrade to Budapest, Bobby took with him, besides his personal effects, also one, or better said one more, suitcase full of unbridled hatred.

Although in the match announcements, probably to quiet the conscience, it was hinted that 150,000 dollars would be donated to charity, which probably never happened even in spite of the fact that the subtitle of the event was "match of friendship", all of that was far from reality. From the outset it was absolutely clear that the "revenge match of the twentieth century" was to have its chess face shown to the public, and that my privileged place was to offer me the chance not only to get to know Bobby Fischer in close detail, but also to watch up close that thing called politics and to observe future history from a distance of three feet.

Vladimir Dedijer was a "famous" historian, the biographer of the president of the geographically large and internationally significant Yugoslavia, Josip Broz Tito, with whom he was a comrade from the war, and he was also a post-war dissident. Once he said that politics is a public thing, that it is like a soccer match where everything is clear: the rules of the game, the roles of the referees, and the tasks of the players; everything is clear and transparent to the public. Through this experience I came to believe, and today I know – politics is anything but that.

The eleventh game of the match was another gem which would remind the world of Fischer's genius at chess. It was perhaps the most attractive according to the evaluations of all the grandmasters and the journalists present. As if he knew or intuited, that day Bobby asked that we not go to the match that day by our usual route, but rather that we take a leisurely walk. The end of September that year was warm and sunny. The high heat had passed (it was nicest in the water around noon), while the fairy tale brisk mornings announced autumn, and the roiling seas in the evening testified to the fact that Poseidon had said good-bye to summer. On that September 20, Bobby won playing the Sicilian Defense, for the finale in high style and a triumph in the first part of the match with a score of 5:2.

It was time to move out. The American chess master was satisfied with his results. The organizers as well. The last few days

The Greatest Secret of Bobby Fischer

on Sveti Stefan were spent in leisurely walks and rest (I mean the champion rested), but there are no insignificant moments when you are working with someone whose name is Bobby Fischer, and this would be proven in one more sequence in the film of my memory. One of those days after lunch we set off on a slow walk – Bobby, Eugene and I.

We did not go along our customary route by the sea toward Miločer, but along a path that lead toward the highway and the mountain hinterlands. While my friends were talking, I suddenly saw the possibility of "great danger" approaching us in the form of a "camouflaged" Dimitrije Bjelica. Wearing a hat, dark glasses, a retro look of the fifties, with an unusual beard, in blue shorts, barechested, he was heading right toward us to the slapping sound of his flip-flops. In times long past, this chess journalist and world traveler had been known as one of Bobby's friends, but after their camaraderie and collaboration in Sarajevo in the seventies (on a documentary TV series about chess greats in which Fischer commented on selected games of grandmasters that he thought to be the most important in the history of the game) they came into a real conflict. He then sued Mr. Bjelica because of some articles published in the paper *Plavi vjesnik*, entitled "My Life". With that name, Dimitrije did not mean his own life, but the life path of the greatest player of all time.

The court found the author innocent of the charges. However, already in our first longer conversation after he arrived in Yugoslavia, Bobby named the man who was now drawing dangerously close to us as a *persona non grata*. The path was relatively narrow, we could not get past one another, there were only a few steps to an unavoidable encounter. I stepped swiftly forward in order to prevent the worst and to ensure that they did not see each other. Bobby and Eugene were looking at each other as they talked, and then Dimitrije made a memorable move. Namely, on his right shoulder, the one further from us, he was carrying a blue and red air mattress which completely fit into his styling with the sunglasses. The wily passerby said "hello" quite loudly and when Bobby looked in his direction, he had switched the mattress to his left shoulder and thus hidden the face of the polite "stranger".

One step, a second, a third... Did I manage to count to five? "Nesh," and again that facial expression, "you know that man who just passed us... I think I recognize his voice. That wasn't perhaps...?"

I looked at Eugene whose face had taken on the color of the red t-shirt he was wearing.

"Yes," I said, "that was Dimitrije Bjelica." My protégé said nothing, but I knew him very well and words were unnecessary. Vesuvius just before an eruption. A moment, I was waiting for the reaction, and then it came. "Nesh, please got to the beach, find that... . . and tell him that I answered him accidentally. I don't want him to take it as a sign of my good will." Instantly I imagined myself on one of the beaches, the main one on Sveti Stefan, only hotel guests had access to it, but Dimitrije was not one of them: I'm hopping over sunning semi-naked bodies to explain "the unfortunate circumstance" under which that "hello" was spoken. Perhaps it looked ridiculous or strange, but such and similar trivia always separated people from the uncrowned king of chess, because in that fatal second you turned from being a friend into being a criminal. But, I knew from even earlier that the certainty of my position lay in the fact that I myself held such an important place on the map of Bobby's everyday life that he did not want to lose me. So, he heard clearly my words when I promised that I would pass the message on to Mr. Bjelica that day, and that we could safely continue our walk. So the moment passed, but my ward asked me several times before he finally went to bed that day if I had kept my promise.

The following day was designated for the special "experience" of getting Bobby ready to travel. Zita and Eugene with his wife helped us in the careful packing of seventeen large suitcases.

Behind us was now the first part of the match, the precise result in chess, and a lot of fulfilled expectations. A long line of cars now left empty Sveti Stefan behind and headed for the airport in Tivat. I have been to Sveti Stefan many times since 1992. Sometimes it happens to me during my stays in Montenegro that I feel a strong urge and desire to see the place where all of this happened. I have gone around this enchanting island on winter nights at two in the morning when there was no one around, and when it all looked eerie and sad, or on summer mornings at the height of the tourist season when everything was humming from visitors and crowds. I felt no nostalgia, because time stood still the moment when we took one last careful look around all the rooms and shut the door on villa 118.

The airplane was waiting for us on the runway, a happy and satisfied group of people took off directly for the Serbian capital, to Belgrade, where the second part of the match was to be played and where the entire story would receive its epilogue. If Mr. Vasiljević demonstrated his importance by the fact that we had taken off from the military airport at Batajnica on our way to Montenegro, this time we were "honored" by the fact that no one checked our documents or baggage, and the entire team entered the plane with our weapons on our belts. The flight was late, less than an hour to the destination, and a new line of automobiles with their lights flashing. The fact that we were taken to the Intercontinental Hotel by a Mercedes from the fleet of the president of Serbia may seem to be a piquant detail now, but back then it was quite understandable.

Our dear American guest settled into a suite on the seventh floor, while my room was right across the hall.

We all breathed a sigh of relief when all seventeen bags finally arrived in the living area of his suite.

The time spent in Montenegro and the first part of the match brought an air of exceptionalness to Fischer's comeback, uncertainty in the achievements of chess, a lot of excitement, but in addition to everything, a feeling of Mediterranean gaiety and lightness.

Before us stood a new challenge which was to quickly turn the fairy tale into a story full of twists and turns, then into an action thriller, a political drama, and many years later, with a delayed effect, into the tragedy of a genius.

CHAPTER 10.

RIGGED GAMES

How does one explain the inexplicable, how does one write about the inconceivable? It is right here that we face such a grandiose dilemma. The time I spent with Bobby was highlighted by the aura of our great mutual respect that resulted from my sincere care for the luminary of the game on 64 squares and his understanding and acceptance of that fact. Such, for many perhaps an unexpected, bridging of the generation gap (Bobby was fifty back then, and I was twenty seven years old) and anything else that could stand between us, led to that even from this distance in time, as in the moment when it all took place, for me not even with the patina of time has a single dilemma arisen about the essence of the character and work of what the controversial champion was in life and remained in legend.

Robert James Fischer was not merely one of millions of people around the world who have throughout history, as well as today, moved black and white figures on a board of magical similar-colored squares. It is certain that in every segment of human existence, there is a personality, an individual or a phenomenon that, with its magnificence, creativity and all-encompassing work covers an expanse of material pertaining to the notion to which it is related. In this case: the genius Paul Morphy, Bobby thought, Steinitz, Alekhine, Capablanca, certainly one of the greatest, Samuel Reshevsky, believe it or not, Fischer mentioned him the most, Tal, Petrosian, Karpov, Kasparov—chess-players, minds, magnitudes, paragons, leaders, teachers and giants. But if we were to whisper the term 'chess' into the ears of millions of people worldwide, of all ages, racial, social and cultural backgrounds, the spoken word, the flash of thought, the first association would be, is, and always will be Bobby Fischer.

Certainly, the Brooklyn scoundrel, the hero of Reykjavik, the poor man from Pasadena, the Serbo-Montenegrin rebel, the Japanese prisoner and the Icelandic resident of Valhalla, earns this intransience of name and image with his immeasurable inborn or God-given talent with which he pushed back boundaries, gave new forms, and with virtuosity, like Rubens on a canvas, made the chessboard glimmer like Venus in the night sky above the desert.

Of course the set and sequence of historical circumstances, because it must be said that the match in Iceland in 1972 was more of a clash of worlds in the midst of the Cold war than a battle for chess supremacy, did in no small part contribute to his planet-wide popularity, but it is almost as if this does not bear so much significance for this story. For Bobby Fischer breathed, dreamed and lived chess. Everything else, daily activities, reading the newspaper, books, conversations, long walks, those were irrelevant fragments obscuring the moves, analyses, sudden ideas, winning combinations under the spotlight, opposite a powerless opponent who concedes defeat.

Look at him, at dinner, suddenly, over a half-eaten steak, in the middle of a conversation with those present, he deftly takes out of the left pocket of his leather jacket a small, folding chess set, his favorite one, magnetic, in leather binding, where instead of black figures, red ones oppose the white, and wanders off in thought, swiftly moving pawns, rooks, kings and queens. His grimacing and wide eyes, aloof from the din, tell us he has sailed off to the high seas of chess theory and practice. Twenty minutes later, with a thoroughly rehearsed motion of his left and right hands, the set in in his pocket once more, and the conversation resumes where it was interrupted.

Would I over-exaggerate if I were to say that Fischer's entire physique was predetermined to play chess? Huge feet gave him a particular stability, immensely strong legs and back readied him to play hours-long games with ease, strong shoulders and arms resting on the table looked dominant and visually imposing against usually far more delicate opponents. His fingers were another story altogether. I spent hours watching that one game from his thumb to the little finger as they danced over the figures. A reflection of his thoughts and ideas. Each one carried out a function in this enchanting dance. The thumb moved the last line of larger and more important members of the royal elite and weaponry mostly horizontally; the index finger pushed pawns forward, without raising them off the board, the ring and little finger carried off captured members of the opposing troops, and the middle finger came to aid the left or right side of the hand that would certainly captivate Michelangelo with its size and perfection. Sometimes, both hands were in action, and from time to time, playing against a weaker partner, he would use his left hand exclusively, while in his right he would hold a transistor radio or a newspaper and casually read it, while a few of the grandmasters who by some means obtained the privilege of playing against the undefeated world champion would feverishly brainstorm how to stave off the inevitable checkmate for as long as possible.

When he was alone, he would lower his head to be level with the board and look at the starting position for a long time, as if he were savoring those moments of perfect order before the fanfare has announced the start of the match. And if someone were to happen to knock over a figure, Bobby would slowly and tenderly clean it with the palm of his hand, almost caressing it, and then gently put it back on the table.

To my protégé, chess was tantamount to talent, to primordial impulse, to scintillating inspiration. He never underestimated hard work, training, analysis, practice. But talent, talent, talent, that was the word Bobby used to describe the basis of his own or someone else's success in chess. He did, after all, return to the public spotlight bringing to the world a new take on the ancient game which would return it to its roots, to its very essence, the giftedness of the player himself. There, he was on sure ground, the comfortable cradle to which he gravitated. This new chess was to be played with the "old" type of figures. A computer would set up the starting position of the back row for each player individually just before the start of the game. Rook next to bishop in the middle, king on one end, queen perhaps on the other, and so on, arranged by random. The entirety of chess theory up to this day, millions of matches played, "tedious, thousand-times-played openings" leading into inevitable middles and logical endgames.

All that was waited for was merely a drop in concentration of one of the players, an incidental lapse. Cliché, monotony, Bobby would say, end, checkmate, a triumph without relish. When all of the previous theory is discarded, cast off to the times gone by, creation, ideas, and of course, inspiration, once more emerge to the light of day. He said, "Then the world will again see who the real master of the board is, who His Majesty, "the Chess Player" is.

Adding to this the new method of keeping time, represented by Fischer's chess clock, the new-old chess would again become an endless field of improvisation, imagination, creativity and skill. In the decades he spent in his voluntary isolation, Bobby developed to minute details this concept, which was at the time poised to fascinate the world.

Apart from his desire to fundamentally reform the game he loved and lived for, Fischer had another strong motive and a superhuman inspiration to turn his idea into a new reality. Namely, even before the start of the match, he had proclaimed he would, after the end, write and publish a book which would expose to the smallest detail and completely unmask the hypocrisy and malice of the chess establishment, of all leading chess players, a bunch of phonies, as Bobby would call them, lightly speaking, and which would finally uncover to the world the real past and present of the game.

The extensive personal documentation and the analyses of matches played before and after Fischer's zenith, especially those of Soviet grandmasters with an accent on those they played against each other, remained at that moment in the modest apartment in Pasadena, from where my protégé set off into a new life. Yet every detail of his convictions, which he would often supplant over the chessboard facing one of his opponents, he bore with him in the vault of his brilliant memory.

Namely, Robert James Fischer claimed that nearly all games and matches of ex-USSR players, and of those from the countries

The Greatest Secret of Bobby Fischer

of the former Warsaw pact, were meticulously colluded, literally from move to move, fluently rehearsed and acted out like a theater play. Analyzing countless such chess duels he would prove for hours on end that in a certain position, it was only logical to play a better, more purposeful move. With particular fervor, he authoritatively and firmly offered solutions which in his opinion had to have been noticed and applied. However, they were not, as they did not fit into the prearranged agreement.

Grandmasters who had access to the greatest player of all time before and after the match on Sveti Stefan and in Belgrade, were "forced" to at least verbally and out of principle accept these unreserved stances if they were to "survive" in Fischer's vicinity. It seemed to me that over time they themselves, understanding the strength of his arguments, more or less genuinely and fundamentally began to adopt such convictions. The champion's associate and long-time friend, the Serbian legend, grandmaster Svetozar Gligorić, was mostly quite reserved toward these forceful outbursts of passion transmuted into assertions. This lack of enthusiasm to uncompromisingly join the battle against a lack of principles in chess stemmed, in Bobby's opinion, from Gligorić's wish "not to antagonize anyone in his waning years". Eugene Torre, his second in the match, a wonderful, level-headed person very loyal to Bobby, supported such an outlook on the reality of the game on 64 squares, but without any particular euphoria, which was neither felt by a frequent guest to Belgrade in 1992-93, Argentine grandmaster Miguel Quinteros, who was also privileged to Bobby's time. There was no strong support for this track of thought from any other grandmasters I had an opportunity to meet at the time. Did this mean that Robert Fischer was not right? I certainly cannot say, but I can testify about moments in time.

Let us turn our attention back to the Fischer-Spassky match, Sveti Stefan, Belgrade, 1992. Bobby won the first game played on the gem of the southern Adriatic Sea and the Budva Riviera. Bobby tackled the beginning of the second part in an especially relaxed mood. After the serenity and the beauty of the Mediterranean, the capital of Serbia and Yugoslavia at the time, known for its cosmopolitan nature and spirit, presented an unusual playing field for this chess-master. A particularly positive atmosphere and a feeling of perpetual holiday were accentuated by the arrival of Ms. Miyoko Watai, with whom he shared a specifically close and multifaceted relationship.

Chess, then, was all but forgotten. Outings, walks around the city, lavish lunches and dinners that often ended with champagne made us all into a merry company whose leader appeared to forget his role in the ensuing events.

Many times, I tried tactfully and cautiously, with Mr. Vasiljević's help, to steer the course back into sport, the competitive track, but all efforts were in vain. The second part of the match began in the magnificent conditions of the Sava Centar, which was for this occasion transformed into Fischer's wonderland, into an environment he had always asked, hoped and wished for. But his form was not at the expected level. Mirth turned into anxiety and impatience. It was as if old specters reemerged from the blackness to cast a shadow over the magical Land of Oz. A crisis was looming. During the match, it was evident on Bobby's face, in increasingly frequent and longer-lasting glances toward the audience shrouded in darkness. An index finger, raised high in the air several times over the course of the match, was another sign that something was bothering him, as was his characteristic grumbling as he walked through the long hallways with echoing footsteps to his hotel room after the game.

Naturally this would not last too long, and the competitive pace would be reestablished, mainly with the help of Mr. Torre. But in this situation, someone else was waiting for an opportunity. It was Boris Spassky. If his ambition were focused on victory over the chess board, or on the desire to overtake publicity and attention, this story would be quite reasonable and legitimate. However, Boris wanted something else.

The Soviet chess-player with French citizenship had a completely different rhythm of life during the match. There was no pomp surrounding him, even though the organizers gave him as much attention as they did to Fischer. Minimal security, leisure, and nonchalance.

The Greatest Secret of Bobby Fischer

A short swim in the morning, either on the Sveti Stefan beach or in the Intercontinental Hotel pool, white shorts and shirt for a mandatory daily game of tennis, no particular requests or specific demands, a youngish, good-looking wife, all this completed the picture of the outward balance and harmony of Boris Spassky. Seemingly, the perfect gentleman. Decent English with a heavy Russian accent, polite and kind towards everyone, of steady, slow movements, reduced mimicry and gesticulation.

Such a "perfect gentleman" decided one morning to call my room's phone number. I was quite surprised when I heard his voice and introduction. Mr. Spassky and I, namely, had only a superficial and courteous relationship. A faint smile and an offered handshake in passing, two or three colloquial words, and that was mostly that. When he would occasionally ask me something pertaining to Bobby or the match itself, I would answer him tersely and with restraint. This was not only a matter of loyalty to Fischer, but also the fact that I already had too much work to do all day long.

To my surprise, Boris asked me I had the time to talk in his apartment. After a few moments of thinking, aware of my responsibility for the entirety of the chess spectacle, I accepted the invitation and said I would be right there. With Bobby still asleep, I left my faithful associates Dane and Voja on our seventh floor, and set off to the floor below to see what this particularity was. With a slight motion of the hand, Boris Spassky showed me where I should sit. A comfortable chair by the window across from which the famous Soviet grandmaster took a seat on a queen-size bed. Beige trousers, a yellow shirt and a simple sports sweater, with tennis shoes on his feet, would present an everyday morning casual look in days when matches were not being played. But the posture and facial expression of my host reminded me of a protagonist from one of Chekhov's stories. You know the moment when the wise but sly character has something to say (which he knows is neither true nor fair), but the goal is of higher importance and must be reached with no room for error. One could say that to that intent, the following picturesque description would be best: a facial expression akin to confusion (a child caught in theft before having stolen anything), eyes shifting back and forth, trying to see the invisible and determine which direction to turn to, head tucked into the shoulders (preemptively apologizing), a slight slouch (I may be a big star and an important person, but you are now more important since you can carry out my will), hands clasped above his knees (if he were a salesman, I would say it was to keep his palms from sweating, but he is a chess-player of the old Russian school, regardless of his French passport), so it seemed to me that he was hiding them, keeping me from reading something off them, and legs crossed, for his calculated openness to show its other, hidden, closed face. We were alone in the spacious room when Boris spoke, "You know, Bobby's form is not really that good".

I nodded lightly, more nonchalantly than quizzically or in agreement.

"He is playing at a very low level", continued my host and raised his eyebrows slightly more awaiting for my reaction. As I nodded again, saying nothing, a string of short sentences took shape, "I could win every game and very quickly end the match."

My temperament began to object, so I finally let out "So, what are we to do then?" with irony.

"It's simple," I continued, "If you can win, win. That's how you will prove your supremacy, history will record that Reykjavik might have been a coincidence, you will surely earn a lot more money in future matches and benefit in every way."

Energetically, quickly, as if he wanted to take flight, Spassky spread his arms, "Oh, that won't do, not at all."

"Why not?" I asked.

"From what I understand," said Boris in a raised voice, "this match was organized in the first place to break the media blockade of Yugoslavia, to show the vitality of your country and people that, despite all misfortunes, have strength, the interest and readiness to invest in such a spectacle.

"I certainly understand that all of this is also a proof of power for your political leadership that so defies the international community and demonstrates a willingness for inter-political exploitation. To that purpose, Fischer is far more interesting and 'usable' in the long term. I wouldn't want," Spassky pointed "to ruin such a machination."

Although there was truth in such a description, I could not accept it at that moment, but to lay the whole concept bare, I directly asked Boris, "I understand what you said, but what do you actually want from me?"

His body returned to its initial position, and he said quietly, "Three hundred thousand dollars more."

I could not believe my ears.

I had not made any movements, and had not said a word, so he added, "But I will settle for two hundred thousand dollars. Of course, I expect that from the organizers, not from you."

I stood up quickly, left my host where he was, and with a quick step, I headed to the door.

"Goodbye, Boris Vasilievich."

I did not get a response, or perhaps it was drowned out by the sound of the closing door. I said goodbye to my dear friends from the security of the man I left behind, and with swift steps that took me to the elevator, I seemed to want to escape from a place where someone had "struck a child, or killed a swallow."[44]

At that moment, money certainly was not the main problem. The match was well under way, having drawn the desired attention around the world, fulfilled expectations for the most part and broke through the media blockade of my country, attracting the attention of the sports, chess and general public. It is clear that no reasonable man would risk any kind of turbulence or disruption for a "prosaic" couple hundred thousand dollars.

My disbelief in all I had seen and heard stemmed from the discovery that the Russian-French grandmaster felt neither gratitude that this financial opportunity of a lifetime had even arisen, nor contentment that he was basking in the light of fortune at the close of his career. Because things could have been different. The main character in this whole story was, of course, Bobby Fischer. Even before the match, there were theories that the opponent of the American grandmaster could even be some other

---

[44] Erich Maria Remarque, *Shadows in Paradise*.

chess player of the newer guard. In that case, this event would not have been called "the revenge of the twentieth century," but the goal would have been accomplished either way.

A prize of five million dollars was waiting for Fischer, and Spassky would certainly accept an immeasurably smaller sum than that which was eventually paid out to him. Knowing that chess purses before the raising of all possible standards were in the tens of thousands of dollars, anything offered to him would be an unexpected and welcome windfall. But Bobby Fischer would not be what legend tells of him if he did not ultimately demand: the winner would get 3 400 000 dollars, and the defeated would get 1 600 000 dollars. After much insistence and many discussions on fairness, fair play and insanity, he accepted. He would get the winner's share, and if he were not to win, the opponent would get the defeat sum in any case. Of course, there was more money in the game than expected winnings coming from television rights, the new chess, Fischer's chess clock and so forth. Be that as it may, Spassky had gotten a gift from the heavens right before his retirement from chess. And now…?! More money!

Had I not heard anything up until then, not one of Bobby's stories of colluded games, deals, directives from the communist authority from the Kremlin who, arranging every segment of reality, wanted to determine even the precise moment of castling, this would seem to me like an attempt to rig the match or blackmail. "I can't believe it, I can't believe it," the hotel rooms and hallways seemed to ring.

The greatest trick the Devil ever pulled was convincing the world he does not exist. I had borne witness to reality, the truth that was unbelievable. Let us examine it logically and explain it thus: perhaps Boris wanted some more money before retiring into sports history, perhaps he wanted to feed his chess player's ego, perhaps he was inspired by something else, or… Perhaps that was the first and only time in his career when he in his later years tried to engineer an outcome outside the chessboard.

Witnessing that moment in time I say that it all seemed like a habit, practice, precisely that which pained Bobby and what he detested: undermine the quality, destroy the talent, strike a deal, prearrange things.

The epilogue—Bobby won, Spassky still sat at the edge if his bed spreading his arms at his chess past (some said he got the money after the match through other business means),[45] some believe it and some do not, as the lights go out and the buzz of the cameras gently blends into the whistle of the wind above water, saying: once upon a time there was, as if it never had been.

Several months later, Budapest became our new home. The Gellért Hotel, by the beautiful blue Danube, wonderful Buda and magnificent Pest, the tourist heart of the old continent, and a very special evening.

We walked through the city bathed in light, Bobby Fischer, Eugenio Torre and I. Across a massive green bridge near our abode (which is still today, as are all the bridges of the capital of Hungary, the pride and epithet of architecture), we slowly walked toward the city center, to the arranged place, a restaurant in which another legend would be waiting, Lajos Portisch, a luminary of the chess game from the country I visit often even today and love very much.

A measured, yet cordial greeting, a choice of food and drink, and the conversation began. The reserved but friendly voice of Bobby, the voice of Lajos, a talk about old times, memories, comments on history and the present of the game, the art that connected them. Everything went smoothly over a cold fruit soup, got more serious through words between mouthfuls of piquant wild game with gnocchi and cranberry sauce, every gulp of mineral water was a step closer to danger, and at last, over a scrumptious Esterházy cake, instead of desert, bitterness. Because we had come to Fischer's favorite topic—rigged games.

Softly, "Lajos, have you ever had an order or a directive of some kind to lose a game you could have won against a Soviet

---

[45] Another version says that Spassky got 250,000 dollars from Mr. Vasiljević that he was supposed to give Bobby as part of the reparations for the TV rights that were never agreed. Bobby Fischer never received that money.

player, or has anyone asked you or your Hungarian colleagues beforehand to lose?"

It was as if all was silent. Was the Danube still flowing? Portisch refused, Bobby attacked, raised his left hand, pointed a finger at our guest-host.

"Those days are over, why hide it," my protégé said.

He quickly took the chess set out of his pocket. Memory recalled an example moving the figures on the board.

"Couldn't you have," he tells Lajos to his face leaning over the table, "played this then? Was that just not logical?"

A dance on the light and dark squares. He attacked. Example two: "Was this not the right solution?"

Example three.

Four.

"Why did you let the Russians win?" he bellowed. Five. Portisch was sweating, squirming in his chair. Sixth game. Eugenio looked on silently.

"Wasn't this easier for you?" the figures yielded to his fingers, conviction became belief, restaurant guests, the jury, the prosecutor stronger and stronger, harsh words, bull's-eyes, and the moves... Moves became evidence.

The rhythm of the presented conclusions, and the "defendant" finally motioned to speak.

Eyes wide open ready to see, ears pricked to hear (Fischer was sweating too, wiping his face with a napkin), like a seasoned negotiator he folded his arms over his chest, waiting without a word, or a breath or a sigh.

Did he really open his heart to us (I do not know), or did he only want to end this (I do not know), or would he as a good host tell his guest anything to keep them satisfied (I do not know), Lajos Portisch exclaimed, "Alright, alright. We did play such games," then more softly "I played them too." We heard it, I heard it (that I do know). The waiter brought tea with milk for the "chess players". I had an espresso.

The river flowed once again, violin music was heard in the distance, real, Gypsy music, the kind that ends lives or gives life back. The great Hungarian chess-player talked of the times when one was FORCED to do a lot in the countries of the Warsaw pact (and where was one not forced to?), of communists blackmailing people (and where and with whom is it any different?), then how one had no alternative, on social benefits that could be lost (and much more could be lost as well!), on the need to protect one's closest, and much more.

The legendary Portisch did not attempt to justify himself, he explained and seemed to grow, now it seemed this relief did him good too, as if the truth about chess spoken before the greatest player of all time healed and soothed the soul.

Now an easy, calm, confessionary conversation that lasted for a time. There was no sign of triumph on Fischer's face, Eugenio slowly joined in, and the light from the opposite direction made Portisch's face shine with a whole new glow.

They parted far more cordially than they had met.

Bobby hugged his Hungarian colleague. We returned to the Gellért hill and the hotel that seemed to emerge from it. My two friends talked about what they had heard. With sympathy, with understanding, no judgment or condemnation (and who was to be judged?), step after step they bore with them (real or otherwise?) a confirmed discovery: colluded games were played, especially among the Soviets. Their land brought forth a large number of top-tier players, so it was easy for them to "cooperate" and, with a little hard work and effort, to reach their desired goal.

We sat in the apartment until morning. I listened to the conversation, the same topic, a retelling of the previous night. Has there, and to what extent, throughout the history of chess, been such manipulation and deceit, staged shows, prearranged winners, false champions? The undefeated champion of the world, Bobby Fischer, believed with every fiber of his being that the conspiracy held firm in its clutches the game he loved so immensely. He was ready to, at any time and any place, uncompromisingly, and seemingly with a wealth of arguments, explicitly prove it.

We live in a world where various everyday affairs, from rigged soccer matches, boxing matches, musical competitions, and even parliamentary and presidential elections are a proven part of our reality. Could we believe that only the game of 64 black-and-white squares was spared of such impurity? Could only it be and stay a haven of all-encompassing "honesty" and "honor"? One man long ago stood up and raised his voice with the belief in the strength of his own talent, raising the flag for the love of truth and justice for all in chess. He was at the time a great American patriot, and he loved his country dearly.

"There are many truths, and they do not agree amongst themselves," the legendary bard Meša Selimović would write.

"I can't believe it, I can't believe it," the rooms and hallways of the Intercontinental Hotel in Belgrade still seem to ring.

The greatest trick the Devil ever pulled was convincing the world he does not exist, we will repeat once more for the end.

I believe it.

I believe.

CHAPTER 11.

AVALA-AVALON [46]

Here we are again in Belgrade, the capital of Serbia and the Federal Republic of Yugoslavia, where the second part of the story would take place under the title of "the revenge match of the twentieth century". But, now everything was somehow new and different. This feeling did not arise only from the difference in surroundings, but also from the fact that changing places also introduced changes in every other sense and aspect. The Belgrade Intercontinental Hotel at that time was the most exclusive and prestigious place in this city at the confluence of the Danube and Sava. It won hearts with its elegance and functionality, but most of all with its exceptional kitchen and professional, kind staff who knew how to satisfy even the most demanding of guests. At the time we arrived, it became the central scene of all events which would portray and give direction to the time and happenings before us.

Bobby was once again enthralled. The two-room, spacious suite offered him everything he wanted. Some slight changes in the furniture arrangement, just enough to make room for a large chess table and two comfortable armchairs. The day after our arrival, we carefully unpacked and placed everything so that it was easily seen and available to the champion.

A certain number of our collaborators came with us to Belgrade, people who had worked in the organization and security of the match on Sveti Stefan and in Miločer, and now they were our honored guests. After seven days they would go back home, but we would retain our lively host from Miločer, Mr. Risto

---

[46] Avala – a mountain near Belgrade. Avalon – the mystical island in the legend of King Arthur.

Radenović, who was to take care of the food and beverages in Bobby's relaxation room during the entire rest of the match.

Just so that the first day might also be interesting, the events of the last evening in Montenegro made a contribution. That evening, in honor of the symbolic closing of the first part of the event, a special dinner was held at the Maestral Hotel. The introductory, ceremonial part passed in restraint, but as the evening progressed, most of those present allowed themselves to relax and dance to the music. At one moment of exaltation, Bobby's usual foot tapping to the rhythm under the table and humming of old hits that he loved grew into his actual participation in a traditional Serbian round dance.

Indeed, my ward could not resist the wish of one of the match hostesses who invited him to expose his body to the fast rhythm of the music. Quietly, on the way to the dance floor I asked him if he was sure he wanted to do this, to which he gave a carefree wave of his hand, thus expressing his relaxed mood. And he had a good time.

That moment of light dance steps and the smile on his face was to cost us some time and conversation the first day in Belgrade, and that is because he responded positively to that hostess from *Jugoskandic*, satisfying her desire for him to enter the dance, and it almost made him lose his head.

When we had set up everything in our new "temporary home", we all took a well-deserved rest. While the chess master was resting, I was paging through the daily papers and magazines. After I had looked through everything, having seen some photographs from that evening, I had no choice but to wait for his familiar voice to summon me. That happened quickly.

Propped up on his bed, he was staring at a journal with the latest news and with his picture where he was smiling and holding hands with two women in the dance. He moodily hissed, "I look ridiculous here. I don't know how to dance.

Especially not those traditional dances of yours. What will people think? You know..." His monologue full of remorse would have gone on forever if I had not interrupted him, "Do you agree that I warned you?"

He looked at me, "You did, but..."

Then, for the first time I stated the motto which, it seems to me, he learned well, although he did not respect it to the end of our work together, "You can do whatever you want and I will always try to make certain that you are all right, but I will accept responsibility only if I incidentally make a mistake, something done because of advice I gave you." Bobby nodded in agreement.

"And now let me see what I can do about this." I immediately called my friends, influential journalists and editors, and asked them to use those photographs as little as possible over the next few days.

My efforts were not in vain.

That same evening I informed the chess genius and unsuccessful dancer of Serbian traditional dances that he could rest easy because "there will be no more damage."

He was very satisfied by that.

A new form of events would also be lent by the arrival of Bobby's friend who we had been "looking for" in the first part of the match and successfully found, and now we were able to wait for her arrival. On one of the last days of September, Miyoko Watai came to Belgrade.

I had many opportunities to observe Bobby and Zita. Even though she was so young, she was absolutely dominant in their relationship. The image that remains in my memory was Fischer's mirth, enthusiasm and his almost boyish actions and expressions. Outside of their rooms, they were like best friends in school who communicate in a language known only to them and play their games in a hermetically sealed imaginary world. Through her influence, Miss Rajcsányi maintained the bond of rationality with the outside world, which was spoken by Bobby's voice.

The very arrival and appearance of Miyoko showed me a different man, a different male. Elegant, of perfect lady-like posture and behavior, closer in years after all to the hero of this story, with her measured steps down the hotel corridors, she brought not only the spirit and soul of her homeland, but also the opportunity to see the reflection of a different Robert Fischer, better or not. It is inadequate to say that her arrival meant a lot to him. I remember how he looked at me when he introduced us. It was the expression of a mature male who was aware of his worth; he was holding a gem and he wanted to preserve it. My ward never told me in detail about the history of their relationship. When he talked about her, he called her his "old friend". But his every movement (Bobby suddenly pulled out his guest's chair before supper, helped her with her coat) spoke of his respect and admiration for her. On the other hand, I could feel it quite well, there was the enormous affection that Miss Watai showed Bobby. Even when it was not shown openly, it could be felt like a fluid, everywhere and always, and it was unambiguous power and the inviolability of emotions.

Even though at that time Zita was his "official" partner, Fischer's relationship in public, his friendship with Miyoko put an especially strong wind in the sails of the American chess player, a wind which blew from the impressive soul of this woman.

Our Japanese guest captivated everyone with her etiquette and reverence of everything Bobby respected. She always greeted people with a bow of her head, in the traditional way of the country of the Samurai and geishas, and when she later returned again to Belgrade, she actually brought some symbolic, but emotionally precious gifts to me. Once, certainly doing so as a symbol of her gratitude for the care I was taking of her beloved friend, she brought me a sports watch, again more as a gesture to be remembered than something expensive. She came with Bobby to my room to present the gift to me. That scene was witnessed by my best man, a famous athlete and teacher of generations of Judo enthusiasts, Munir Šabotić, who had come to visit me at the time. After a while, between her two visits to Yugoslavia, Bobby received a gift from the distant island nation. He brought something intended for me, a jar of healthy algae, some special vitamin candy, and a box that had "For Nesh's friend" written on it. It's not hard to guess, it was a lovely sports watch. There are things that cannot be bought. Actually, everything that is worth something cannot be bought.

The Greatest Secret of Bobby Fischer

People often spoke and wrote about Bobby's sexuality and relationships with women. Males often detect domination or inferiority among themselves. I must say that the greatest chess player of all time really loved women. But, like in everything else, those relationships were very specific, a little strange and unique, requiring a special description for each. It is also a fact that Eros did not hold a primary place in the life of Bobby Fischer. He sought for the erotic and physical within the whole of his life journey and within his relationships as such.

During the match, Bobby also had a remarkable masseuse. She was a medical doctor who had done her postgraduate work in China.

The skill of shiatsu was turned into unrivaled art by her fingers. She was able to bring out certain, quite powerful emotional reactions just by touching a certain part or point on the body. I can testify to her knowledge and skill directly because I was the only one, apart from Bobby, who had the privilege of experiencing her medical touch. In our time together, she told me that during their sessions Bobby would often get an erection, but that he would immediately ask her to stop and leave the room.

Thus, she never experienced any kind of unpleasantness or rudeness from her patient. This would be understandable if we were talking about a short plump woman in her fifties. But in addition to her knowledge, skill and education, Sonja was five foot nine, with legs as long as the Yangtze, a slim waist, and all the rest simply superlative.

From future events we will understand that, without context, Fischer did not care a great deal about the physical and sexual, though he sometimes talked about it as a banality. That is why the relationship with Miyoko was different in this sense. It had all the elements of the strength of a deep friendship and the mutual respect of two grown up people. Here there is just one small question mark missing behind the words "grown up", if we understand that the term has a connotation of maturity, at least when Fischer is in question.

The Greatest Secret of Bobby Fischer

If I had an artistic gift, there would be two images from my memories, two moments I would certainly like to paint because of their content in terms of energy and potential, or even better, if I had the magical power to recommend them to one of the great painters of the past.

For the first theme I would choose Francisco Goya, and judging from his biographies I would I have to pay a lot of money for it. For the analogy to be complete, he was a court painter, and here he would have to eternalize the king of chess with oil on canvas. One day in the late afternoon, Bobby announced to me his wish to have supper in one of the town's restaurants. I made the reservations and soon Dane, Voja and I were ready to depart. I went to get Fischer and knocked on his door. I heard a voice beckoning me in. And what I saw when I entered is the picture.

Miyoko was lying on the bed, gracefully leaning back on a large cushion, perfectly dressed (a Coco Chanel outfit, elegant high-heeled shoes), discretely made up, her back to me on her left side, looking at me over her shoulder. She had probably been waiting for Bobby to get ready, so she had decided to do so in a relaxing position. In the background of the picture, some thirty inches from the bed stood Bobby, now ready in a new suit, also looking straight at me. For a moment silence, the room bathed in greens and browns. I remember that image, a grain of sand in a sea of events, but also a sort of strange, completely unbelievable energy in the room. In all the time I spent with Fischer I never felt such tension, harmony, synergy and closeness between my ward and another person as I did at that time between these two beings. A wonderful moment. But still just a minute.

"Let's go," I said. With those words I broke the thread, returned Goya to his own time (imagine it, that genius ended up mad), and we left for one of the better restaurants in town.

The second part of the match was to be held in the congress hall of Sava Centar which is practically one with the Intercontinental Hotel because they are connected by a passage that allowed us to reach the hall quickly, without going outside. The management of this building had plenty of experience in putting together large events like this. In addition to many manifestations in culture, concerts of domestic and foreign music stars, important film and other festivals, and in the history of this place there had also been great chess duels and tournaments.

While Miločer offered a special, exotic exclusivity, Sava Centar would give the event spatial grandiosity.

The large stage, properly and tastefully decorated, the technical characteristics and performance (sound and temperature insulation, the possibility of placing the cameras discretely and without sound), the glass wall of unbelievable dimensions that separated the players from the public, the comfort and visual field available to the audience, all of this brought the world what was certainly the best possible framework for playing one of the greatest chess events in history. We looked over the place many times. Never once did Bobby have a single complaint, nor did he find any fault with what he was offered. So it seemed to me that those "inspections" were more of a chance for the champion to enjoy what had been achieved because he had been fighting for such conditions his whole life, both for himself and the other grandmasters, giving his ego a stroke in his complete satisfaction. Sava Centar could hold about 4,000 visitors. In a visual sense, two to two-and-a-half thousand people in the audience gave the impression that the place was full. In this case there was no worry about the number of visitors because the interest was enormous, and the organizer had decided to make entrance free. The times for the games were harmonized with the working hours of most of the population of the capital, so that fans of chess, but also others who were interested could come after work to watch the match from the comfortable, blue armchairs in the magnificent hall. It is especially interesting that the congress of the ruling party at the time (the Socialist Party of Serbia), whose president was Slobodan Milošević, was announced to take place on October 3 and 4. Just how important the chess match was is indicated by the fact that the summit of the largest and strongest political group in the country was moved, or better said, rescheduled.

While everything was ready in an organizational sense, satisfied with everything that had been achieved, Bobby almost completely forgot about chess those days.

The Greatest Secret of Bobby Fischer

During the first part of the match, when Spassky took the lead 2:1 after Bobby's initial anthological win and three draws, Bobby had a small crisis in his game; the newspapers and media reported that Bobby changed his life rhythm on the doctors' recommendation, that he controlled his newly acquired habits, regulated his diet and introduced recreation as a daily requirement. It was believed that such a turnabout drastically changed the rhythm of the duel, and that he, thus refreshed, easily captured the next three wins.

I must testify that this was not true. The whole time we collaborated, he carefully guarded his remarkable appetite, and when advised to eat smaller, less spicy meals, he responded by continuing his habit of salting his watermelon; recreation, especially swimming, he always loved anyway.

Hedonism was the name of everything that happened from our arrival in Belgrade to the beginning of the continuation of the match. At that moment Bobby forgot about the essence of why he was where he was. Day-long walks, visiting practically all the most famous restaurants in town, with the heaviest possible accent on gastronomic exaggeration, brought a lot of satisfaction with good company until the wee hours of the morning.

As Fischer intensively rested, interest in the match was revitalized. This statement is related mostly to the domestic and foreign media who had slowly drifted into routine reporting after their initial euphoria. Press conferences, although they were attended by a lot of people, slowly became everyday meetings of those involved in the match, without a lot of turbulence or dynamics.

Again there were crowds in the lobby, a lot of people, guests and journalists at the reception desk checking in, as they were in all the other hotels of the capital, the telephones were ringing, people asked for passes, for interviews which radiated with the desire to be as close to the epicenter as possible.

In the quiet of the left wing seventh floor of the Interkontinental Hotel, closed to the other guests, Bobby did not take much interest in all that.

The Greatest Secret of Bobby Fischer

The match's patron, Mr. Vasiljević, often came around to ask about the state and mood of his favorite, but when he would get a report on that, an unbridled nervousness would overwhelm him.

At the time, Bobby still did not have his own money. Upon arrival in Yugoslavia, he asked for 20,000 German Marks for his basic needs. He did not carry them around, nor did he ever pay for anything during the whole time we were together. I got a weekly allowance for the champion's needs from the organizers, but it was not a part of the calculation of his contractual payment for winning or losing. I kept careful evidence and turned my report into the owner of *Jugoskandic*, and he would look at it and generally accept it without commentary. In a country where inflation had brought the standard of living for most people to the very brink of poverty, 5,000 to 7,000 German marks for Bobby's personal hotel bill and an additional couple of thousand for expenses – that was something to think about. But no one paid much attention to that, because the knowledge that this was a question of national interest directed everyone's thoughts to making sure the event met the desired goals. Thus, Bobby lived like a king, without a penny in his pocket.

His winnings would come much later, with a lot of uncertainty, dramatic moments, and with a happy end for him. In conclusion, far from chess and training, Fischer was completely unready for the continuation of the match, the twelfth game of the duel with Spassky.

Twenty years have passed since 1992, and twenty-two more before that since the greatest talent of the black-and-white squares made his new Belgrade move, because before the event we are talking about, deeper in time, there was a match to be remembered in 1970. The Soviet Union against the rest of the world. Fischer mentioned that moment of his personal history to me with a smile on his face, because he let the Danish grandmaster Bent Larsen play the first board for the West. He did so without vanity in the duel with the chess players of the East, because he soon fed his ego by showing everyone who "the first board of the world" was in 1971, when he wiped out the Dane 6:0 and then proved it again in Reykjavik against Spassky.

The Greatest Secret of Bobby Fischer

The main entrance would be open to the public at 2 p.m. and the hall itself at 3 p.m. The games would start at 3:30 p.m. I was to receive a lot of recognition and congratulations from various people while the match went on, among other things because of the fact that my ward was never late to a single game or press conference. In the light of all the preceding decades of experience the world had with the whims and wiles of the main hero of this story, that fact was almost unbelievable. But the consensus between Bobby and me meant that this was to be a matter of fact. October 1, Spassky was to go first, the Russian-French grandmaster was playing white.

We had to arrive on time for the start of the second part of the match. The hall at Sava Centar had long since filled to the hilt by an audience who was excitedly and impatiently waiting for the arrival of the stars of the show, above all for their favorite, Robert Fischer. The arrival of the great chess player on the stage and his appearance under the lights on the grandiose stage caused a roar of heartfelt, honest enthusiasm among those present, who got up from their seats and shouted their approval, applauding loudly for the only American they considered to be their own at that moment. Bobby, truth be told, from the very beginning of his career, had been a favorite of chess fans all over Yugoslavia, but at this moment that love burst forward when his visit to the "Satanized" country was understood as support for the people and country by the majority of the population.

Somehow awkwardly, shifting from foot to foot, passing his visor from left hand to right, back and forth, on the instruction of Mr. Kubat, he went out in front of the glass wall in the auditorium. The frenetic support was shown by all 4,000 people to the point of exaltation. An unforgettable and unrepeatable welcome, unbridled honesty. Does the world of chess remember all that to this day? An emotional experience *par excellence*, hard to repeat.

But, so that the day did not end in syrupy sweet triumph, Boris Spassky appeared somehow quietly in the arena behind the star of the moment, and also received wild applause. To my surprise, he brought a visor to the first game of the continuation, almost identical to Fischer's, but of a different color, white. For a second,

Bobby did not know how to interpret this gesture: was it necessary or was it a provocation? Those were well-known moments for me, lasting as long as a clap of the hands, in which the champion did not know how to react. However, as if he was expecting or intentionally creating this small ambiguity, Boris said a few words about the bright lights, concentration, so that the American pointed at his opponent and nodded his head. "All right, then," but soon this would be interpreted differently as well.

For the first time in the match Fischer opened a game with c1 – with a pawn. Commenting in front of the monitors in the hall, the experts interpreted this as an expression of the champion's insecurity, because retreating from his favorite 1. e4 (which usually announced his victorious ambitions) indicated exactly that to people who knew. Internal turbulence and his leisurely life outside chess in the pause of the match were highlighted by the fact that his opponent that afternoon had some brilliant moments. In the endgame Bobby sacrificed a knight, attempting to achieve a draw, but the game was already lost. A new dimension of the match, now with an uncertain score of 5:3. While the rhythm of the given musical score sped up in the new circumstances, the notes on the paper, which looked as if they were indelible to the uninformed observer, were now suddenly sliding from the staffs like falling stars into the abyss of the everyday, while the untrained ear heard this cacophony like a symphony. Namely, Belgrade in 1992 and 1993 was doubtlessly one of the "most lively" spots on the planet.

The city looked like a compilation of fragments of a Lisbon port at the beginning of World War II, as it was brilliantly described by the novelist of emigrant fortune, Erich Maria Remarque, plus the fatalist sin without a tomorrow in Foss's "Cabaret", the ghosts and specters around holiness, "Christ Carrying the Cross" by Hieronymus Bosch, above an omnipresent impoverishment and a fall from heaven of edified harmony. "The ship for the promised land" would never sail into the harbor of the city on the Danube and Sava, as if into ball of twine, irreversibly connected by their interests, there were all kinds of people waiting in hope and hopelessness on the docks of fate: politicians (domestic and foreign—barkers, heralds, emissaries, peace-makers, warmongers), popular and high culture (or high popular and lower culture – either way it was the same), criminals of sorts, civil and military intelligence services (agencies and offices of all colors, shapes and descriptions). Refugees from the war zones with varying monetary, educational and other kinds of profiles, searching for their place in the new surroundings. Opportunities for getting wealthy quickly and easily haunted everyone, while the offers of possibly profitable jobs were as colorful as the Devil's notebook.

Cigarettes, smuggled from Neverland into Wonderland, crude oil from the north went south, weapons of all calibers without a place of origin (everyone needed them and they were looking for a buyer without patriotism), diamonds from Central Africa – all were arriving from Hong Kong, medicines from Switzerland arriving in barrels made for derivatives, fish flour from Chile, a lot of artistic works and gold which still had the smell of the nearby war zone, and a lot of other things in true and false stories, in dreams, but also in waking. Like a magic curtain, all of that covered the chess spectacle, turning slowly into the essence of events at the moment the lights were going out in a room without doors and windows. Extra-institutional levers of power were, hierarchically placed according to significance in their "daytime" activities and "night time" manifestations, primarily in the hotels, cafes and restaurants of the capital of Milošević's Serbia.

Thus the Mažestik Hotel, a famous decoration of Belgrade's downtown, formerly the favorite gathering place of the Yugoslav intellectual elite when visiting the capital, became the meeting place of the third league captains of Serbian destiny and the transfer of power. Bobby really liked the renovated apartment where the famous Croatian writer, Miroslav Krleža, used to stay.

The successful qualifications of those who had some luck and the sought for "abilities" would "promote" them across the Sava to the *Hyatt* hotel. A very strong second league of influence and power sprang from that sacral elegance, along with the first of numerous murders in an endless series of deaths. And finally, the then imposing Intercontinental. In passing, for coffee, lunch, supper, everyone and everybody, the leading party and the opposition. Emissaries of the UN and people with global influence, businessmen from all over the world. However, there were also those for whom Baudelaire says that "they have more fun than a polite soul can even imagine". The news came and went, human faces, too.

Footsteps in passing, knowledge and discovery remain. Whatever is up is also down, whatever is outside is also inside. Let us return in front of the curtain, because the audience is waiting.

The second week in Belgrade (for Fischer incognito) we were to be visited by the president of FIDE at the time, Florencio Campomanes. The scent of money could be smelled from far away, and in the world it was followed by the wish to push one's name as high as possible into the black and white heights.

The first man of world chess came on a short, content-full visit, as I was told later that day by an influential banker of the time.

Namely, Fischer's comeback was giving a new, surprising possibility for the popularization of the game on 64 squares, but also a brilliant opportunity for the all-encompassing advancement of chess. A path into the future was being sought for. On one hand was Campomanes, flexible and ready for compromise, and on the other was Jezdimir Vasiljević whose motives were the personal promotion and world fame accorded to the man who had financed the comeback of the mysterious champion. For the start, the upcoming final match of the candidates for the world throne should be relocated from Linares to Belgrade. The reason – the winner would receive a million dollars from Mr. Vasiljević. The difference was enormous, because FIDE had foreseen 100,000 Swiss francs for those purposes. But more importantly, the question of all questions: how to arrange the real spectacle, a match between Fischer and Kasparov? It would be a long road, full of obstacles. In the first place, did Bobby need be to coaxed back under the flag of FIDE? Mission impossible. Or perhaps? Jezdimir Vasiljević was to sponsor a FIDE competition while Campomanes lobbied so that the world chess federation recognized that future clash of worlds and generations as the match for the world title. A short meeting was held in one of the two large restaurants of Belgrade's Intercontinental, and even though it was full of understandings, plans and hope, it proved to be in vain.

The Greatest Secret of Bobby Fischer

During the visit of the FIDE president, Bobby was not to be allowed out of his rooms. I was asked to make sure of that. But the Devil never sleeps, and that would be proven this time as well.

Just as the conversation was going on, Bobby suddenly got the desire to eat lunch early. I tried to direct our conversation toward the possibilities and advantages of room service, but my ward insisted – to the restaurant. The corridor, the elevator, the above-mentioned partners in conversation at *Rotiserija*, which one reaches by turning right. For a moment we stopped in the foyer. I turned left, hoping that Bobby would follow me by inertia into *Braserija*. He did just that, but after a few steps he stopped, "Nesh, shall we get a steak?", pointing with his thumb in the direction we were not supposed to go. I said quickly, "I have a surprise for you, I'll order something special." To my great fortune, the encounter with Campomanes was avoided due to the excellent lamb liver wrapped in vine leaves, which my friend could not pull himself away from for a long time. So, Vasiljević was prepared to offer amounts that the world of chess could only dream about until then. The banker loved chess. He often "played" against Bobby. The grandmaster with a smile, talking, sometimes eating, would make his moves, while Jezdimir sweated and smiled. Usually the placing of figures lasted eleven or twelve moves. To the uninformed, Jezdimir would smile and crow, "I held out till the twenty-second move!" However, his motives for such grandiose support of chess certainly did not lie only in his love for the ancient game. To the only question asked of him by the journalists at the press conference on Sveti Stefan, why did he organize and sponsor the match, he answered, "I love shows." And he really did love them. But the real thing was about to happen. Or better said, the time was ripe.

Just one day earlier I was told that Bobby needed to be ready to visit Slobodan Milošević. It was a day off, so our entire focus was on that event.

The morning broke in special excitement which shone like an aura around Bobby's face. As he prepared, with visible stage fright, he kept asking and stating things "to get it all right" in his knowledge of the life and work of the president of his host country. Beyond all doubt, the American grandmaster was completely prepared because the "training" had gone on for a long time and had been quite thorough. Namely, since his arrival in Yugoslavia, Bobby had shown great interest in the history of Milošević's political activity, his rise to power, and his technique and means of maintaining it. All of that had turned into unreserved respect for the man he was about to meet. He was absolutely delighted with the "decisiveness" and readiness of the so loved and so hated Serbian leader to courageously and uncompromisingly resist the "new world order" and all the "unjust" pressures and extortions of the international community.

Fischer was also impressed by Milošević's "firmness" in domestic political relations and the way he managed events. He sought for signs of the correctness of his views in the analysis of events, the discussions, and also in the president's confident stride and sharp gesticulations which could be seen in the media.

It should not be forgotten, and he should not be blamed for this, Bobby never took sides in the Balkan wars which were raging at the time, and it seemed that they would grow into a real conflagration. That story did not interest him as much, and his neutral position (the very fact that he was in Yugoslavia at the time was reason enough for condemnation) was simply a logical consequence of his thinking about and understanding things, a product of the champion's very character. Therefore, in Milošević, Bobby Fischer sought for and found only those elements that would confirm his image and experience of the world, and that in the achieved common denominator of overlapping views and opinions he would find support, reinforcement, and thereby suppress that terrible Don Quixote feeling of loneliness in his jousting at the windmills of the dark world forces and ubiquitous injustice.

However, this grandiose but only thematically limited, peculiar adoration was to receive an adequate response after Mr. Vasiljević's departure from the country.

Simplified through time, Slobodan would say to him, "You got everything you asked for, we got everything we wanted from you.

The Greatest Secret of Bobby Fischer

We're not asking for anything more, we're not giving you anything else."

But that day Bobby, carefully dressed in his most elegant form, went to meet his "main" host, the man he so appreciated. It seemed to me that Fischer experienced Milošević like one of the superheroes of his favorite comics who, gifted with virtues, was battling against global evil, guarding his best secret weapon for the victorious end. On a lovely sunny October day, we quickly arrived at the Old Court, the place of the encounter, located in the very center of town. Announced by the protocol officer, we stood in front of Slobodan Milošević. Sincere, smiling, speaking good English, he indicated that Bobby should sit on "the sofa" where all the important world leaders and politicians would sit that year and in the years to come, as if on a conveyer belt. The relaxed air of his host, the "renowned banker", did not help Bobby much; with a confused smile he struck what was for him a rather unusual pose on the couch, his arms stiff at his sides, leaning back, as if he were trying to glue himself to the back of the wooden frame of the antique piece of furniture. A photograph was taken as a keepsake and for the archive. Since Mr. Vasiljević had announced a conventional half-hour conversation, and since I knew all three of the protagonists, it seemed to me that I would best spend the time talking with my colleagues from the president's entourage.

Heading back to the hotel, I had the experience that an automobile can run without fuel. As if excitement and joy had been pumped into the tank. At least that was the way Fischer was acting.

This did not surprise me because Milošević's charm was not resisted even by his most adamant opponents, domestic and foreign, who experienced "enlightenment" in that very same place. For instance, a prominent opposition leader, the president of one of the strongest anti-regime parties, a man who had often been arrested and harassed by this man, would look straight into the camera of the state television after one such session and announce that the president was "an exceptionally charming and interesting man." The storm of satisfaction that came about after this audience should thus be understood, because Bobby had positively gotten a confirmation of his expectations toward Milošević. The next day that feeling would be the central rhetorical inspiration of the uncrowned king of chess. It was obvious that new energy and additional certainty were flowing like adrenaline in his veins. Having caught a good wave on the open sea, Fischer elegantly surfed through the sixteenth game of the match, playing black.

He chose Benoni's Defense and imposed his own rhythm from the very start. Since Spassky got into trouble with time, there was no dilemma about the result already after twenty moves.

In an excellent mood, Fischer could await the continuation full of confidence. On the other hand, Boris Spassky was experiencing some difficult times. Because of a kind of psychological fatigue caused by his oversights and struggles in the sixteenth game, he asked for the second time in the match that the next game be postponed. The medical committee approved the request. Bobby and Eugene trained hard all night. In the early morning I saw Torre coming out of the champion's suite, visibly tired and with his eyes bloodshot. With a smile and a gesture in which he dramatically wiped the sweat from his brow, he showed me just how difficult it had been physically and psychologically. Obviously, a new enthusiasm had arrived.

The delay of the game certainly did not make Mr. Vasiljević happy. Those days it became clear that the expenses of the match were increasing rapidly. Rough estimates said that they were exceeding 50,000 German marks per day. Investment or loss? Everyone still believed that it was an investment in the future.

And it appeared again in a brilliant perspective. The focus of the first match after Spassky narrowed and went in the direction of Judit Polgár. It would be truly interesting – the female wunderkind from Hungary against the American chess legend. The gem of the jet-set on the French Riviera, Monaco, would be the right place for twelve attractive games and a prize fund of 2.5 million dollars.

In our conversations, Bobby relatively often mentioned the Polgár sisters, with a strong desire to "see how things stand there". However, to my inquiry about Judit as a potential rival, his answer would be undefined and uncertain. It was the kind of risk he would gladly accept because of the media attraction and the money certainly, but he was aware, though he was ultimately self-confident, that a loss of even one game would endanger his authority in the chess world. So, several times he told me that even in a rapid chess variant, in which twelve games would be played in three days, the prize money would have to be significantly higher. Money as a means to refuse. Still, the Polgár family was really interesting to Bobby whatever the case.

Also, Anatoly Karpov, distancing himself from Kasparov, said that a comeback after twenty years demanded courage, and that Bobby should be congratulated for it. Another door was, therefore, open.

The seventeenth game of the match brought a slight surprise, because Fischer self-confidently headed down a line for which he considered Spassky a great expert, especially playing white.

He demonstrated his superiority in chess and once again showing remarkable talent.

The weather in Belgrade was lovely. From the standpoint of meteorology, but also on a personal level, Fischer was enjoying himself. Mostly working at night on chess with Gligorić and Torre, daily swims in the hotel pool, enjoying the remarkable food at the Intercontinental, we often went for long walks along the Sava or among the buildings of Novi Beograd. He was in exceptional physical and mental condition. He carefully followed events in the media, and often talked about them with me at length. His hunger for information was enormous, he gathered it from everywhere, along with his favorite analysis and synthesis. Our Japanese guest, Miyoko Watai, was still there, while Zita was temporarily absent.

On the eighteenth day of October, Bobby was visibly upset. In the daily press and radio and television broadcasts, he saw and heard the news about how the elite troops of the republic Ministry of Interior Affairs (Milošević's lever of power) had seized the building of the Federal Service of Internal Affairs (ultimately under the control of the federal premier, Mr. Milan Panic). Even before saying hello he asked, "Nesh, is this a coup d'état?" When I explained to him that this event was not nearly so serious and that the whole thing would certainly end peacefully and be "forgotten", he calmed down. Over supper he asked for further information and explanations, and with a conspirator's facial expression he silently congratulated the president of Serbia for his decisiveness.

In everyday communication, Bobby often switched from English to Spanish, but while he stayed in Yugoslavia he made great advancement in his knowledge of Serbian. He understood almost everything, often with my help he read the Cyrillic letters in the unavoidable newspapers, and he could even put together a few sentences with a little effort. On the wings of his enthusiasm and good energy, he walked lightly into game eighteen. While his loud laugh echoed in the hotel lobby and followed the rhythm of our steps that led us to the ever full hall at Sava Centar, Boris was still going through an obvious crisis. The doctors could not find any significant health problems (except with his prostate) which were so significant that they would influence the outcome of the match. Fatigue was the problem, and it could clearly be seen on his face. In spite of that "advantage", the game did not produce any significant creations, so Fischer playing black easily agreed to a draw.

Press conferences were held according to the normal schedule. How interesting they were varied depending on the excitement which the previous game produced, on events in the surroundings, but also on the inspiration of the journalists present. Their number varied greatly. Besides the domestic, constantly present ones, there were others from Russia, Spain, Italy and the USA who were accredited throughout the entire duel. A number of journalists came and went to check the pulse of exclusivity, but now they were already expecting a possible quick finish. As time went on, as I got to know my fellow travelers of the pen, I often drank coffee with them, without talking about Fischer, the match or chess at all, of course.

We were quite available to some of them whenever they needed any kind of personal favor or aid. I really liked the lovely and kind English chess player and journalist, Cathy Forbes (now Warwick), who had a whole series of "colorful" and memorable experiences as she was traveling to her destination, but also during her stay in Yugoslavia. She took them all in with a smile and with a positive attitude she got through them. That is why she "deserved" my help that last evening on the Montenegrin coast, the one that Bobby so enjoyed and then regretted; she got to play a quick game of chess with Fischer. In a small booth, while the band entertained those gathered, smiling Cathy experienced great joy which could be seen on her radiant face, a moment to be remembered forever, while she made moves on Bobby's little pocket set and exchanged a few words with the great of the game. From today's perspective I feel sorry for some of the representatives of the Fourth Estate and for people known to me in my private life, because I used my protection to get them an autograph or photograph from Bobby after many requests and tearful pleas. With complete confidence in me, the chess master agreed to those things, and those very same people would later use those photographs or simple photomontages to represent themselves as great friends of Bobby, or they even put those autographs up for sale. A position in which you can make somebody happy is truly beautiful if there is honesty present which should be understood and enjoyed. Cathy knew that.

For me and my team, the most interesting were the so-called stars, domestic and imported, who came for their share of the fame and for affirmation of their own vanity, full of self-confidence and unhidden arrogance. Some of them called by phone in my room-office with the expectation that, certainly, their name and the hissing of the long-distance line would give them direct access to an interview with Bobby Fischer. Others, still, were easily noticed and recognized. One or two vans pull up outside the entrance. The superstar approaches the reception desk with a dapper light step. An entourage of assistants carry the luggage, while the camera and sound men try to tame their equipment which resists harnessing at high speed. Check in as an introduction and preparation for the "unstoppable" approach of the marked "victim". From this temporal distance, it is almost impossible to understand how fame, affirming or obtaining it, could have produced a documented conversation or interview with our returnee to the chess arena. Without the slightest exaggeration (aware of the fact that the news has the importance and lifespan of a butterfly) there were actually few such challenges in the media world as the realization of these possibilities.

We would always follow these rituals and demonstrations of importance with a smile, because everything was clear. The road to the top had to go through me and it was unconquerably high, especially for the brash and brazen, regardless of who stood behind them, and at that time it could not be anyone stronger than the authority of our supporter. Especially since that was Fischer's wish, carved into my mind through his words. While some might be able to open that door with sincerity and honesty, we kept it locked for the immeasurably self-loving, whose ritual we would watch again after a day or two, with indifference and even a grain of irony, as they passed by the reception desk and got back into the van or two that would take them into the future. But no matter how clever you are, no matter how hard you try to be wise, mistakes are possible in places of high responsibility. I have already mentioned some of them, but the worst were those that happened with an emotional connotation.

The evening after game eighteen of the match. In the "red" hall of the Intercontinental, in the far right corner, Bobby, Gligorić and Torre. Just next to them, at another table, Dane, Voja and I. Loud comments on chess, dinner had reached dessert time. Cake with fruit, the elegant hostess gently but decisively stopped a tall heavyset man at the door, looked back at me, while Voja was already a step away from the entrance. I walked over to him, politely greeted our "guest", who said loudly, "I'm going to see Bobby." No ambiguity, no alternative. It is an understatement to say that he was dressed humbly.

Long dirty hair and beard. If it were not for the smell of alcohol wafting from him, in a strange, distant, and hinting way, he might have reminded me of my protégé before he came to the country where he was now staying. I politely asked him if he had an appointment, doing so without sarcasm, though I knew of course that something like that certainly had not occurred. "I don't need an appointment," he said, "I beat Fischer at an official match." Since Bobby was facing me, he saw that something was going on. I went over and whispered to him, "A grandmaster...would like to see you." Without a moment of hesitation the champion stood up, as did Torre, while Gliga turned to see who was arriving. And then he stood up. I accompanied our guest to the table. Handshakes. Bobby explained everything to Eugene who laughed sincerely, while Gligorić already knew the whole story. Yes, that was the man "who defeated the king of chess." The conversation lasted less than five minutes. I was standing nearby, just next to my ward, who pulled me a couple of steps aside at one instant.

"Nesh, should we offer him dinner?"

"Dinner is over, Bobby, maybe dessert, tea or coffee, but I wouldn't recommend even that." I did not say this because of a lack of hospitality, but because of the fact that the general state of our visitor did not please me. Namely, not rarely did it happen that Bobby overlooked certain facts, certain obvious things in the real world either intentionally or not, desiring to meet expectations. In order to avoid the regret that was so likely to come later, I gave him my advice. Bobby turned toward the table, then stepped back to me.

"He doesn't look so good. Should I offer to help him?"

"What did you have in mind, concretely?" I asked.

"Well, let's say money. I could give him a hundred dollars." There it was, discomfort. The world champion. The prize money – millions of dollars!

A guest at the wrong moment. Bobby wanted to show respect and to help the man, and to do so without insulting him. And, after all, what did the humble looking grandmaster expect? "OK, we'll do it. Let me handle it."

The brief conversation was over. They shook hands in farewell. I followed the Yugoslav chess player toward the entrance of the hotel. In broken words, with holes in his memory, he was talking about what might have been if only... I took an envelope from the reception desk and discretely put three hundred dollars in it. With a long introduction and a lot of rhetorical beating around the bush, I tried to explain the meaning and the amount to him. But the speed with which the envelope disappeared from my hand showed me that no such "caution" was necessary. Until late in the night, Bobby commented on the entire event with Eugene and me (including the details that I also shared with him). Should one do good deeds and hope for good things, or do good things and wait for evil in return? The Devil exclaims: Vanity, my favorite sin. To this very day I remember the feeling which is only now clear to me as the moral to the story. I defeated him, and today he plays for millions. That means that I could have done that, if only... Adoration and love, hatred and envy. Rise and fall. Among those of us entangled in life, how cursed is that thin line that divides virtue and vice, sadness and laughter. If I give, what do I give, if I feed the hungry with real food, is what I call good really good, or do I sink into folly no matter what I do? Whatever the case, two days afterwards a large headline appeared in an influential daily newspaper: an interview with Fischer. Bobby could not have been more disappointed. He swore and cursed, unable to believe it. Without getting into moral questions and without judging anyone or anything, there is one thing I am certain of: Fischer's clumsily shown respect was honest and pure and, most importantly, not a single word in that "interview" was spoken that night.

But it is unimportant, because who really cares about the truth?

The price for this event was to be paid in a certain way by a certain pompous Spanish journalist. For days he could be seen everywhere, in the hotel, at the pool, and in the hall when the games were being played, where he wondered among the rows like the phantom of the opera or one of Shakespeare's ghosts. We were headed for the game nineteen of the match, and there he came right after us. Down the hotel hallway, elegant, ocher suit with crimson pinstripes, a shirt in the same tone as the suit, his tie the color of the pinstripes. A fast pace in new brown shoes, his glasses and hairstyle like the vicious lawyer in "Carlito's Way", masterfully played by Sean Penn. "Mr. Fischer, Mr. Fischer," he called after us as Bobby quickly walked ahead with Torre. Four guards and I. "Mr. Fischer, Mr. Fischer," he called in a falsetto, "just ten minutes for an interview." I saw my ward and the expression on his face. I stopped to ask the energetic journalist to understand the reality of the situation. But, as I blocked his view and all perspective with my body, he jumped on me as if he did not see me, and kept shouting, "Mr. Fischer, please, Mr. Fischer, please." At a fast pace my group arrived, reaching us at a run. As they pulled him away he reached out for us with both hands, "Stop, just stop for a second." Bobby looked at me. The lights went out. Bobby, Torre and two bodyguards went on ahead.

The nineteenth contest saw a long and exhausting battle in one of the most unusual games of the match. The tension grew in the seventh hour of the difficult struggle, with alternating advantages and possibilities to win, but the game ended up in a draw.

To the greatest chess player of all time, security was of great importance, perhaps because, to his own feelings, he never had any. He enjoyed rituals before bedtime.

Namely, at the end of the day, just before going off to sleep, he expected an inspection of every nook and cranny of his two room suite. This precautionary measure was taken every day of our work together. Was it perhaps too much? Even perfect security measures could not safeguard Bobby from his trepidations. That was what I really had to struggle with. One evening, just as I was preparing to leave his living area after my check, Bobby asked me to look one more time behind the curtains and drapes, and also under the bed. When he saw my inquisitive look, he sat down in an armchair, spread his hands and confessed something, which relieved him. "You know, Nesh, that I'm mostly worried about what Mossad or the CIA might do to me, but I have one other great fear." I sat down next to him, ready to hear him out and do whatever I could to overcome this challenge. With a sigh he said, "I am, you know, really afraid of Komodo dragons."

In addition to all the other things I had to account for, now this as well. And then, a monologue.

Many times he had watched nature stories and travel shows about this fascinating reptile with its fantastic abilities to kill. This relic of prehistory lives on the Komodo Islands, and my client was always haunted by it in his dreams and nightmares. With a lot of sympathy I had to accept this exclusive feeling, aware of the fact that rationality was not going to be of much aid here. It was superfluous to say that these evil reptiles did not exist at the time either in the Belgrade zoo or in private ownership. Even though you would think the same thing that I did then, that the transformed signals from the corners of the mind, gathered from who knows where and who knows when, can take on such strange forms of reading and recognition in reality as the personal stamp of the individual, then there certainly will be surprises.

Many years later, while I was reading an interview with the Hollywood actor Billy Bob Thornton in *Playboy*, I learned that this hero of the silver screen had a peculiar kind of fear in real life. In disbelief and enthrallment, laughing at the happenstance, I found out that Komodo dragons are a source of great psychological suffering for Angelina Jolie's ex-husband. Welcome to the club, Billy Bob. And even now I am wearing a smile, because of a great idea for a business. Like a *Betty Ford Clinic*, why not open a center for rehabilitation from the fear of Komodo dragons...

Games twenty and twenty-one were like images in a warped mirror. In the first, Spassky easily, routinely capitalized on his advantage. It was if Bobby did not even exist in it.

In the second, the situation was reversed. Fischer again demonstrated his strength. After reaching a draw position, Boris made a fatal mistake which the American grandmaster turned into victory with a steady hand.

Game twenty-one saw the appearance of a heralded, but now obvious and visible, tension between the players, one that had been hanging in the air since the beginning of the second part of the match. Spassky's arrival with a visor at the first game of the Belgrade part of the chess match had been accepted by Fischer at that moment as a need of his opponent, but after a couple of days in conversation with him I figured out that the winds of doubt had entered his mind, bearing the idea that the Russian-French grandmaster was making fun of him. At this stage of the game, Boris used his rest area unusually often. He explained that this was because of chronic fatigue and slight health problems.

Though we had reigned in Bobby's exaggerated dubiousness about the "illegal" use of that room by checking it regularly before every game, this habit and practice really irritated the American grandmaster. After the twenty-first game, because of that he quite angrily demanded that such "ungentlemanly" and "unchesslike" activity cease immediately.

The opposing team explained this as a necessity and inevitability, in no way a wish to create tension or disrupt the concentration of the former world champion. But Bobby could not accept that. Even outside of this specific moment in the duel, in life terms defined as the "revenge match of the twentieth century", the relationship between these two chess greats was quite interesting. As already mentioned, Bobby Fischer differentiated Boris Spassky, although not completely, from the other Russian chess players, which in his personal worldview was certainly a compliment.

While being bitter rivals, they had seen each other three or four times during Bobby's exile from the public scene. According to Fischer, they talked about the good old days on those occasions. Driven above all by a feeling of the importance, history and the greatness of the Iceland drama, the long awaited returnee practically did not think about any other candidate for the spectacle he was preparing, though he had absolute choice of freedom. He thus directly made it possible for the player ranked 101 in the world to unexpectedly make a lot of money. Naturally, the prize amount was thus adequately justified by this alone according to the measures of the organizers and financiers. Still, what was surprising to me was the absolute lack of any sort of manifestation of gratitude from Spassky, even in public. He left the impression of latent confusion, feigned awkwardness, but also kindness toward everyone. Boris mostly agreed with Bobby on sensitive chess questions or those of a political nature in which the king's external character was manifest. Certainly, the mentioned "favor" did not have to mean absolute agreement on all things or single-mindedness, but also not...

Return into the past. Sveti Stefan. The morning of an off day.

With their entourages, Bobby and Boris meet at the gate of the bottom of the ramparts of the resort. Their accidental encounters during the duel were mainly in passing, quite brief and conventional. It seemed to me that Fischer was slightly afraid that Nikitin, or especially Balashov, might appear from somewhere, while Spassky was simply going about his business. That afternoon, after a couple of exchanges, each group headed in their own direction. We went to the beach while they headed for the center of the island. To everyone's consternation, Boris suddenly turned and followed Bobby, and after ten steps he began to imitate the quite characteristic gesticulations and gait of his "benefactor". He obviously wanted to make everyone laugh and to play a practical joke. Fortunately, my protégé did not see him. When our faces all took on the same look, mildly said – very serious, Boris quickly turned in the direction of the safety of the walls. Since the security of both these greats of chess was practically under the same coordination and command, that evening we all agreed that this wannabe Chaplin imitator had gotten away with murder. To my surprise, during the whole period there were also famous and important people who, in their ignorance, considered Fischer's personality, or some part of it, as something available or acceptable for mockery. Generally, it is a known fact that the relationship between security agents and the people they protect are mutual and exceptionally strong. And I have to say that I, like my friends, was loyal like a Samurai and sensitive in a special way to him, especially because of Fischer's so visible and commonplace "awkwardness" in real life. Each and every such improper and tasteless joke was immediately and dramatically placed in a framework which showed that such things were not tolerated. The lengths to which we were ready to go and just how far we were actually allowed to go is indicated by the case of the already mentioned federal premier, Mr. Milan Panic. With the express wish to spend time with Fischer, he arrived unannounced many times at the Intercontinental. The explicit desire of our ward was that no such meeting was to take place. An accidental encounter in the lobby. While the premier waved hopefully, Bobby turned his head away, and let our dear colleagues in Panic's entourage know that no meeting was to occur. On one such occasion, returning from our afternoon walk, just the two of us, I noticed some familiar vehicles in front of the hotel. It was an old Mercedes stretch limousine which had once been the pride of the president of the SFRY, Josip Broz Tito.

The Greatest Secret of Bobby Fischer

Now it was being used by the American Serb, the pharmacologist, businessman and disposable premier, Mr. Panic. When he saw this antique beauty, Bobby smiled and said, "Nesh, do you know the engineer who 'parked' this 'train' in front of our door?" I smiled to, and we went in through the back door to reach our suites in anonymity and unavailability. One meeting of these two protagonists was to occur sometime later, but that was because Fischer desired it to be so.

Politics, power, money – on paper they are only words of profound or shallow content, depending on how you look at it and who is looking, but in reality they are represented by people. Those people sail the seas of their times and events, driven by the winds of their interests, by their open or hidden motives, and create and even shape those times and events.

The seventh floor of the Intercontinental where Bobby had his suite was truly an interesting place. The president of the Bosnian Serbs, Mr. Radovan Karadžić, was often present and stayed there with his entourage. Visitors: Mr. Krajišnik, Mr. Koljević, Mr. Buha, Mr. Zametica, and the parliamentarian Mr. Kennedy (the Englishman in the role of counselor and support from the land of Proud Albion).

The president (premier) of Montenegro, Mr. Milo Đukanović with his entourage. Natural, elegant Lord Owen, seen walking the hotel corridors with a stack of documents in his hands, while the sympathetic Mr. Cyrus Vance walked there as well, bringing messages of the world for the Serbian politicians of that time and thus leaving his own trace on that place as well. Numerous quite influential businessmen and "businessmen" whose companies and enterprises bore strange short names, seen in the spy movies. Lawyers from all over the world, Mr. Giovanni di Stefano, Arkan's best man, was especially active and ready for openness and communication, but so were people on "the other side" of the law (in retrospect it is almost impossible to determine which side of the law was which, where the line was and if it even existed in those years), also influential on a global level.

The telephone rang early one morning in my room. A well-known voice was asking for Mr. Vasiljević. The leader of the

The Greatest Secret of Bobby Fischer

Serbian Radical Party, Mr. Vojislav Šešelj, wished to speak with the banker. The newspaper headlines indicated that such a thing was possible, that it was the wish of today's Hague prisoner to have today's inmate of the Belgrade central prison on his list of candidates in the upcoming election. That intention of Milošević's bitter opponent, later coalition partner, was refused, because Vasiljević was to enter the upcoming Serbian elections on his own. One of the "icons" of the opposition struggle and renowned writer, Mr. Vuk Drašković, as a confirmed lover of chess, visited the match and played a couple of games in the foyer of Sava Centar. The head of the General Staff of the Yugoslav Army, Mr. Života Panić, who had "honored" the grand opening was often seen there, as was Mr. Frenki Simatović, commander of the "Red Berets" (later the Special Operations Unit), who would drop by the hotel for coffee. Certainly, there was the unavoidable Željko Ražnatović Arkan, who would make the rounds in his pristine and pressed uniform, with his beret elegantly tipped, complete with his weapons and his entourage. And there were others…

That was the environment Bobby Fischer stepped into each day when he closed his hotel room door behind him. And it was not easy to answer all of his questions: who was who, who was with whom; nor was it easy to comment on his statements or defend his complicated mind from the winds of the fatal thoughts which might have an effect on the very reason why we were there.

With Mr. Karadžić it was easy, because Bobby never showed any special interest in him. The usual "hello" in passing when they met, without introductions or conversation. Only sometimes, thundering in laughter, the bard of world chess would comment on the long, shaggy hair of his "neighbor". "It looks like a lion's mane," he would say. "Why doesn't he just get a haircut?"

Games twenty-two and twenty-three saw a division of points. The twenty-third contest between the grandmasters was especially exciting, as they traded possibilities for winning the game. After the exhausting battle, everyone agreed that the outcome was fair.

However, Bobby was sometimes also quite upset because of someone on the colorful palette of the hotel's customers. One day we were sitting in the hotel restaurant outside the hotel entrance.

The Greatest Secret of Bobby Fischer

Bobby liked the comfortable armchairs and he often stayed there beyond all measure and quite commonly napped in them for a few hours. This time we were talking quietly when, from around the corner, from the elevators, came the rather short slim figure of an important Israeli businessman, straight at us at high speed. When he reached us, or rather to the entrance of the closed restaurant (through the glass you could see the staff setting up the tables), he gave the door a hard kick because he could not get in. The rudeness of this gesture really upset Bobby, who naturally noticed the background of the "lively" businessman with the characteristic Yamulka on his head. When the maître d', keeping to protocol, went out into the foyer to explain to the guest that he would have to wait a few minutes for lunch, the obviously irritated chess player sharply and loudly commented on the arrogance of the gesture. This, in accord with Bobby's beliefs, brought about a lengthy monologue on the privileged status of the people to whom our momentary hero belonged. Thus I heard, among other things, that my ward had gotten information that the American police did not react when, during a regular check, they found a Mossad agent, armed to the teeth on the territory of the USA. He sought for chances to confirm the conspiracy everywhere and in every place, such that in his "efforts" there was no such thing as an unfathomable or inexplicable detail or event.

In our immediate vicinity, a well-known French "philosopher" and "humanist" had a room, having come to visit Belgrade in the middle of the month with his better half. During the day he visited the hotspots of the Serbian capital where he was a regular visitor, with his statements about the uniqueness and greatness of the Serbian people who ought to die strategically to the last man as they defended European civilization; he spent his nights in nasty arguments with his better half, who everyone around recognized by her perfectly designed elegance. Bobby often asked me to quiet these stormy outbursts of "passionate anger", accompanied by shouts, screams and the sound of things breaking, or to have the French couple moved to another floor so that he could rest. That was certainly done, but it was not the end of the scandals because the "humanist" almost lost his head over an affair with a beautiful

The Greatest Secret of Bobby Fischer

Serbian woman who, to make the story more interesting, was already married. Her furious husband, in accordance with traditional Serbian customs, came to solve the problem right there at the hotel, with an armed entourage of his relatives. Just how important "foreign guests" were in those days is best proven by the fact that, from the eternal loss of philosophical orientation and humanist practice, the Frenchman was saved by members of Serbian state security. Whether one of them was even the best man at the future wedding of the "captured Serbian princess" and the representative of "the European spirit", I honestly do not know. However, as one of the main "puppeteers" of the political scene here, an invisible architect of the events, a mysterious Belgrade dentist, a lady of enormous influence, said it best those days, "The Serbs are a nation of people who are terribly grateful to anyone who loves them." There were all kinds of things in the country in which, in those days, there was nothing. Bright colors and broad brush strokes, of personal vanity and interest, the canvas – they presented the framework in which the match was held. Such vibrations and sounds crashed above our heads.

No matter how hard I guarded him from events and information which would upset him, by his own will Bobby Fischer boarded the ship of light and darkness, heights and valleys, which today even without him still sails with a new crew, under a different flag and with a different captain and officers, on the same sea above which the same winds still blow.

Game twenty-four of the match did not bring much excitement at the board, so that the delegates of the Socialist Party of Serbia, who held their congress in the smaller hall next door, did not have much to see during their coffee breaks.

The rhythm of the match and the intensity of the games seemed to slow down in comparison to the part on Sveti Stefan. The reason for that should mostly be sought in the broken rhythms of the players themselves (Fischer's above-mentioned leisure during the break between the two parts, the fatigue and slight health problems of Boris Spassky), and on the other hand it seemed that the entire event had fulfilled the reason why it was being held, and everyone was expecting Bobby to be victorious in the end. In the sweet feeling of satisfaction because of the achieved thoughts, expectations and hopes, people had already gone far ahead in new matches, big plans and expectations.

Suddenly, game twenty-five saw the real, inspired Fischer. After Spassky's initiative at the opening, he came back from not such an easy situation by moving his knight to b6. Bobby's well-known resilience and love of the fight brought him victory over his confused opponent, to the thundering applause of the audience.

Completely consistent with his selective reliability, so typical of his sudden changes in stream of thought and reflection, on the October morning after that victory Bobby informed me that he would go have lunch that afternoon the with federal premier, Mr. Milan Panic. My surprise was not so much in the fact that this contact had "gotten by" me, but rather because his constantly expressed animosity toward the Serbian-American businessman had now withdrawn before some new sort of internal impulse. Among other things, that also was Bobby Fischer.

Besides his unwavering fundamental opinions, everything else was inconstant, wavering and indicative of the chameleon syndrome. At first glance, it might seem like a practical calculation. The elections were looming. On December 22, 1992, Mr. Panic and Mr. Milošević were to find themselves in a direct contention for the position of president of Serbia. Milan Panic was pro-Western, democratically oriented, a lion without real strength, in the jaws of power, with the secured support of the first man of the SR Yugoslavia, the great writer and accidental politician, Mr. Dobrica Ćosić, and thus all of those who wanted change. In the public media, Bobby could see the analyses of the voters shown through the prognoses of the analysts, who showed the likelihood of victory as: Panic – 37%, Milošević – 31%, (others – 32%), giving significant advantage to the businessman who had such remarkable vitality and energy.

Taking Fischer's reality into account (the threats of the American administration) such a "sitting on the fence" could be practical and existential wisdom. Perhaps there was some influence from the outside? Or a sudden curiosity? From the way he announced the event (somehow shyly, not looking me in the eye), it seemed to me that the stimulus for such a gesture surely must have come from outside our circles. Perhaps from Mr. Gligorić? Whatever the case, elegantly dressed, at the appointed time Bobby awaited his guest at the hotel restaurant. When I saw the approaching group, I warned him that in the premier's entourage, apart from the bodyguards, and protocol officer, there were also "courtiers" in the form of the editor of a respectable Serbian magazine, his better half (at that time life and journalistic), and the most well-known photographer of that time who was sporting a typical moustache on his drawn face. Since the chess player showed no signs of distress, the merry group was allowed to approach. Mr. Panic approached the table with a quick energetic stride, his arms stretched out wide and he was smiling from ear to ear. All the others behind him. Lunch passed in a merry tone, including a couple of quick games of chess between the champion and the premier, played on the pocket chess set. Without much hesitation, Bobby also allowed photographs to be taken. Sincere handshakes in the end, and parting waves from both sides. I remember the slight feelings of bitterness I had at the time. So many empty words, the hostility (it had turned out for no reason) and his explicit demands that encounters and meetings with the premier were to be avoided, and that the press and photographers be kept at a distance. And then, a *salto mortale* without explanation. The impression I had did not arise from any sort of political connotation, but appeared as an internal indication of what would happen later.

Namely, Bobby was prepared (he had it in his character and in the make up of his personality) to change his opinions, his thinking and views, to sacrifice everything and everyone on the altar of his self-satisfaction. He said nothing on the walk back to our rooms. Silence. My doubt in his honesty. "And what will stop doubt when it appears?"[47] I checked out his room. In one second, I imagined the scene that would occur if I were to say at that moment that, according to my information, there were agents of Mossad staying at the hotel who had just lost two Komodo

---

[47] Meša Selimović, *Death and the Dervish*.

dragons, all so that the staff would be occupied with catching them while Israeli special forces finished him off. I closed the door and inarticulately add in my thoughts, "Bobby, my team and I just quit."

I smiled at my own thoughts as I left. The champion wished me good night. Shalom, Bobby.

Just when everyone was expecting a quick finish, game twenty-six saw another turnaround and Spassky's victory. Thus the Russian-French grandmaster took his fifth victory in the match and ensured its extension for a while. This was confirmed in a draw in the next contest.

While things at the chess board were like that, there was no certainly lack of excitement in the capital city of Serbia and the SR Yugoslavia. Thursday, October 29. In the Hyatt Hotel (a few hundred yards from our Intercontinental), the first of a hundred or so unsolved murders occurred in an unbroken bloody series that never ended, nor has the light of justice ever reached them till this very day. Namely, when the maid went to do her daily routine behind the locked door of room 331 she found the lifeless body of the twenty-one year old king of the Belgrade streets, Aleksandar Knežević, a.k.a. Knele. Gunshots had thus ended a short, stormy life, marked by its all-encompassing speed and danger. That same afternoon two close friends of the deceased, in an attack of anger and pain because of the loss of their friend, expressed their broiling emotions by breaking chairs, tables and planters and other things in the rich inventory of the Hyatt.

When they finished that, their road took them to a place which for them had been *terra incognita* until then. Through the force of their grief, then with the force of their hands and tools, several expensive automobiles were damaged, among them, unfortunately, the new Mercedes of Mr. Vasiljević. Seeing this, some of the security personnel were already in the parking lot fully armed, while one of the "uninvited" visitors (who is also no longer among the living) held his gun pointed at the oncoming danger. When I ran out of the hotel, I saw the moment before the storm, a second before bloodshed. Both sides shouting and threatening (better emptying of the ego than of the pistol clips), but we still managed to bring the incident to an end (happy endings that year would not happen). We all went into the Intercontinental together. The conclusion: according to the stormy convincing and apologies of the perpetrators, it turned out that Vasiljević's Mercedes was damaged as co-lateral damage in a sad situation. Since I incidentally knew in a certain way the two "hot-blooded" young men, the thing was completely clear. A coincidence. Clear explanations, coffee, then a peaceful departure gave birth to the hope that this chapter was finished. Still, all of us on Fischer's team were gathered and on guard till the next morning. And just so that sleep would not happen that night, nor on the next few, the newspaper headlines lent a helping hand.

The men of the pen, all of them, meaning the journalists of the daily papers and magazines connected these two events. "Was Jezdimir Vasiljević involved in Knežević's murder?" The sequence of events from the last evening which could connect the two hotels without reason or rationality by blood, did not get a different connotation even now. From the media, announcements and public information, more dangerous and ominous was the pulse of the steaming city which was whispering from ear to ear, taking on, like an echo, new forms, making an unrecognizable sound from the first voice, which sometimes reaches the target only after the bullet materialized the word.

Early morning, the lobby is packed. The semi-circular booths filled with familiar faces. "Underground" and "overground" Belgrade. All feeling summoned, few invited. Hunched over ("in position by teams, without uniforms", but everyone in their place), the messages went from group to group in hushed tones. Was there going to be a conflict between the two different worlds? Of course not. The participants the previous evening's attack on the property of the main organizer of the match confirmed it. But in a certain way, Fischer was also a target, worth millions. Could someone, in the heat of passion, possibly endanger the chess spectacle? There were voices, hints, threats, but it was all short-lived. My protégé, sensing the excitement all around, asked me for a detailed report. I spent a lot of time explaining the event (the part that had to do with us), the relationships and connections. He was quite interested in all of it, down to the last detail.

"Where shall we eat?" I asked him. "Perhaps here in the room?"

"Of course not," said Bobby, then added with curiosity, "let's go downstairs." As if onto a stage, the champion stepped into the crowded foyer.

More a demonstration of elegance than of power. My closest team, now reinforced by an international one.

I remember three days and three nights without a wink of sleep. All doubt was removed. If there had been impassioned words – they were withdrawn, if there had been threats made in haste and ignorance toward the powerful banker and his chess darling – they were forgiven. The "undefeated world champion" once again got a confirmation of his power which did not come from him, but was reflected through his being, which enjoyed it.

A life was lost.

The Mercedes was fixed.

In the cold eye of the observer, everything could be seen like this.

Campomanes, the president of FIDE, arrived once again in Belgrade. Continuing agreements and negotiations about future plans with Mr. Vasiljević. The confirmation of old ideas and new concepts for the planetary chess perspective. At that moment, however, another arrival was to be far more important to Fischer. Long awaited, grandmaster Miguel Quinteros arrived in Belgrade on a visit with his better half. In the early days, Bobby often mentioned him to me in various stories and anecdotes, highlighting his popularity and importance in Argentina. Namely, Miguel was very close to the now deceased son of the Argentine president at the time, Menem, and was a respectable and respected member of his country's establishment. As a spicy detail, Mrs. Torre (describing how handsome the long-awaited guest was, especially with his dark beard and moustache) gave me the information that the South American chess player had dated a gorgeous Philippine girl for a while, who had "confirmed" her looks at a competition for the most beautiful woman in the world. So, our newly arrived "member of the company" was a

The Greatest Secret of Bobby Fischer

remarkable refreshment to us all because of his merry character and his energy.

And we finally saw the end. After two draws (in game twenty-nine, Spassky had good chances to win), so that the symbolism could be rounded off at number thirty, the victory finally occurred. Boris dragged out the endgame through an attempt at sacrificing his knight, teaching patience to the audience and the organizers. But the inescapable finale had to happen. In the return match, twenty years after Reykjavik, 10:5 for Bobby Fischer.

The champion came out in front of the glass wall to the ovation of over 4,000 fans who cheered him joyfully. The match organizer, Mr. Jezdimir Vasiljević, slightly confused, put a wreath around the neck of the new-old champion.

And it all might have seemed like a triumph.

It reminded us of happiness.

Or of solace.

If any of that exists at all, or if we can understand it.

CHAPTER 12.

THE HUMAN TOUCH

It is not easy to say at what point the feeling of loneliness, persecution and perpetual existential vulnerability in the life of the chess genius and the tragedy of his everyday life was the hardest. Up to his return to the wider world, the public spotlight, in that now distant year of 1992, and up to the realization of the spectacular "peace match" or the "revenge match of the twentieth century", the repeated duel of the knights of Reykjavik, the lowest and hardest point had been, in Bobby's experience, a seven-day stint in the jail in Pasadena. This traumatic experience of complete helplessness which he described in detail in his author's brochure left an indelible mark in his mind and memory. Erroneously arrested, his identity mistaken for that of a bank robber's, physically mistreated, humiliated and degraded, in that year of 1981 he got another painful confirmation of the focusing of evil on his mind and body, his entire being. The world champion, the possible pride of his country, derided, strangled, left nude in a cold solitary confinement cell, without food for an entire 24 hours, no right to a phone call, forgotten by everyone, according to his experience, he barely saved himself in the station where he was held without due process. Adding to it, another horrifying threat that struck on his deepest fears. The threat of being detained in a mental institution.

On one occasion, while quite fatigued, I made one of my few verbal lapses in the course of my work with him. Namely, wanting to remind him of our previous conversation, I used the following formulation: "Remember your stories about your minor inconvenience in the Pasadena jail?" Bobby was visibly disturbed at the mention of the term "minor". I had certainly not done it on purpose, but the slip of the tongue betrayed the possibility that I thought the victim had overblown the experience, influenced by sensitivity and grievance, but also regarding the fact that the words "torture" and "torment" had a completely different connotation in the Balkans at the time. We quickly resumed the conversation without consequence. The dungeon of Bobby Fischer was far narrower than the one he bore in his memory.

His prison was the girth, weight and height of his own body. In that tenebrous despair and chasm, much of it, yet also nothing at all, was imprisoned behind bars of doubt. Being overcome with feelings of pain, bitterness, fear, palpable in the damp darkness or a bare void, emotionless white emptiness or a collection of shattered mirrors of memories. A casemate with no escape route, unless that escape was self-isolation or death. Thus, Bobby's illness, his curse and his destiny, were definitely diagnosed as a permanent, all-encompassing inability to recognize feelings and emotions, or more precisely, the lack thereof.

Even his self-love and egocentrism were not so strong, nor did they go so far as to do him good, and neither were they so grave as to lead him to self-destruction. An endless flat line, sometimes up, sometimes down, but always like a ball buoyant in the coldness that governed his life. There were moments when the image seemed like suffering and manifested itself on the surface with symbols of pain. Sometimes it seemed like joy, the sight and sound resembled happiness, but a swift return to the circus tightrope of an alienated life without a safety net, back to the cage which the bird of his soul flew into in his early childhood.

I remember the sunny day by the river Tisa. A mystically beautiful river, the scent of linden trees and a breeze from the northeast, a breath from the faraway steppes and birch forests seemed to bring with it wistful Russian ballads.

One could cut the melancholy with a knife, and in those moments, we enjoyed it. We sat on comfortable chairs on a sandy river isle, in silence. There was no one around us. And suddenly, out of nowhere, a girl of around three years of age, beautiful as an angel, with ribbons in her dark hair. In her Sunday clothes, wearing red lacquered shoes (let us say she was in church with her

The Greatest Secret of Bobby Fischer

parents, or visiting friends or relatives), she approached our hero with an innocent smile, the one only worn by children, whose souls still remember God's purity. Bobby jerked up and looks at the sudden visitor. His faint smile disappeared in a moment, and he turned his head away. The parents ran up to us and apologized for the disturbance, then softly warned their darling not to leave their sight again.

As they left, she was still looking in our direction over the shoulder from her parents' arms. There are few people who would not even briefly and out of courtesy play with the amiable visitor, or at least offer a polite smile. One of those people was Bobby. During the match, there were many similar situations, and the same reaction.

In "guarding" his worlds, he had difficulty understanding pure and noble intentions. Of course, evil and evil-prone people were abundant in his life, but surely throughout the years, people had come and gone bearing honest wishes and intentions, caring with an open heart for his wellbeing. Many of them I do not know, but can I attest to some.

There would certainly be no return of Bobby Fischer from anonymity and the oblivion if the mosaic of events and time did not bring together several personalities and unanimous resolves. First and foremost, Zita Rajcsányi. She was the impetus, the hope, a new life for the aged genius. She did not meet him in abundance and wealth, but in material destitution, the somewhat forgotten chess player who could only count the days to the end in the Pasadena apartment in his life's twilight. An honest admiration, strength coming from untainted feelings gave birth to new horizons. She breathed a new breath into his lungs, "loosed" his feet to run again and helped in his chess rebirth, to the joy of millions. Intelligent and proud, in the end she felt, saw and knew that he had clumsily, yet arrogantly marginalized and hurt her. Having pushed her away, she left him at the storm reach of self-sufficiency, because his disregard was too great, and her grievance too deep. Bobby's powerful remorse did not help matters. He then lost, or more precisely, pushed away with his actions, not only the

The Greatest Secret of Bobby Fischer

woman of his life, but his best friend, one full of sympathy and honesty. The director of the match, Janos Kubat, once said, "I know what you gave him, but I certainly gave him a chance to make money". Both in a metaphorical and literal sense, that was absolutely correct. If it were not for this, in every sense of the word, extraordinary man, Fischer would probably carry only one dollar bills in his wallet for the rest of his life.[48]

Janos never presented himself as Fischer's manager. For the media, as well as privately, he always commented that he stood for a group of people interested in new chess investments, new spectacles and improving the conditions for the ancient game and those who play it. At the time he wisely sought the best paths for the chess of tomorrow, diligently and earnestly stressing that in the end, "All Fischer's decisions will be his own and the American chess player will absolutely autonomously and of his own free will select from what is offered, with his final word acting as law." Immediately following the start of the match, our hero began without reason to express his doubts towards the man who provided his new life opportunity and had a crucial influence in the ascension of what had been until recently a poor man of a brilliant mind for chess, to a millionaire with a sound material foundation for a blissful future. However, as a token of his "appreciation" Bobby completely stopped seeing him and gave those around him the sign that it was his prerogative and final wish. Janos Kubat continued to work on the perfectionism of every aspect of the match, with intention of making his dreams come true in the coming days. One further rejection of honesty, respect and concern.

A chapter of its own, Mr. Jezdimir Vasiljević. Today, when he is surely going through difficult times, beset by a serious disease (in addition to everything else), it must be said that he loved Fischer uncompromisingly, to an extent that bordered on the excessive, and that he wholeheartedly strived to fulfill all of his favorite's

---

[48] The story claims that when he was arrested in Pasadena, he had a couple of one-dollar bills in his wallet.

wants and needs. To their last days together, he stayed true and responsible to all the promises he gave and the contract he signed. The fact that two important items, the TV rights to the match and usage of the newly-patented chess clock, by circumstance, were not in truth implemented to the end, was compensated by the fact that in the duration of the match (while the banker was in Serbia, and after his departure, i.e. escape) Fischer received significant amounts of money which he, upon later reflection, mysteriously forgot about. Truth be told, the chess player himself admired his patron, but the finale was to be expected. Jezdimir Vasiljević thus became one of the leading players in the conspiracy, the man who "defrauded" him, the man who "abused" his talent and skill. Immeasurable hatred, waves of resentment with nearly 4,000,000 dollars in his pocket. In Fischer's mind, the Serbian businessman was, following his address to the nation from Tel Aviv, cast downstream into the muddy waters of absolute abhorrence.

This is how Robert James Fischer fought on his battlefield and on the map of his permanent "warzone" strewn with intercrossing trenches, with love, caring and goodness. Brave when he knew nothing could and would happen to him, particularly courageous when, much later, the money from the match arrived, it was almost touching how and how frightened he was. If in his walk down the street, a little dog would go by and bark at him, he would quickly recoil and "run" for his life. When on his insistence I took him to the shooting gallery so he could watch me practice shooting, after the first sound of a gunshot, he would seek shelter in the next room, fearing he would get hit by a stray bullet.

Bobby's resolve manifested itself, therefore, in hurting and rejecting those who loved him. The existence of goodness would shatter his view of the world, bring into question his whole life up to that point and pull whatever ground he stood on out from under his feet. Going from his experience and emotional scars he received in his youth, having adopted it as a model without a model, because he had no other, we now have a man without a role model, a picture without a frame.

And God? What about him? Fischer was not a truly religious man. He thought that "somewhere up there, there must be something" but it wasn't the Maker from the Torah, the New Testament, the Koran, Bhagavad Gita or some other comprehensive book on civilization and religion. Even his joining the World Wide Church of God was merely a fruitless search for identity, refuge, or a hiding place. In that sense, he was neither particularly informed nor educated.

When to the invitation of Prince Tomislav Karađorđević,[49] who was present on Sveti Stefan and often at the Intercontinental, we visited Topola and Oplenac, with particular pride the descendant of the Serbian royal family showed his American guest around the church holding the crypt where his ancestors were buried. Frescoes of Orthodox saints, the interior filled with glistening light and the flickering of the candles left no particular impression on Fischer. He did on his return, however, vocally praise the traditional Serbian meal the dignified and, in his modesty, exceptional Tomislav Karađorđević which had been arranged for us in his home in the vicinity of the church. The blue-blooded host extended the well-known Serbian hospitality in its true form and essence. It was not, therefore, easy to walk the world with a closed heart, preemptively judging and condemning others, far from one's self as from God who gifted the "walker" with enormous talent and a call to brilliance and to the mission objective.

"What goes around, comes around," Bobby exclaimed when the Twin Towers burned and thousands perished. His last words were, "Nothing heals wounds like a human touch." A contradiction, or... The great Serbian theologian and philosopher, Holy Bishop Nikolaj Velimirović on one occasion said, "Even the worst of men must three times in life remember God: when he sees a just man suffer for another's guilt, when he himself suffers for another's guilt, and on his deathbed."

Bobby, everything could have been different if you had let the people who loved you truly touch you. In such a world, at least for you, nothing would go around, nothing would come around, and

---

[49] Prince Tomislav Karađorđević, the son of Aleksandar Karađorđević I, King of the Serbs, Croats and Slovenes.

the God you could not grasp would always be close by, so you would never be alone.

CHAPTER 13.

THE END OF A NEW BEGINNING

Finally, the match was over. Finally, especially from the standpoint of the organizer who, because of the length of the chess duel, was now almost every day remarking on the expense which accompanied the players' "inefficiency", but also because of the ubiquitous belief that the media significance of the event had long since passed its zenith. Besides his sincere concern for his ongoing investment, the accusations of Mr. Vasiljević about the financial aspect were more of a smokescreen for covering his desire that the rhythm speed up as it led to the end because of his big plans for the upcoming events. However, there was certainly no relaxation before Fischer proved his primacy in game thirty. Satisfaction overwhelmed everyone involve in these events when we toasted with champagne as the stage lights went out, as the hotel slowly emptied and the expected sunset finally came.

A lot of people came through my office that day. We bade farewell to those who had worked in various positions in the organization, to the match visitors from the whole world, to the accredited journalists who had spent a couple of exciting months in our proximity. A defeated but quite satisfied Boris Spassky also left the capital of Serbia.

Eugene Torre headed home with his family so that he would be temporarily absent. The vacant corridors, Sava Centar empty. The sound of footsteps could be announcing Bobby and Zita, Svetozar Gligorić, Quinteros with his wife, or ever less frequently, Mr. Vasiljević who was always in a hurry. In my vicinity, Dane and Voja, always available, but now doing shifts, spending their evenings off at home. The wind had stopped blowing, the sea grew tranquil. But the scenario foresaw no such calm, so this was just an illusion that would only last a couple of days.

How and what next? Whether some people wanted to admit it or not, this match with a little good fortune could have been a turning point in the history of chess. The most important thing had occurred: Robert James Fischer was back. That fact, together with the just finished spectacle, had focused the attention of the chess public, and not just them, on the game itself, on the sport. Equally important, big money had appeared on the black-and-white board. In the joining of these factors, people with vision saw a great chance for new, exciting adventures, the moving of longstanding borders and the conquest of new areas of success. Possibilities were being sought. A lot of activities at FIDE and by its president Campomanes, who had found in Mr. Vasiljević, or it seemed at the time, an adequate and financially powerful fellow traveler on the road into the future of chess. Through contacts, the directions and alternatives were sought through the world chess federation, the establishment of the *Jugoskandic* association, but also through secret agreements on benefiting the players and the game. Other wealthy fans appeared, also prepared to invest. A Dutch businessman, Joop van Oosterom, wanted to invest a million dollars in women's chess. His name appeared in the wings also in the final calculations of the prize money for the matches being talked about, together with some famous business people who also had a passion for chess.

The speculations were varied and interesting. The list of Fischer's potential opponents was long, with different material eventualities and places of play, and the names in circulation were: Judit Polgár, Anatoly Karpov, Ljubomir Ljubojević, Nigel Short, and finally, or primarily, Kasparov.

However, as the possibilities grew, the number of barriers multiplied.

Above all, the arrogance of Garry Kasparov. In the name of the Russian Chess Federation, he demanded the exclusion of the Yugoslav team for the European championships in the Hungarian town of Debrecen. Even though the Russian chess players and their organization distanced themselves from such statements and bad intentions, the bitterness remained. However, Mr. Vasiljević, who was mentioned as a possible financier of the FIDE match for the title of the world champion, from the shadows of course, did not allow this to stand without an adequate answer. "Garry Kasparov's play is worth one dollar," he said on one occasion, "and that's exactly how much he'll get from me."

A new turnabout. Kasparov and Short refused to play a match under the auspices of FIDE in Manchester. Their announcement was made together in London: the two of them were forming a new chess association, with the explanation that FIDE was for "amateurs". Nigel added, "FIDE often oversteps its rights and it has not shown respect toward hopefuls for the title." They announced that they were expecting financial offers in the period of March 10-19, and that the decision about the venue for the match would be made on March 22. Kasparov passionately and publicly showed animosity toward the Serbs, and decisively stated that he would never play for communist money. He was probably referring to Jezdimir's dollar. Defending its rights, FIDE was to forbid the match, and on March 25, Kasparov was relieved of his title as world champion. From the comfort of his position in chess, Fischer was carefully following all this.

Just to make sure he was not at peace, already in December the Federal Grand Jury of the USA and the American public prosecutor officially brought charges after the warning in September, saying that Robert James Fischer had broken the law by which American citizens were forbidden to have commercial dealings with Yugoslavia. At a press conference in Washington, American prosecutor Jay Stevens made the threat concrete: 10 years in prison, a 250,000 dollar fine, but also a new caveat – *his winnings from the match were to be seized!* He offered Fischer an alternative, either to return to the USA and stand trial, or *to remain forever in Yugoslavia!* This naturally included an extradition petition.

In order to vent the tensions caused by the newly arisen situation, Mr. Vasiljević announced to the media that Fischer was staying in Yugoslavia, registered as the director of the *Jugoskandic* chess federation.

The Greatest Secret of Bobby Fischer

He added, "The money is still in the country, in a safe place." Here the organizer meant the money which was supposed to be paid to Bobby as his prize for winning the recently ended match. However, Fischer still did not have his own material means, because the promised prize was still far away. The merry nature of Miguel Quinteros fit perfectly into the post-competition period, and Bobby, relaxed, went on enjoying himself. Back in America he had heard of some of the spas in Serbia which are quite famous for the medicinal qualities of their waters and for their positive effects on people's health. He chose Kanjiža on my recommendation, without even thinking about it. We prepared for the trip and headed off, to Fischer's great delight.

The exceptional surroundings, the kind medical staff, the comfort of the hotel itself all pleased the new guest. The town has a largely Hungarian population, typical central European architecture, and was to offer us an unforgettable time.

Pools with warm water, massages with hot mud, long walks along the River Tisa fit perfectly into Bobby's affinity for a healthy life. There was little chess playing. With Miguel he talked more about a variety of topics than he worked on his playing form. From the outside, Bobby and Zita's relationship was still harmonious, without palpable or visible turbulence. And while we were enjoying ourselves in northern Vojvodina, the outside world was burning with political fever resulting from the elections in Serbia and Montenegro. Perhaps there would be no place in these memoirs for this episode if its result and consequences had not so dramatically affected the further developments in Fischer's life and career.

Namely, the political situation "in the country in the mountainous Balkans" in 1993 took on a new dimension, precisely because of the fact that there was a huge regrouping of forces on the political scene. The pro-Western federal premier, until recently quite alone, was now in the race for the Serbian presidency and he received unexpected but powerful support from all sides. Once it was shown by the president of Yugoslavia, Mr. Dobrica Ćosić, he got the support of almost the entire opposition and even the government of Montenegro. Thus, with a fair wind at his back, fully confident, Mr. Milan Panic went into battle against his only real, undefeated until then, competitor, Mr. Slobodan Milošević. Still, to make the elections "more interesting", Mr. Jezdimir Vasiljević "had to" get involved in the seven candidate race.

Regardless of later events, it must be said that Jezdimir was a charismatic man. That charisma came from simplicity, directness and sincerity in his behavior, which left no one indifferent. Funny in a "folk" way, gifted with the skill of finding ways to do things and with his experienced instinct for survival, full of stories and anecdotes, he was always an interesting partner in conversation. Since we were people on assignment and were thus separate from his business affairs, we had the opportunity to see him exclusively when he came to see Bobby, or when we were coordinating and planning things related to the undefeated world champion. I had only one opportunity to enter the central offices of the *Jugoskandic* empire. An enormous room, moveable cubicles and the simplest of office furniture. When I left the room after a few minutes, I easily defined my impression – it is all temporary.

Now with his energy, which simply seemed to poor from his rather small plump body, he was campaigning under the slogan "Man of Change". Already at one of the first pre-election press conferences, he distanced himself from Milošević, and noted the fact that he would finance his own campaign to the tune of 250,000 dollars. Eloquent Jezdimir had one particular Munchhausen-like characteristic. Namely, quite often, not intending to lie, at least that is the way I took it, he would tell a story that was the fruit of his imagination, a projection of a wish or a simplified Marquez-like phantasmagoria. For example, in the middle of December he announced to the media that Bush and Fischer had come to terms. Further, the American president had sent a letter in which he apologized to his chess genius countryman for the pressure, while Bobby had expressed sorrow and contrition for spitting on an official document of the most powerful country in the world (?!). At the same time he announced a Fischer—Ljubojević match, and a duel between Judit Polgár and Spassky, set for January 30.

The Greatest Secret of Bobby Fischer

Events in the capital city were becoming very interesting, so we decided after our rest and relaxation in Kanjiža to focus our observations closer to the epicenter of events. Snow covered the plains, ice rimmed the Danube, and we returned "home" to the Interkontinental. Fischer kept far away from Serbian politics, of course. Still we walked down to the smaller hall of Sava Centar a couple of times, where the banker was making his pre-election advertisements. Bobby smiled sympathetically while he watched Jezda in his elegant blue suit, with a hefty pipe in his hand, and then in conversation Bobby would analyze him and thus search for symbols, causes and effects. From the outside and inside, everything still seemed to be going quite well. Since we were in Belgrade, Mr. Gligorić started coming by again, so that training in chess became a more intense topic of interest for my ward.

About that time, Mr. Lothar Schmidt, the referee at the match both in Reykjavik and in Yugoslavia, called us. He was sincerely worried and he warned Fischer to take the threats seriously that were arriving from the other side of the Atlantic. Bobby was grateful for such concern and care. However, all danger of that type seemed far away and benign to him so that, in conjunction with periodic consultations with a lawyer, Mr. Miljević,[50] the red lights did not light up on our alarm system. While Mr. Vasiljević with his escort in a convoy of expensive automobiles was cruising around Serbia on his election campaign, which was based on the promotion of private initiative and animosity toward the National Bank of Yugoslavia and Mr. Panic, Bobby was living his comfortable Belgrade life. The media moratorium before elections, December 17. Elections on December 22, 1992. The result: Milošević – 56%, Panic – 34.2%, while Jezdimir Vasiljević obtained 1.38%. As soon as December 30, the parliament of the SR of Yugoslavia gave Milan Panic a vote of no confidence and he slipped into political oblivion, while Milošević reconfirmed his absolute power once again. Although he had distanced himself from the new Serbian president, that same evening Vasiljević came

---

[50] Vlada Miljević, the lawyer who played a significant role in the administrative framework for Fischer's comeback to chess.

The Greatest Secret of Bobby Fischer

to the Interkontinental, in a good mood and ordered a round of drinks for everybody, then toasted the winner. Fischer, who had been invited, also accepted a glass. While the crystal was raised to celebratory heights, Jezdimir added his votes out loud to those of two other candidates, obtaining a sum of 6.52%. "We took those from Panic," he said. Bobby was merrily chatting in the relaxed atmosphere with the winning loser, while late into the night the telephones were ringing in the surrounding suites. I saw some well known faces trotting from room to room. "Politics eats people alive," as the folk saying goes from the Serbian countryside. Authority. Power. But Bobby Fischer described it like this, "When you see that flight into vanity, then you must wonder who and when those people got the chip built in, the one that can be used by a powerful and distant hand to manipulate their destiny or, if so wished, after they've been used and played out their role, to 'turn off their vital functions'." We could hear the sound of glasses clinking in honor of passing this-worldly glory and prestige. Santé, cheers, *živeli*!

One more episode in the series of the necessities of fate was complete. And then Bobby's sister, Joan Fischer Targ, came to see us.

It was not hard for me to recognize her at the Keleti train station in Budapest. She arrived from France. Though she did not look like her younger brother, her specific inner energy led me right to her, and I easily recognized her among the hundreds of passengers who stepped out onto the platform. I introduced myself to her. She had heard so much about me. I thanked her and returned the compliment. Light blond, almost white hair, an energetic middle-age lady, looking younger than her documents stated. White sweater, brown jacket and pants of the same color, hiking shoes for traveling and not a lot of luggage. An American woman in Europe, just like the Lord made her. I took her to lunch at a nice restaurant in the center of the Hungarian capital. She talked quietly, measured and dignified. If Bobby had not told me that Joan, under the influence of the media information and stories, was a little afraid of coming to Serbia, I would have felt her slight nervousness and discomfort before the journey. But when we got in the car being driven by Dane that day, I noticed that I was helping her to relax through conversation. The highway to the border with no stops, slight trepidation from the back seat. However, when our guest saw my friendly conversation with the Serbian customs and border control, and the official pass of my colleague with his passport, all barriers dropped and she fairly happily continued our conversation till Belgrade. I did not obey Bobby. It was not easy to hide the identity of our guest, so at the reception desk we checked her in with an accent on her married name. According to my own instincts, I settled her into our hotel, on the same floor but in a different wing.

I knew it would be easier for me to control the demanding situation here, according to the facts I had heard from my protégé, because I would have the Fischers in proximity and under watch. It did not surprise me that Bobby was in no hurry to see his sister. He accepted my explanation about the practicality of having a common "home base", and then asked me to go get her only later when he was ready for dinner later that evening. Since we arrived in Belgrade around 4 in the afternoon, 9 in the evening, according to his measurement of time and "closeness", was the proper moment for their first meeting after many years.

I went to get Joan (she had just changed her hiking shoes for something more appropriate) and led her to Bobby's suite, entering it with her. Her brother was waiting for her in leisurely attire, in his old leather jacket, ready to go. They shook hands, no embrace. A cold "hello", no smile. I left them like that.

After ten minutes we went down to dinner. A sentence exchanged here and there at the table. The only sign of care was seen in the fact that Bobby, as a "good host", recommended which dishes and delicacies she should try. Over tea and dessert he read the paper while Joan stared in front of herself at her fruit salad.

I observed them from the side. I felt, regardless of their interpersonal relationship, great joy in seeing and getting to know another one of the Fischers. As I looked at their profiles, I was surprised that they really looked alike, and my thoughts led me into the past and I imagined them as children. Quickly in my thoughts I made a film according to the scenario I had from what

Bobby had told me of his memories. I managed to get to that feeling, to mystically step over the threshold of time and to enjoy the images I saw.

Regardless of Bobby's doubts that his sister was coming more on a "business" visit and in search of money than in the desire to see and visit him, I invested quite a lot of effort in taking care of Joan. When she wanted to see something of Belgrade, I accompanied her so that she would feel as comfortable as possible. She knew that I was completely available to her at all times and for whatever reason. Joan showed, at least to me, humility and an unusual gratitude for the attention I gave her. I suppose that Bobby's coldness and hostility awoke in me the need to compensate for her sake as much as possible because, regardless of the situation; to me she was the sister of the man I was taking care of. Perhaps one of the nicest rewards I got was received at the moment when we parted, somewhat later in Budapest. This time at the airport.

She stood in front of me and looked me right in the eye for a moment, and I saw tears on her cheeks. She gave me a long, gentle hug. "Thank you, Nesh, for everything you've done for me," she hesitated a second, "and for my brother."

Wanting to go on enjoying the healthy waters of Vojvodina, Bobby wished this time for us to go to the Junaković Spa, near Apatin. So we went to the west, to a town known for its breweries. Again, lovely surroundings with lots of woods and the famous hunting grounds full of various wild animals. But the proximity of Croatia and the battlefield was to bring Bobby a sort of surprise. On arrival and in the first few days of our stay, he saw a great number of young people missing arms or legs, or with some other visible physical handicap. He asked me quietly, "Why are there so many invalids in Serbia?!" I glanced at him to make sure he was being serious. When I saw his expression of actual wonderment, I explained things to him. During our further stay, several times he initiated conversations with some of these young men, with good intentions but without much empathy. I translated for him. By asking questions, he carefully tried to find out more from them about the war and their lives and suffering. His curiosity was the reason, and as a result he ended up being quite upset. The stories we heard were told with the trembling voices of young men who were forced to grow up too soon.

We spent our days as one should in such a situation. But there were surprises after all. One evening, Joan asked me to come by her room after I had seen Bobby off to sleep. She waited for me kindly, with a story about herself, about her brother, about their relationship and the relations in the family. I already knew most of what she told me, but I still listened to her carefully. Then the conversation turned from her intimate confession to the culmination which was coming. Namely, Bobby's sister asked of me, or through her questions actually demanded, as much information about her brother as possible, about his general state, but especially about his financial state. With all respect, I talked a lot, but of course I told her nothing. With a gentle smile, Joan told me that she and her mother had long suspected that "The Russians briefly kidnapped Bobby and cruelly experimented on him, encoding his conscious." At first it seemed like a joke, but the seriousness on her face convinced me that there would never be a lack of excitement or surprises with the Fischers. On one occasion, later, carefully with chosen words, I told Bobby about this sequence of events, and he confirmed that he knew that his mother and sister believed in such a story.

Except for this short excursion into the "twilight zone", I spent a lovely evening talking with Joan and once again understood how far away from each other they were as a family, how little they knew about each other, and that the coldness of those long past, days of youth had definitely turned into an eternal winter in their lives.

Joan headed home from the spa near Apatin. I saw her off to Budapest, and once again I witnessed their restraint in their conventional way of parting.

And then, we went back to Belgrade. A pile of mail awaited us upon return. Generally speaking, during his entire stay in Yugoslavia, Fischer got an enormous number of letters from all over the world. His fans wrote to express their respect and support, but there were also those who believed that they were

The Greatest Secret of Bobby Fischer

connected to the recipient via some special, mystical thread. On a couple of occasions we carefully analyzed the handwriting and contents of those letters which, in addition to the graphic and spectacular quality of the handwriting, contained things that also made Bobby worry. In this, two ladies were the frontrunners, one from the USA and the other from Canada, whose letters (I still have them today) Bobby did not even want to read because those small masterpieces of Gothic calligraphy scared him so badly that he did not even want to have them in his room.

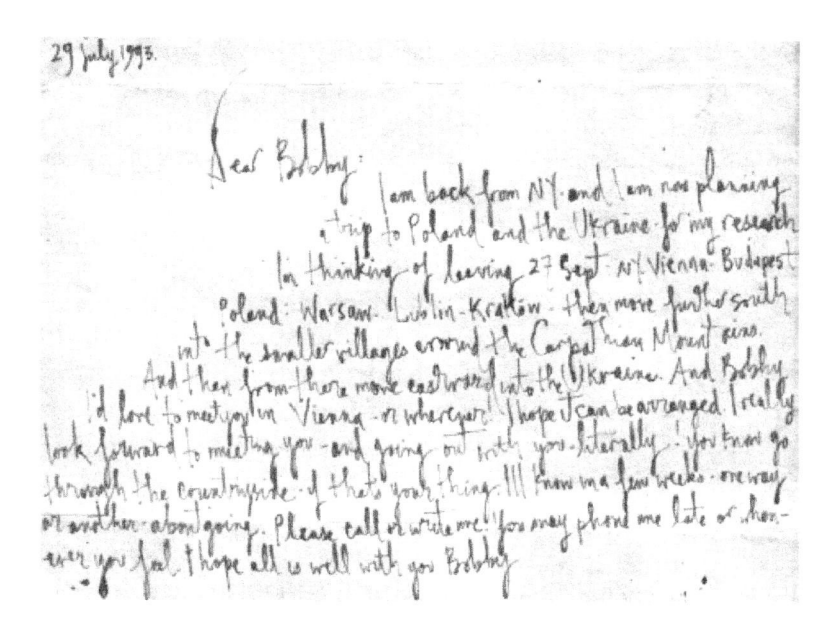

However, there was also news that did not arrive in the mail. In the media, and then in conversation with Bobby, Jezdimir announced a match between Judit Polgár, who was seventeen at the time, and Boris Spassky. The duel of genders, years, perspectives and careers would be held in the period from January 31 to February 16, at the Budapest Interkontinental. The match was to ten victories, Fischer's clock would be used. The prize was 200,000 dollars, of which 120,000 went to the winner and 80,000 to the loser. A curiosity was announced: Zita Rajcsányi was to be the match secretary. Of course the financier was Mr. Vasiljević, while Mr. Kubat, as always was to be the alpha and omega of the event.

It could not be said that Fischer was overjoyed by such a sequence of events. He, of course, was not ready at that moment for new efforts in chess or matches, nor did he want them. Still, this slow change of focus from him to Judit and Boris did not please him, to be sure. In addition, although the prize money was not that much in comparison to the previous announcements and expectations about new investments in chess by Mr. Vasiljević, it brought about a special kind of uneasiness in my protégé because of the fact that he still had not been paid the money promised him for the match he had played. The organizer gave him various explanations about the obstacles he faced in carrying out his promise and fulfilling his contract, which was still possible at that time because Bobby still believed him.

In the newspaper he read an article about the introduction of his new chess clock in practice. Even though several such announcements had been made, this one seemed to be fairly serious to him. The patent for the future of chess would be produced in Japan, with the emblem of *Jugoskandic*, with a first run of 100,000. Additional security that led into the future. In Budapest, mid-February saw victory for Judit Polgár over Boris Spassky.

For beauty and youth, and of course, for skill at chess – 5.5:4.5.

On the other hand, Kasparov was struggling with great difficulty to get full financial satisfaction, besides his verification as a player. In that sense, the heights Fischer had reached in Yugoslavia were too high for Garry in more ways than one. This obvious fact spread quickly throughout the world of chess, so that the Swiss *Schachwoche* proclaimed, "Kasparov can get serious money only through Fischer." However, the extent to which providence is incomprehensible to the human mind, or to which destiny is unpredictable, was to become evident in the stormy events that were starting at that moment, or were just becoming visible.

The Greatest Secret of Bobby Fischer

The beginning of March, except for announcing spring, did not hint at any providential events. A normal evening in Belgrade. The chess master was in his suite after supper with Mr. Gligorić. My colleagues and I were having late coffee and a chat. The telephone rang, "What's Fischer's headquarters up to?" asked the voice of Jezdimir Vasiljević.

"Everything is under control," I said, a bit surprised.

"Come down for a drink," he said in a commanding albeit joking tone. An unusual time for a visit, a surprise invitation. We went downstairs and saw the banker in one of the booths with his bodyguard, and there was a bottle of whisky on the table. A strange sight because Jezdimir did not drink, apart from an occasional glass of Ballantine's, or some champagne from time to time. The customary Havana cigar between his fingers. I had seen him many times before that, but never like this. He spoke quickly, then slowed, changing the rhythm of his words, the intensity of his movements, opening up various topics only to quickly close them again. His face was ruddy, though the bottle was just there for show because he only drank a couple of sips, like the rest of us; he got up from the table nervously, paced back and forth, came back to the table, and he kept doing this over and over.

The businessman suddenly insisted that his ever present bodyguard go home to get a well-deserved rest. My two friends and colleagues went up to our room to take their shifts, because some strange feeling was circulating the room, as if the uniqueness of the moment could be felt. We were left alone in the empty lobby. He was wearing a beige suit, blue shirt and a light scarf. His overcoat and briefcase were lying to the side.

"I can't take this anymore."

I looked at him in curiosity. It was clear to me that the unavoidable was coming with unstoppable force. He wiped the sweat from his brow and added, "They're robbing me! Everyone! From my family to the government!"

I remained silent.

"I have to get some rest, to get out of here for a while." And then he explained his plan, "I'll go to Budapest. Press conference.

It will be just before March 9.[51] Dissatisfied bank clients in the streets. And if a few windows get broken at my savings banks, it won't be terrible. That will put enough pressure on the Serbian leadership, especially on Milošević, to make all of this stop."

I was listening and thinking. This was all we needed. I was looking at his familiar face. He really was worried, and for the first time I felt his fear and great uncertainty.

On March 7, he headed for the announced destination, waving from afar, with his son Stefan in his arms, with his wife and his usual entourage. And indeed, there was a press conference in Budapest. Numerous journalists from Yugoslavia published his promise, "I'll be back on Wednesday." A lot of Wednesdays would pass before Jezdimir Vasiljević would return by force of chance, by force of law in his homeland. In the streets of Belgrade nothing significant happened on March 9. There were no dissatisfied clients, no anger or fury because of the collapse of the pyramid scheme. On March 10, the banker was already in Tel Aviv.

Like an ironic number game, the ball on the roulette game of life, led by coincidence, stopped on the number 3. Then the skilled croupier threw again... Nine... Then one after the other: 1, 9, 9, 3. So, 03.09.1993. Bobby celebrated his fiftieth birthday, half a century, half a life, we hoped and wished for him. We ordered an enormous cake for him, and the hotel put together a special dinner as a symbol of gratitude and so that everyone there could enjoy it. Birthday wishes came in from all over the country, the telephone rang from all corners of the world, a lot of nice wishes for the upcoming years. Zita was especially gleeful and her face was shining with satisfaction.

Over the next few days, Fischer spoke very carefully about ongoing events. He asked few questions, as if he were afraid of the answers. He was in a sort of strange state which ranged from firm belief to disbelief that such a bad confluence of circumstances

---

[51] On March 9, 1991, there were huge opposition demonstrations in Belgrade. For many years afterward, opponents of Slobodan Milošević marked that date with gatherings in the streets of the capital.

could occur after such an "idyll". Jezdimir left on his trip into exile without saying good-bye to Bobby.

According to the information available to me, they never met again, nor did they ever talk over the phone. To this day I have the distinct impression that the banker was slightly ashamed of the way he had to leave the country, while Fischer's hatred and loathing, born later, were an unbridgeable obstacle for someone to explain the inexplicable to him.

A couple of days after the departure, we received a video tape from Israel on which the "fugitive" explained to the nation the reasons for his departure, exile, banishment. After watching the recording, Bobby reacted angrily for the first time,

"Nesh, this is a bunch of nonsense."

The next day the tape arrived at the Belgrade TV station, Studio B, which broadcast it during prime time. That evening, as we sat in the comfortable armchairs, a messenger from the reception desk came over to me, "Telephone call."

"I tried to reach you in your room," said Vasiljević, "but since I didn't get an answer, I thought you might be down there. How's our boy?" he added with clear honesty which showed how much it meant to him, "Please try to explain things to him, to get him to take it easy. Take care of yourselves for a few days. The money will come, tell him not to worry. I'll call."

Precisely that "I'll call" was actually all that was left.

By chance, Bobby asked me already the next day what we should do, because according to him, he only had just a couple of hundred dollars. Knowing his character, I was quite sure that his habits were not going to change, so we both smiled and agreed that such an amount would be enough to cover his expenses over the next fifteen minutes or so. Therefore it was necessary to immediately find an alternative. My protégé certainly would not go uncared for in a country where the people loved him so much, but searching for a solution was going to be a truly demanding task, there was no doubt about it. Sure enough, an example.

Precisely in those days, inspired by the visible and clear indications of Fischer's difficulties, representatives of the Yugoslav Chess Association and the Crvena Zvezda (Red Star) Chess Club

The Greatest Secret of Bobby Fischer

came by and offered a respectable and workable solution. It was quite concrete: to the end of his life he was offered housing, a regular salary, then a position as a player, trainer, or counselor, with absolute freedom of choice. Bobby listened to them carefully, while these chess activists and his fans, full of energy, positivism and sincere good intentions, tried to show their unhidden concern and to explain this elegant way out of the momentary situation.

When they finished, in a dramatic moment of silence, they looked unblinking at the champion. They were expecting an answer which would make them happy and which would mean that he understood their efforts to please him. After a couple of second came a series of sentences. Once again, a completely uncertain future. With no money in a country from which he could depart only at enormous risk, with the ballast of a truly rigid address from the president of the country where he was, indicted globally, potentially exiled. And then he said, "Well, people, you must be joking with me. You are offering me to play for or be a trainer for a club that has a red star at the top of its emblem. Don't you know that I have been open anti-communist all my life? There is no way this is going to happen!" Shock on the faces of all present.

The last days of April offered Bobby one more exciting event and a new confirmation of his deepest beliefs. Tragic events in the little town of Waco, Texas, where more than eighty followers of David Coresh were killed in an attack by law officers. Koresh was the founder of a religious sect called the *Branch Dravidians*, and Bobby could not have been more upset. He talked for days, based on the information available to him, about this being a confirmation of the vulnerability of anyone who was different in the territory of the USA. It was interesting that he was not "bothered" by the banner of this religious group which had a Star of David on its blue and white background.

Thus, such an unenviable situation could be made even worse by Fischer's whimsicalness which was manifested in such ways as well. As a backup plan, I prepared two apartments in Belgrade; one was mine, completely renovated in a style that seemed to me would suit my protégé best, and another one was rented in an elite part of the capital, with an excellent layout that also offered room for security personnel. Likewise, new vehicles were obtained for transportation needs. My personal financial resources at that moment meant that Fischer had some time, at the present rhythm of monthly expenses, to find a solution for the days ahead. Our assistants were also ready to go on working as volunteers.

Days passed, the bills at the hotel were multiplying. A couple of times I had conversations with the management of the Interkontinental, with people who were kindly and professionally interested in future relations or, more concretely, paying the bills.

Since Bobby had never signed a single bill during his entire stay in Serbia and Montenegro, either on those after lunch/dinner or on the general monthly ones, it was I who became the man with probably the largest number of "autographs" in the world which marked the influx of cash into the accounts of the large hotel chain. At that moment, I did not even think about the amount of my possible debts. When the uncertainty had started to slowly take on serious dimensions, a phone call came. Vasiljević. The money for Bobby and his expenses was prepared. These were not finances from the prize money, "but just taking care of the chess genius".

There was enough for a couple of months, so that an illusory financial peace was bought for a certain time. Even though our financial security was in question, my protégé did not deprive himself of a single pleasure.

In spite of that, in our conversations ever more often he called the fugitive banker a dastard, a bandit, and he clearly saw signs of Jezdimir's participation in the overall conspiracy and the anti-Fischer lobby. Thus in the hierarchy of the conspiracy, the organizer of the "revenge match of the twentieth century" quickly advanced to the very top.

The relationship of trust between us in such a situation took on a new dimension. Despite the fact that my colleagues and I had no kind of material reward, the general consensus was that we could never leave Bobby in such a situation. Loyalty and fidelity were, and still are, at the very top of my internal list of positive character traits. On the other hand, for the truth to be complete, my motive and inspiration besides that was also a vision of future matches, of open perspectives and chances that I hoped for – these were a secondary, but powerful motive at that time. However, Bobby was becoming more demanding in every possible way, because his attacks of depression were occurring more often and more intensively. When he talked – more and more words of hatred, and they were becoming stronger, yelping sentences, curses and threats. A lot of reminiscing, connecting various events in the past into an explicable theory without a basis, conclusions that caused him pain.

Then, the drop that made the cup overflow. The grain of sand on the pan of a scale that is tipping toward the abyss.

While the match was going on, Fischer saw many beautiful women around. Some were attracted to the legend and his personality, or rather to an image they had created in their hearts of the chess master; some were attracted to the glamour of the spectacle or the smell of money.

He had the opportunity to see how different variations of the male-female relationship came together and split apart before his very eyes. Sometimes he was boyishly enthralled by the skill which some of the men around him showed in dealing with women, with the tendency to change partners quickly, to enjoy the human body. Clumsily, if something like that exists in the betrayal of affinity, Bobby made a step in his desire to go down that path. Namely, on the last evening on Sveti Stefan, in Bobby's now famous round-dance, he met one of the hostesses of the match, a heavy set, medium height and, with my apologies, not overly pretty lady. During March and April, this woman from Belgrade came to the hotel at the request of the chess master and very quickly ended up in his suite. For all of us in Fischer's proximity, things were clear. Zita was his girl for the future, the sacrosanct "owner" of his spirit, Miyoko was an old friend and a person of special trust and closeness. And now there was this new "heroine"...

Certainly my job description did not include commenting on or attempting to manage Bobby's private life, but this time I had to do so out of friendship. Namely, this young lady who appeared in the story was well-known for her "happy character and nature".

The Greatest Secret of Bobby Fischer

Since we did not deal in gossip as well-informed people, this news was empirically proven and shown among those of us in the inner circle. Her scanty and fairly vulgar way of dress caused the staff and guests at the hotel to giggle but Bobby, "carried away" in his pleasure, did not notice this when he took his new "chosen one" to lunch or dinner in the hotel restaurant. According to his explicit wish, we "had to" take her with us on a one-day excursion to the gem of Serbian tourism, the Vrnjačka Spa.

So, I took the freedom of warning my protégé for his own good about the possibility of being "compromised" by having such a relationship in public, and as a man I turned his attention that the news of such a public display of the Don Juan syndrome might even reach Zita. I was satisfied by the fact that he listened to me carefully, that he did not take my advice in the wrong way, but it I certainly was not pleased by the fact that he did not listen to my suggestion.

Once again, a moment came when the straw broke the camel's back. Bobby knew that Zita was coming. Regardless of that fact, he invited his "new pet" to supper. When I saw that all three of them were going to the restaurant, I knew that things would not turn out well.

An image to be remembered: Zita with a frozen smile, a grimace on her face, Bobby clumsily walking between them and shoving his life into the abyss, ripping the silk in two and nonchalantly shattering the mirror of the future into tiny pieces. Zita spent that night in her own room and the next morning she left the hotel early. The gates of hell had opened.

After a couple of days, when he saw that he had done irreversible damage with his awkwardness, banality and direct approach, he quickly ended his "Belgrade" affair. But his calls to Zita remained without answer, or at least without the answer he wanted. He invited me into his suite ever more often so that we could talk, but all the conversations started and ended with a sigh of pain, defined in the words: Zita was angry.

"How is that possible?" I thought cynically, because I was expecting exactly such dramatic consequences. All of this was intensified by Jezdimir's departure; the series and confluence of unfortunate circumstances made a mush of confused thoughts, undefined feelings which could not depend on the solid ground of stabile emotions because, like a stretched out fishing net as it dries, they allowed the breezes, storm winds and hurricanes of life's blows to get through.

As winter turned to spring, the crisis grew deeper and deeper. Now completely exposed, Bobby Fischer became an easy target for a few nervous and "disappointed" bank clients, who hinted at the possibility of a more dangerous variation of having their debts paid off. They tried to attribute their disappointment and expectations to my ward. We somehow easily solved that problem in the end, so that particular wave did not have an influence on the already demanding situation.

There were several offers that either directly or indirectly presented chances for me to make an extra profit. From the simple journalist type, to articles written relying on first-hand information, the co-authorship of books, or perhaps an interview which I could tape secretly. However, "more serious" possibilities also opened up.

A famous businessman, famous for the wide spectrum of his activities, came to me with a prepared construction. As a well-informed person who had detailed knowledge about the fact that the Fischer clock would never be widely exploited, over coffee he made a rather direct offer.

My task would be to take the prototype of the instrument for the new means of chess time measurement from Fischer's room and to give it to a technical team for a couple of hours in the room next door. Experts from the land of Dostoyevsky would quickly make the necessary "observations" and millions of dollars would soon be paid. The business visionary, reputed to be fair in his agreements and contracts, proved it here because the agreement presupposed that Fischer would get a cut. With a smile I listened to this proposition to the end, but today, when hundreds of varieties, or better said counterfeits, of this idea are in circulation, it is clear how great a financial loss came about from the lack of well-timed and legal exploitation of that prototype; more important is the extent to which Bobby's concept has been degraded as the years have passed.

Naturally, not even from this perspective and with all these facts, I would not have acted differently, but to this very day I am sorry that one more of Bobby's ingenious ideas was blown away like gold dust in the wind, as if it had never existed. While we thus kept control over most things, the chess master sank daily ever deeper into his dark worlds, or more precisely stated, he went back to them along new paths. Instead of our former dialogues, more and more often I listened to his monologues. The list of conspirators expanded both upward and downward, all events from his arrival in Yugoslavia were now painted in a new manner of retrospective and in dark colors of perception, they departed left and right, while in the middle the new-old Bobby Fischer turned on his own axis.

The worst of epithets were now aimed also at many people who had earlier been seen through the eyes of respect and satisfaction. The very peak had to be reached on the steps of deepening and expanding hatred. The only bright spot, the trace of new hope was offered by Zita's surprising one-day visit. Good preparations had to be made for it. Physically, Bobby did so by going to the hotel barber, getting a haircut and a beard trim, and then by carefully choosing his wardrobe and shining his shoes long and hard. In order not to stand before his "queen" empty-handed, in his desire to try to get things back into balance, he prepared some special propositions.

My deep conviction was that Fischer was actually afraid of a redrawing of the world map, of new realities, of new arrangements of the figures on the board. With her hands and will, she had already and anyway set up a position which was unknown in his game of life. Zita was the only thread that tied him to his now disturbed, tottering security and balance. That was why he wanted her back so passionately. Again because of himself and because of his "royal" ego. Can that be bought? Not this time. The nicely wrapped gifts were: Bobby was to propose marriage, Zita would choose the city and club where they would live and play together, she would get the exclusive rights to writing and publishing his biography, and a million dollars.

That day came, and passed. Lunch together, Zita stayed briefly in Bobby's suite, and then I saw her passing by me with her typical secretive smile and firm stride, heading into a new life. I knocked on Bobby's door. His shirttail out, he was lying on the bed, silent, as if drowsing, pale, almost unable to speak, he indicated that I should sit down. Several times he tried to start up a conversation. They remained only as attempts because he slowly fell asleep. After something more than three hours he slowly woke up. Difficult moments when a sleeper, who is being cruelly punished by life because of his omissions and committed acts, realizes that, unfortunately, it is better in his dreams even if they are nightmares than in real life.

Muggy, almost sap-sticky, days set in. There was no talk about his future in chess, about matches or about business plan. We lived for the moment because that was all we had. Money was still arriving but at an irregular rhythm and in varying amounts. The immediate future was also not clear in this aspect either, because his prize money was still far away and out of reach.

The first point of uncertainty was whether Mr. Vasiljević would even fulfill his end of the contract, and the second, equally important, was whether the US government would block the payment of 3.6 million dollars earned in a country under sanctions. In the overall gloom of his spirit and tempest of thought, Bobby became irrational to the utmost in practical matters that were not his strong suit even in his "lucid" days.

On one such occasion, after the financial crisis that lasted some ten days, 50,000 German marks reached Bobby. In reality, those financial "refreshments" involved much effort and exposure to dangers of all sorts, since in those years, one of the favorite pastimes of criminals was hunting for "no one's money" that entered the country in the guise of assorted "investments". Therefore, Bobby was the ideal target. But then I saw the scene in which he was on the edge of his bed, dressed in pajamas, counting to fifty. Thousand by thousand. When he finished, he began counting again, this time up to twenty six. Twenty six thousand deutschmarks. Then he told me, "Nesh, you'll hand this over... Namely, a friend of ours has been bugging me for days, asking for money to have his teeth fixed here in Yugoslavia. I can't take it anymore."

To my understated ascertainment that for such a tidy sum of money, one could repair and make perfectly beautiful a set of mammoth's tusks, Bobby shrugged. A repeated insistence to think it over, if for no other reason than for the sake of his financial situation, yielded no results. It is then completely redundant to mention the risks I exposed myself to, above all in the context of Jezdimir's statement and warning spoken over the telephone, "Take care of your money, because people in my milieu are not too pleased with the fact I worry about it so much."

To consummate my horror, as I exited the room, at the door I heard Bobby's voice clearly indicate the whole meaninglessness of all his reasoning at the time, "This isn't even my money, anyway." I fulfilled his wish and deposited the envelope at the specified address, or more precisely, the hotel room number. As I left the area, I heard the joyous screaming and squealing of the lucky recipients of "no one's money" in the hallway, and I understood full well that we were beginning to sink into quicksand that was sooner or later to swallow us whole.

Bad moods become bad decisions, for in the uncertain present and foreboding future the most unreasonable thing is certainly finding fault with the president of the country that had thus far shown so much affection to its dear guest. The entire situation gains gravity when that man's name is Slobodan Milošević.

Namely, wanting to find a scapegoat for the current state of his logic pathways, the chess player came upon his former hero. Weeks prior, that one bullet point pervaded our conversations, but with no clear indications as to how far it would go. In his usual manner, Fischer then saw in the president of Serbia a "communist disguised as a nationalist". For this secret role he was "qualified through his close friendship with the former US ambassador in Yugoslavia, Mr. Lawrence Eagleburger, and through his pre-political banking engagement, in Yugoslavia as in the US, where Slobodan lived and worked for a time". Considering that everything to do with finance and money transactions was, according to Bobby, under the auspices of the secret rulers of the world who controlled all monetary flow, and for him it was completely certain that the same connection had to exist here as well. "That's where he was recruited," with energetic hand motions he confirmed his discovery, "there is no dilemma that he is behind the savings banks pyramid scheme. Even if he isn't their outright founder, as president, he would have to know what goes on in his own 'backyard'."

The result and incarnation of this manner of thinking soon came in the form of a direct address from Robert James Fischer to Slobodan Milošević. At the end of the day, after our usual long walk and a rest, I was called over to "hang out" some more at his apartment.

"Sit and hear me out!"

Then he took a handwritten note off the table. A letter to the president. And without any evasion, directly, conclusion to conclusion. The match was held in Yugoslavia, part two in Serbia. The organizer, the well-known and acclaimed banker, under patronage from the state. A step further. Bobby, on the trail of Mr. Vasiljević's stories of the sale of TV rights, demands an additional two million dollars.

His debtor is the state of Serbia; more precisely, its president. So, along with all the accusations comes a direct financial demand. The chess player asked me what I thought of it. Without going into deeper descriptions on what suicide looked like, I simply said we would do so if that was what he wanted. With an absolute understanding of how unproductive of an act that was at that particular moment, but with acknowledgment that my task entailed protecting Bobby from himself, the only thing I could do was to mitigate this situation to the utmost degree.

I entrusted a person of complete confidence with the task of typing out the text. Bobby carefully examined, read and put his signature underneath the text. Despite the risk of this gesture, I had to be sure the president received the letter, with an additional verbal comment, and that he would unavoidably study its contents. For that kind of specificity, the best contacts are those of

The Greatest Secret of Bobby Fischer

low intensity, yet maximum efficiency. Thus, to aid us, I asked a person who in their line of work spent a good deal of time with the president of Serbia, without being involved in politics.

After an hour of waiting in front of the Interkontinental Hotel, the well-known BMW arrived. In a gray suit and a cream-colored topcoat, the man who would guarantee a safe delivery. An A4-sized envelope was handed over and, after some thirty minutes, I received confirmation of it arriving into the hands of the recipient. I notified Bobby of it. He was pleased with the stern and direct tone of the letter and proud of himself, ready to count the hours to the response.

He would never receive it in writing. But it's non-existence in printed form was clear enough.

Several days later, Fisher asked me to help him write in red felt-tipped pen the full address of the presidency of Serbia on an identically sized cream-colored envelope, and address it to the Serbian president. This time the chess-player insisted on the formality. He took the sealed letter to the reception desk and sent it via regular mail. A few hours later, as we were sitting in the foyer, he suddenly jumped up from his chair, slapped his forehead, and exclaimed, "Nesh, I forgot to sign the text!"

My agony continued with his insistence to find the letter and return it for editing. However, it was already on its way to the central Belgrade post office. I resorted to a simpler method, convincing Bobby that this mistake and embarrassment would never even reach Milošević. Events and terrors blended together, old ones and the new, made stronger by listening for sounds in the silent shadows and looking for light in words that bore darkness.

Like many times before, Bobby would not leave his room until I went to him. But now, even nights were a formidable challenge. Afraid of being left alone, he lingered in the hotel lobby, talking to me or napping until morning. I would greet new days in one of the comfortable lobby chairs, or on his living room sofa.

I remember a certain event from that period. The setting spring sun shone through green panes of glass and lit up the hotel flora and scant visitors, while we sat in an oval booth furthest from the reception desk.

The champion wandered the expanse of his memories, napped or stared despondently at the empty table in front of him. It was as if we had used up all our words for the day. The silence was broken by the jovial laughter of two young men who sat in armchairs next to us. Both were around thirty years of age, of frail build, not too tall, with modern hairstyles, dressed in sports-elegant clothing. They were in a good mood, talking loudly, in what I easily recognized as Czech. From time to time Bobby would turn towards them. He looked at them intermittently with aside glances. I asked if they were bothering him. "No, it's alright," he said. After some ten minutes, one of the two young men slowly turned around, looked in the chess-player's direction, and asked in English: "Excuse me, are you Bobby Fischer?" I sat up, awaiting a reaction. At a decent distance, my two associates, ready for action. Our ward, however, motioned me not to worry.

"I am," he answered. The usual short conversation, admiration, respect, short answers, and even a smile here and there from the legend. Almost as if the champion savored that modicum of unexpectedly expressed respect. In the end, the elated happenstance speaker said, "Imagine, when we set off from Prague, our neighbor, Mr. Steelman, who is a big fan of yours, asked us that if we met Bobby Fischer in Belgrade, we should give him his best regards. And what an incredible fortune and coincidence to meet you and have the opportunity to give you his message. Unbelievable." They then stood up, saying their goodbyes, and with swift step left the hotel. In a moment, as if jerked awake from a dream, he continued his conversation with me on various topics, ending in the usual long walk. A late evening routine, leading up to our retiring to bed. Finally, we went to our own rooms. My door, as usual, open, and I, still dressed, in a comfortable recliner, resting, looking towards the hallway. Three hours after midnight, the witching hour. I heard footsteps in his room, bathroom, water, shower. Hours passed. The night grew old and perished in sunrise. I closed my eyes for a moment. Sounds on my threshold. I saw him, in his pajamas and his favorite old bathrobe. Barefoot, white as a sheet, sweaty brow, messy hair; with a finger on his mouth he signaled me to be quiet. I approached him silently, as he offered me a slip of paper. I read it:

Nesh, those two from last night were sent to kill me.
First: I don't know this Steelman.
Second: he surely doesn't exist anyway.
Clear message: 'steel', 'man'.
Steel man: they want to pump me full of lead.
They will shoot me.
Third: Czechoslovakia, the land that is no more.
Therefore, they want me gone too.
Fourth: I want you to find them and bring them to me.

I read a line, then looked at him, line, look, line, look. Eyes wide open, he nodded in confirmation and gestured for silence, so that no one could hear or record anything. I motioned that everything would be alright. My associates arrived, with another Fischeresque day ahead of us.

For the sake of my peace of mind as a professional, I checked hotels, the local internal affairs office – department for foreigners. I informed myself from all my sources. Considering nothing illegal had been done, and that Bobby had in fact allowed the two inquisitive men to approach him, my task was again focused on the mind and the consciousness of the potential target that was to be protected from demons and spooks. We spent several hours commenting on the previous night's events. I advised him then that he would have to be more flexible or drastic if the suspicion arose immediately. I managed to placate him, but I expended a volcano of energy choosing my words, playing the mind game, leading this non-chess match, move by move, to my victory and his temporary tranquility. I must brag that I regularly won (which is why I stayed with him for so long); the only trouble was that I had to play ever more often, and the starting positions were ever more difficult. All circumstances considered, I thought a vacation in the north of Vojvodina would do him good.

Destiny whispered softly. For the first time, we set off to Kanjiža and packed all his belongings. Paintings, a chess set and heavier portable details were moved into my room which, we kept booked. Once more in the north of Bačka, this time in longer and warmer days. The organizer and financier of Fischer's comeback never did call me again. Borne on his fortune, from Israel he would sail off to Latin America, and then who knows where until the epilogue. In relaxing and usual spa activities Bobby sought an outlet, but the weight of the happenings was too heavy for anything corporeal to calm the tempest in his mind. Apart from a brief look back and a glance at his pocket chess set, he had nearly taken his essence off his list of priorities.

It is certain that in that special moment, for Bobby there was little reasonable hope to return to his suggested grand plans and challenges embodied in future matches. There was a possibility that in a positive turn of events, there could appear a point that would turn the course of reality toward new potentials, and which could become one more new opportunity. It revealed itself in the form of the concordant and globally-known Polgár chess-playing family. The continuity of Fischer's interest was expressed through fervent curiosity in the pedagogical methods László used to guide his daughters to chess, for the careers and success of Judit, Zsuzsa and Zsófia, and all the other details related to the new worldwide stars.

One delightful sunny day that reminded me with its remarkableness and excitement of bygone events, the famous chess-playing family, previously announced, came to Kanjiža. We expected the visit in morning hours. It took two hours of driving at a moderate speed from Budapest to our residence.

The Polgárs arrived at the expected time. Modesty, though not indirectness, but above all an evident harmony, captivated our attention. Even a less-than-astute observer would immediately notice that under the wing of their father's authority and inviolability, three powerful, yet subtly different characters had grown up and developed.

From the aspect of chess, Bobby was most interested in Judit, but in our later conversations he would mention Zsuzsa most frequently, who, as the oldest, spoke the greatest share, and as the most competent English speaker interpreted for her family. Mrs. Polgár and Zsófia were somehow the most reserved, but certainly equally important in the entirety of their impression. The creator of this project, László, casually intent with every word and every move, covered in his nonchalance what was certainly prepared ahead of time. The day was wonderful, the pleasant company and the conversation steered Bobby in the direction of a good mood after quite some time. Following lunch, a conversation in Bobby's apartment. My greatest expectations were focused on the possibility of Mr. László Polgár filling that void, the vacuum of authority, of leadership, which was left with the departure of Mr. Vasiljević and the inability of Mr. Kubat to continue to influence Fischer's chess career.

In the late afternoon, a cordial farewell ended the meeting of the greatest chess player of all time and the most influential and successful family in the history of the game of 64 black-and-white squares. Until late into the night Bobby commented on details, gave his opinions on the mutual relationships of our guests, and sorted out his impressions. However, as early as the next day, things returned to the awkward everyday routine in which there seemed to be neither solace nor hope. On one of those nights Bobby announced we would be holding a very important conversation. He waited for me in bed, his bed, in a position characteristic for the time and his sharp emotional descent. He was decisive, accepting no alternative: "I want Zita back. If she won't come on her own free will, bring her by force." And as an order: "I want you to bring her to me in any way and under any circumstance." After all I had lived through with him, I could not say I was surprised.

Namely, during the time I spent with him, Bobby was utterly convinced (on multiple occasions he stated this in his letters or in direct communication with certain people) that my friends and I could, like Hollywood movie heroes, do whatever he desired. Such a feeling arose from the actual fact that up to that moment, it had been so. Never in guarding his person from all manner of emotional self-harm did I verify information about any plans that my ward gave me directly. I trusted him. But in those days, intrigued by the ringing of the telephone and loud conversations coming from behind his door, I decided to check the locations of incoming and outgoing calls.

My curiosity yielded confirmation and justification. Specifically, Bobby's self-initiated investigation was underway on rumors that had reached us, that in her "new life" Zita had a new relationship. He dialed numbers, asked, pleaded, but also threatened. I, of course, had complete information up to that point on the life of Fischer's former queen, and now his potential "victim"; on the other hand, that kind of intimacy, however interesting to my protégé, was not allowed to be part of my work.

There was no real danger of him carrying out his wishes and plans, since at that moment, he was absolutely helpless in a gravely dangerous jungle, in which his desire to turn from prey to predator overnight was a fairytale without whimsy or a happy ending. To avoid an even more disadvantageous turn of events, I asked Zita's father, Mr. Rajcsányi, for a meeting at the Kempinski hotel in Budapest.

Having up to then had exceptional cooperation in every sense of the word with this respectable man, it was not hard for us to keep any set of unfortunate circumstances merely substance without potential. My worry also related to the conceivable moment when Bobby might get his millions of dollars, and when in such a situation, financially fortified, he would be hellishly more powerful. How far he was ready to go in his intent to burn all bridges and roads he had crossed, with shaky ground beneath his feet, he then expressed through an absolute and shameful resolve to reach the very edge. So great was his irrational ability to forget who he was talking to and what he could offer to whom without any potential, and in a blind aspiration to "motivate" me to act, completely sure the kidnapped Zita could successfully be kept for him, through a cynical sneer he said that SUCH AN EXPLOIT WOULD BE AN OPPORTUNITY TO SHOW THE LOCAL HUNGARIANS WHAT WOULD BEFALL ALL THE PHONIES. Surely he thought that in that moment, along with Mr. Gligorić, his only friends on Earth, his Serbian followers, would do Zita's new friend and compatriot harm, and in doing so fight for his convictions at the price of waging a "new war". Thus for his own

The Greatest Secret of Bobby Fischer

good Fischer would have to be foiled so the boomerang of his selfish desires would not then come back to hit him; Zita and her chosen one would receive timely information on the arrow that would never be fired. This was for me a further confirmation of the signs that I could read, the advance notice that was becoming ever clearer, that in his self-sufficiency, weakness outside of chess and increasingly frequent cynicism, he was ready to sacrifice everything and everyone for his faulty perceptions and judgments.

In the next few days, the Hungarian grandmaster and journalist, András Adorján, arrived in Kanjiža. After settling into the hotel, he aggressively and markedly attempted to approach Fischer. On several occasions he tried with skillful acting to play out an incident in which he would be the victim, hoping that in that congruent, yet multinational environment, he could divert attention to himself and get his coveted publicity. However, we did not allow him to do that, by elegantly avoiding the provocations that left us in peace and quiet, and saw him off on his way home.

We had stayed in Kanjiža for far too long. The comfort of a Vojvodinian down pillow, stuffed with an all-embracing weight of dreams, delayed the inevitability of facing reality. Where to, and what next? We had to go somewhere, to some new grounds, because these inner ones, as well as the outer ones, had become cramped and crowded.

For the first time in the previous year, I separated from Bobby. I went to Belgrade to prepare my departure from Yugoslavia. After all consultations, contacts, still unconvincing promises, false hopes, we concluded as least uncertain: Budapest, Hungary. I returned to Fischer two days later. He agreed. From Kanjiža, under my arm, instead of postcards I carried an issue of the German *Stern*. Forty eight hours of my absence were enough for a photo-reporter of this well-known magazine to covertly take a picture of Fischer taking a walk. A reflection of his exceptional deftness, or a lapse in someone's capability and loyalty? We arrived in Belgrade. Bobby was briefly in his apartment. Belongings remained unpacked. Everything we weren't taking with us, we left with Mr. Gligorić. All the bills at the

Interkontinental were paid. We set off, in two rented cars with two hired chauffeurs, on this trip, during which we would find out if the Earth was spherical or a flat plane off whose edges ships fall into oblivion, and for us, that was the border of our northern neighboring country. Robert James Fischer, Eugenio Torre and I. I said goodbye to my two inseparable associates, leaving Dane and Voja behind. In the luggage we were carrying – a US government arrest warrant with drastic threats, allegations against Milošević, dangers of varying intensities from all directions and an all-around uncertainty in every aspect. We had valid passports, and I had brought some money of my own with me. Bobby had taken an empty wallet, without any photographs as mementos.

That August morning would have been like every other. If only it had not been that particular one.

CHAPTER 14.

NISTAR

In search of some excitement for the soul, in northern Vojvodina in a place near Kubat's magical Senta and Kanjiže "Fischer's and Mine", I found a painter and his works[52]—they cause the soul to tremble long after the first shock caused by the visual impression, by the portrayed depths of evil and the heights of good, by the thousands of interrelated characters, beauties and monstrosities.

The paintings of this artist cannot be looked at without you wanting to see them in the search for answers and solutions to decipher them, reached through understanding of the fact that the infinite is hidden in the finite. If I could, I would use words to tell him, or breathe inspiration of the visible and experiential into a paintbrush. Photographs and film would also be insufficient. Acuity is not necessary as much as strength is, the strength to unequivocally grasp the moment in which the object of the search is found. The curse of the inexplicable.

Nistar.[53] It remains thus only in my memory.

The crisp autumn Budapest evening comes in through the open window of the Polgár's apartment. The breeze stirs the curtains, while the dim light of the living room consents and meaning is given to it by a golden triangle of light focused from the ceiling on the chess board on the table beneath, as if lit from the heavens. I am sitting in a comfortable armchair leaning juxtaposed on the opposite wall from the silent city asphalt, and I am looking at the

---

[52] Hodi Ference, painter, he lived and worked in Ada. He passed away at the beginning of 2011.
[53] Nistar – from the Hebrew Kabbalah, a term that signifes the hidden, the secret, or something that cannot be explicated to another human being verbally or in any other way. How salty is salt, what does a rose smell like?

The Greatest Secret of Bobby Fischer

beaming oval face, nonchalantly framed by a beard beneath the balding head of Mr. László Polgár, and also at the pale countenance of Robert James Fischer, pale from all the experience of the past couple of months, couple of decades, couple of lives. The silent gallery consists of a multitude of chess sets which our host has collected but I would not know they were there, peering in from the darkness, if I had not seen them earlier. On the left, his arms crossed over a black and white background, his head leaning forward, is our host.

In the chair across from him, as if submersed in the right half of the board in defense, the undefeated champion of the world. Move after move. Slowly. Word after word. Silently.

László is interested in his guest's shaky, or rather non-existent, plans for the future. On the other side of the table, words uncertain in reply, more curious and concrete when they take up the methodology of an education in chess. If a painter were to portray the essence, from the dance of light and shadows he would have to emphasize the blue blazer of the adventurous spirit, the champions' father, and the brown-green combination of the legend. While the game continues the pieces slide, or they are set down on the board from just above it.

Bobby starts in on his favorite topics. Conspiracy. Victims. Himself. Examples.

Evidence. Words. Movements. The rhythm of the game. Fischer talks. László is silent. Explanations. Solutions. Complaints. The champion keeps adding on. László is silent. The latest proof of evil. There's Yugoslavia. There's Serbia. There's Milošević. There's Vasiljević. And this guy.

And that guy. The Jew, the damned Jew. Everywhere. Always. And forever.

A moment of absolute emptiness. As if in silence. As if motionless. Without a past. Without a future. I would like to have the next scene in a frame, painted by a master's hand, angels and demons from whose eyes the worlds behind the mirror are peering, cities on the bottom of the sea, ships in the clouds, the crucifixion without a cross.

The Greatest Secret of Bobby Fischer

To the right, Lásló has sat up in his chair, leaning over the table, thrust into Bobby's even paler face pressed against the back of the chair, Lásló shouts: "What the hell, what the hell, Bobby. Didn't it ever once occur to you that They, Those who you hate the most, would actually like to help you? Is it possible that you never thought how it would be for you if you had our help?"

God and the haberdasher. The Devil and his apprentice. The wise and the knowing. A secret revealed in an instant. A door unlocked. A curtain raised. Bobby scared to death. Still, nothing.

A moment of absolute emptiness. As if in silence. As if motionless. Without a past. Without a future.

A frame.

The roaring laugh of apa[54] László which can be heard all the way to Buda. As if it were a joke, and what else could it be. As if it were a game with his guest, and what else could it be. As if it were irony, meant to interrupt the paranoia, and what else could it be.

Mr. Polgár thaws the frozen Bobby with his laugh. On the face of the champion there is something like the smile of a patient waking up after an operation, with the feeling that the wound hurts and also with the understanding that the next few days are uncertain, but that he is, however, alive. I have never seen Fischer so tiny, helpless and terrified. We departed soon after, on foot, toward the hotel. He did not speak. From time to time he started to say something but stopped himself.

We cross the Danube, heading for the other side. For which side? Because a river has two sides, indeed. As the poet says, "To those on the other side, we are on the other side."[55] In the fruitless search for himself and his place under the heavens, talented, rewarded, handicapped by the rewards, damaged, Robert Fischer forever remains in the middle of the bridge of life where the vibrations are most intensely felt, where the winds blow the hardest, at the spot above the mainstream where the river moves most swiftly and where, when we look up, the clouds sail by most quickly.

---

[54] Apa = father in Hungarian.
[55] Arsenije Arsen Dedić, famous Croatian poet, singer and songwriter.

That evening, if my friend had only a moment earlier or later passed that way, he certainly would have experienced that mystical cognition that must occur when the moment in the life of the dedicated master intertwines with the pulse of the steel arch above the water. Then he would see himself approaching from the other side in the middle of the night. From the other side of the river. Were he to meet himself so in the middle of the bridge, a short word but powerful, like a bolt of lightning in the flat Pannonia plain, a secret would sink into the bottom of his heart, revealing itself: THAT YOU ARE PART OF THEM, JUST AS THEY ARE PART OF YOU.

THAT WE ARE THEM AND THAT IS CALLED WE.

All of that might have been, if only we had passed there at the right time.

CHAPTER 15.

AGAINST THE WIND

As if lowered from heaven on angelic cords onto the bank of the Danube, the spires of the Hungarian parliament gleamed in the sunny August morning. And so we found ourselves in Budapest. The European prince of rivers connects the east and the west on a thread of thrones – Vienna, Budapest and Belgrade. We pressed northwards and were met with the dulcetly depressing spirit[56] of Central Europe and its, at the time, transitional economies. Majestic Prague and magical Zagreb, there lies the culture we had dived into, and it was there that we found a new ambient, a new scene set on the same old stage, the heart of Europe, that venerable dame.

We felt no dread on the Yugoslav side of the border. In spite of the fierce accusations addressed at president Milošević, the police and the customs officials greeted us just as everyone else. I stepped out of the car to report to those expecting us. No man's land. An air of expectation filled the car. I tried to strike up a conversation to ease the tension, but Bobby and Eugene were content to sit it out stone-faced. The Hungarian officials took their time with our documents, and the minutes dragged on like hours. Luckily for us, nothing dramatic ensued. The worst-case scenario would have had us arrested on the spot. However, there we were, quietly on our way to Szeged. I saw that my companions had begun to loosen up, as they probably naïvely thought that once we cross the border, all danger would remain behind us. A professional knows that only then were we driving on thin ice; that we had been flying over a gaping abyss or diving right into a maelstrom. For if anyone had

---
[56] The words of Jovan Rašković, famous Serbian neuro-psychiatrist and writer.

meant us harm, they would undoubtedly avoid the public nature of border crossings, the media coverage and the scores of potential eyewitnesses.

That is probably why nobody but me in our white *Mercedes* noticed the *Nissan Patrol* with an all too familiar Hungarian license plate, which had been following us at a safe distance from the first widening in the road since the crossing at Horgoš. Although the faces inside the large Land Rover were too far away for me to see in the rearview mirror, I had no doubts about whom it was driven by. It would have been very naïve of me to disregard my own safety while caring for Bobby's. If the Hungarian government was to decide to enforce the U.S. warrant on Bobby, there would certainly be nothing I could do to stop them. But I took comfort and confidence in the fact that no other evil could befall us, under the watchful eye of the four of our "invisible" concomitants. They were the body of men that exhibited all the skills, the experience and intelligence to match my rigor with an all-purpose technological support, not to mention they were also my loyal and trustworthy friends.

And so, without any kind of hassle, we arrived at the Gellért Hotel, which lies in the shadow of a hill of the same name. A residence of Habsburg pedigree, equipped with wondrous swimming pools and Roman baths it had about it a spirit of hedonism. We settled into comfortable suites on the top floor. For a few days, my team had also stayed in a rented apartment nearby. After lunch, we went for a walk through the city center of Budapest, which was teeming with life and tourists from all over the world. It was such a stark contrast to ostracized Belgrade. At the end of the day, I wanted to speak with Bobby. We were by ourselves. By reading the signs and marking certain changes in his demeanor, I was left wondering whether our mutual agreement would remain unchanged. He confirmed it with a "never, there would never be any reason to change it." I reminded him that he could come to no danger with me at his side, as long as he chose to heed my advice. Of course, I would have been completely powerless to stop a potential intervention from the Hungarian government, although through swift preemptive action, we had the means of legally transporting him to a different country, and then further on to safety, were such a need to arise.

Everything seemed in perfect order, as it had been for some time. Then, one day, just as I was leaving the suite that had several floors, I looked back and suddenly noticed his eyes conspicuously following me on my way out. What did it mean? I was about to find out the following day.

I usually got up early. On our first morning there, as Budapest was beginning to stir to the sound of trams and delivery vans, I was accompanied by the nice lady from the reception desk on a tour of the hotel. Together, we carefully inspected every entrance, exit, corridor, hall and dining room as well as the surrounding area. The beautiful park astride Gellért Hill seemed to me like an ideal place for leisure or exercise.

Over breakfast I warned Bobby that the "eyes and ears" of the press were certain to include taxi drivers, maids and restaurant staff, who had surely already upheld their end of the bargain and that, as a result, he was certain to encounter a pair of rapacious press photographers' lenses on the other side of the Danube. In fact, a few agents of the Fourth Estate were bound to be waiting for him right outside the main entrance too. I advised taking the side exit, but as soon as he finished his tea, Bobby went straight for the main entrance. Needless to say, photos of him and me filled the next day's press. It was bad enough having the chess grandmaster's arrival so pompously announced. But now, the text accompanying our photos was copiously riddled with the epithet "Serb". And so the press had officially declared "open season". He leafed through the papers discontentedly. Photos, he had not given them permission to use. Photos of him, that he would not receive a dime for. But for all his complaining and wounded glares, he dared not chide me.

Around that time, I had had great difficulties explaining to my client, that the interest that those gorgeous ladies in the street and at the hotel entrance showed him was not the residue of "magnetism" but that such behavior was in their line of work. Of course, there was nothing I could do to prevent him from making his moves and chatting them up for hours on end. It was up to me

The Greatest Secret of Bobby Fischer

to keep the aggressive, knife-happy pimps from intervening on their charges' behalf and procuring a swift payment for both of them.

All of a sudden, my angel of a chess player developed a taste for the Hungarian capital's strip clubs, places which were at the time already the patronage of Russian "businessmen". Whenever I pressed the fact that every night of pleasure in the company of those lovely hostesses would cost him a few thousand dollars, he took it as a kind of a challenge. As far as he was concerned, there was no reason to tighten his belt, especially now that he did not have anything to save for. By day or night, he would wander the streets of Budapest as it pleased him. As we strolled through the city center, I caught glimpse of many a familiar mug, some of whom, taking into consideration their unlawful past in Serbia, Croatia or Bosnia could well be ideal recruits for blackmail or abduction jobs. Fortunately, though, with a little help from certain people and circles, we quickly re-established the forced "brotherhood and unity" within the Budapest wing of the Yugoslav underground. A deal was also struck with the Russian freelancers as well as the more organized factors. Having such a consensus brokered for him, the "wild-child of world-class chess" was free to make the streets, squares, exteriors and interiors of the dazzling metropolis his personal playground.

So what was the cause of the change in my client? The smell of cash that was almost within reach was enough to turn the ugly duckling into a swan with a touch of a wand. Namely, the three-and-a-half million dollar prize for his victory over Spassky was to be redeemed in Belgrade. Those days, however, the newest concern was transferring the sum from Swiss banks to Budapest-based sub-branches, and that moment was almost at hand.[57] With a fat bundle of cash, even Bobby Fischer was in for an injection of adrenaline, even though it was certain to boil down to false

---

[57] The actual routing of the prize money was actually quite different from what the chess player thought and experienced at the time. The five million dollars had "left" Yugoslavia already before the match in actuality, but the aim of this book is to show the chronology as Fischer experienced it at time. Thus, this segment of the text follows that internal logic and chronology.

confidence. Nevertheless, it was not enough to fill his heart, if he indeed had one.

Apart from Eugene, who was a regular in our group, another great chess player of the old guard, a Hungarian-American by the name of Pal Benko, kept showing up at the hotel. He was usually dressed in short sleeved plaid shirts of various colors and a pair of common dark pants and he always had with him an old leather attaché case. As a result, his overall appearance resembled that of a retired university professor or an émigré doctor. He was also more of a listener than a talker, and would often accompany us on our daily walks around town. The slightly raised dark hair and high temples gave his skinny figure an impression of height while his narrow glasses, lowered onto his nose while he played, betrayed a lifetime of good days, and of bad days, that had flown past him nonetheless.

The move to Budapest did Bobby a world of good even chesswise. Now, together with Eugene and Pal, he spent much of his time training and analyzing. However, there was no doubt that the main source of Bobby's motivation was the Polgár family. The champion's inspiration and desire for company stemmed from his irrepressible need for acceptance and security. Visits to their home became accompanied by the visible effort and hospitality of the hosts, but also the increasing importunacy on behalf of the guest.[58]

As I observed this assembly at the table or the chess-board, I gave myself to deciphering the relations and possible interests. Along with being a source understanding for Fischer's motives, the Polgárs used their nonchalance to outsource any thoughts that their generosity might conceal ulterior interests. Although chesswise they were perfectly well off on their own, such a contact, in the person of a chess legend and a common passion, was certainly most welcome. A coach was, therefore, not really necessary. A match, perhaps? Against Judit? That was a story at least a year in the making, although nobody would mention it. Perhaps Mr. Polgár would like to take an interest in Fischer's career, to offer guidance, if need be? To be honest, I had secretly hoped so. Even if

---

[58] In downtown Budapest, the Polgárs owned several apartments in one building.

The Greatest Secret of Bobby Fischer

there were such intentions, they apparently fooled the eye, or at least there was nothing in the perpetually cheerful mood of that famous family that would imply them. The vegetarian lunches and dinners, the verve and optimism that shone out from that frozen-in-time household enticed Bobby in his continual search for refuge and acceptance.

From the rooftop of the Polgárs' apartment block, we watched the play of fire above water, the Hungarian Independence day fireworks, which lasted for several hours.

And so we came to Nagymaros. Some fifty miles north of Budapest, the Danube curves into a kink with Visegrád, the ancient seat of Hungarian rulers, watching over the far side. On the opposite bank stands a weekend resort, built by the former communist oligarchy, and at the time inhabited by the more opulent members of the new ruling class. Although nothing spectacular, the three small houses next to each other, adjoined to a spacious yard with a view of the river yet separated from it by a patch of reeds and brushwood, constituted the pride of the Polgárs. An extended weekend (in fact a whole week) with Bobby, Eugene, me and a guest from the USA, the young and promising curly-haired Leo. A good mood was shared by all. The pleasant atmosphere helped Bobby get on track, after several eventful months. Field trips followed, along with excursions into the surrounding nature and, of course, a visit to the old town.

However it wasn't long before the rumors that Bobby was there got to Budapest. The first at the door the BBC crew, reinforced by their Serbian branch, in the person of two sisters, twins, that I had been acquainted with. They requested an interview. Although our location had changed, our attitude did not. They left unsatisfied, as they failed to account for their tri[. And then, we found ourselves in yet another storm.

It was ten in the morning. Time for breakfast. We took our seats at a long massive table, set on the porch of the main residence. I sat opposite to Bobby, so that over his shoulder I would have a clear view of the yard and the chain-link fence that separated us from the narrow path and lush shrubbery. Sometime later I noticed movement in the brush. Behind the curtain of reeds I made out a camera on the shoulder of who I was about to identify as the Hungarian national TV's cameraman, a tall man wearing a red T-shirt and a pair of shorts. Next I made out his similarly dressed assistant. I watched them recklessly climb the fence led by the promise of exclusive material. Bobby saw my expression and looked behind. Something like a scream, a howl followed: "Neeeeesh!". I leapt over the table, reaching the small gate in the fence in a matter of seconds, while they made a run for it down the dusty path. I got my hands on one and then the other, holding both firmly by the arms. I felt their fear. Perhaps the "Serbian" thing from the media finally kicked in, as everything bearing that epithet was at the time, owing to the general political climate, considered wild and dangerous. I calmly informed them in English, that they should proceed to the yard to sort matters out like civilized men. On my return, I was met by a roaring applause that I found distasteful, as I felt like some beast fetching the game for the pack. For matching my thoughts in reality, it was my client that I would soon have to thank.

Just after a few seconds of relishing in the sight, the general elation was superseded by caution, as Bobby, in a moment of triumphant delirium, pulled the camera off the cameraman's shoulder. Next he reached for a branch, which was accidently lying there on the porch, and vigorously struck the camera with it a couple of times. When he saw that there was no way to break it, at the top of his lungs he called to László to hand him something sturdier to suit the purpose.

And as the sensible host cooled down while pretending to look for a larger garden tool, Bobby reached inside the camera for the beta tape, pulled it out, threw it onto the ground and stomped it into pieces with his foot. An air of discomfort was all around and only the chess master gloated over the deed. As he was beginning to calm down, the momentarily pacified journalists jumped into action. They demanded that they should be allowed to call the police. The host gave them permission, thinking only of protecting his esteemed guest. The "injured party" agreed, but still demanded "my head" as reparation, stressing the fact that, as Zsuzsa translated, "this is Hungary, after all". I understood their point. They were right, as a matter of fact. But why, then, were they so afraid of me? If one was to stroll into someone's backyard with a camera to film them while they are having breakfast, one should take into consideration the probability of being bitten by their Doberman, or getting caught by a Serb. All jokes aside, a couple of phone calls by Mr. Polgár, a calm talk with the reporters and the police patrol, along with the included reparations saved me from a messy aftermath. The champion's eyes followed me back to my seat with a wordless gaze. When I saw him, it was as if the skin on his face got tighter, the numerous moles and warts more obvious and the eyes had lost their pupils. He stared at me with the whites of his eyes. That is when I realized that we found ourselves in a new match, a new game. The wager – my own head.

So we got back to Budapest. My "fame" seemed to have grown, since my victims found their way onto the morning talk show, where they described in vivid detail the treatment they had received.

The fact that Bobby's little game was still on, was made even more obvious by another curious incident. Sometime around noon we were heading for the city center. Although I had no doubts that it was yet another round of roulette, the champion had in store for me, I still advised against taking Váci Street,[59] which was at that time flooded with tourists with cameras and that there was no possible way of preventing them from taking photos of him. Still, he acted as if he did not hear me, or perhaps he did not want to. After some fifteen minutes of a leisurely stroll he was suddenly "fatigued".

Although he was obviously still in top form, he decided to take a moment to rest from a sudden "frailty" of his lower extremities on a bench at the very heart of Europe's most crowded promenade. I retreated to the side of the street, close to the entrance to one of the many bookstores, pretending to study the titles, as I waited for what was bound to happen. And a couple of minutes later, I turned to the sound of a familiar shout.

---

[59] The epicenter of the capital city of Hungary, the main and busiest pedestrian zone, full of tourists day and night.

A passing cyclist, with a camera at his side got himself a close-up of the tired pedestrian, setting the flash off right under his nose. It took only a second to reach Bobby, who was pointing in the direction of a yellow bike and the shortish, sportingly-clad figure riding it. I pressed my advantage in the crowd, where a pair of quick legs are a bigger asset than the narrow tires of a mountain bike, and in a matter of seconds I caught up with the "impudent" press photographer. Before I got to utter a single word, he began calling for help at the top of his voice. As I was already prepared for another dance with fate, I managed to calm him down and convince him that there was nothing I would nor could do to him. Bobby slowly made his way through the crowd, tottering with each step, before he finally reached the scene of the incident. Just as he was about to speak, I asked my "blameless" victim to be on his way. He seemed to understand a bit of English and got the gist of my gesticulation, and to this day I am grateful to him for not making a scene for thousands of tourists to enjoy – "the spectacular arrest of a ruthless thug in the center of the beautiful city".

And so the day was finally upon us. The money had arrived. Miraculous, but true nonetheless. Truly there aren't many who, sinking under the pressure from their life's ordeals would ever stay true to their promises. However, the benefactor of Bobby's last match (the former banker, who was now both an exile and a target) was such a man. One of the few who, throughout Bobby's entire lifetime, up to its end, always treated him fairly; he was the "bloody, double-crossing, treacherous, dirty Jew, son of a bitch", Jezdimir Vasiljević.

And so, one day, Fischer went on one of his visits to the bank to check on how things were developing. How could it be possible, even after all those threats from the number one world power? Despite the fact that the entire sum was now at his disposal, I advised him not to withdraw all the money, on that day at least, as circulating of rumors of his vast financial power could have the same effect as copious amounts of food on a famished body.

The Greatest Secret of Bobby Fischer

Even so, having reached the desk, in a fit of euphoria he immediately asked for 50,000 dollars. Always alert as we were, this sudden "machination" of his really left me speechless, if that is how you describe total incomprehension of the heights of avarice. Not once did it cross our minds, to bring a bag adequate for the job. So the money ended up in a crinkled transparent nylon shopping bag, which the genius and the "genius" had stuffed into one of his jacket pockets. Then, as if there was somebody after him, he dashed to the car and later from the car quickly back to his hotel room, which he did not emerge from until the following day.

I sat on the balcony, watching the river. It washes everything away, doesn't it? Imagine I could have put everything I felt into a big cardboard box and sent it downriver. What was inside? Something very hazardous – my contempt.

Early in the morning the phone rang. A gentleman of trust disclosed some very disturbing inside information – there was to be an abduction, the conspirators – unknown. We raised our guard and "battle-readiness". I proposed a trip to Szentendre to Fischer, who was reeling from the news. It was quite a picturesque kind of place, the northernmost point the Serbs reached during their Great Migration in 1690. It was a wonderful sunny day and there was much to see in the regal colors of the fall and the warmth of history. My thoughts were elsewhere, though. Contacts, follow-ups, eavesdropping on messages from the shadows and once more an answer of unambiguous ease. The info: there was intent, but the plan was off, and now Fischer was once more out of harm's way.

The next couple of days passed at their usual pace: restaurants, walks, the delight of the cold and warm waters of Gellért Hotel's baths and swimming pools. But what was to come had to come. We were sitting in the hotel lobby: Eugene and Bobby at one table, and I at another, doing my job and occasionally glancing at an edition of *USA Today*, my favorite paper. After a while I got up and walked around for a while, as my companions enjoyed the cushy seats of their armchairs. Not unintentionally, I took a seat closer to the champion and his second in command. Concealed behind a palm, I overheard, "You know, Eugene, these Serbs are one lazy and slow people. Of course, they have good sides, but still…" I could not see a thing, but it was as if I could see him. I am certain that this very moment, without a shadow of a doubt, I could still repeat his gestures. He went on, "Haven't you noticed that even Nesh, who, to be honest, knows everything about everything, has gotten sluggish and lazy, just like the rest of Them?" The feeling was close to being stabbed in the back by your best friend, or when you put a lot of effort into a present that nobody likes.

It was as if… as if I faded into life, and then resurfaced in a flash. Once more I stood firm on my feet, strong and unshaken. I had one last task before me, the most difficult of them all. I had kept Bobby safe from everyone and everything, dutifully and passionately, sparing neither expense nor myself. Then I strived to protect him from himself, which was by far more difficult. And then, the final test of my prowess, the trial of my very soul – how was I to protect him from myself? That was why, with my own wellbeing in mind, this was to be our hour of parting. To my relief, events were unfolding on their own, which I realized when a few moments later Torre whispered into my ear, "Bobby would like to speak with you."

"And I with him, Eugene. Don't worry."

After dinner I was on my way to the scheduled meeting. The Filipino grandmaster opened the door with a smile, although there was much anxiety in it, too. As I went down the stairs into the lower room, I saw Bobby lounging on the red sofa. He tried to maintain a laidback attitude, but to no avail. I realized that that would be no ordinary conversation, since it was not the Fischer I knew, sitting in front of me. To relieve him of his anguish and myself of the pending speech, I said, "Bobby, now that your money is here, all the doors will be open to you, a whole world of possibilities. Therefore, I think my job here is done. Now it's time for us to part." He agreed. That was, after all, what he wanted to see me about. He went on praising my personality and what I went through for him. I cut in, "Dear Bobby, the pleasure is all mine. As is the privilege." Both of us wanted the whole matter over with as soon as possible.

"Nesh, if I recall correctly you spent some of your own money on me over these last few months, and yet you didn't receive any pay from me. Jezdimir left the country more than five months ago, so I presume you didn't get anything from him either. How much do I owe you?".

By then, Fischer had owed me a respectable sum. But with the intention of "testing" him, I said, "One thousand and four hundred dollars".

He reared in his seat and said, "That much?"

"That much, Bobby" I repeated calmly, "I know it's a lot, but that's how much you owe me".

"Fine, fine", his neck twitched as he counted the hundred dollar bills. Eugene, who was standing nearby, knew it was not the case. His experience and dealings with me told him it was a significantly larger sum. I picked up "my" 1,400 dollars from the table, a bit cross with myself for playing the stupid game. I unhurriedly strolled out of Bobby's apartment. I couldn't see my face, but…

After some fifteen minutes, there was someone knocking on my door: "Bobby regrets not having given you a parting present. He says you may keep the custom-made chess sets with his and Boris's signatures. Surely one day, they'll be worth a fortune."

"Thanks," I responded composedly. "Also", Torre continued, "Bobby suggests that you take a walk downtown sometime tomorrow and maybe pick out a watch for yourself. The price is no object, of course." Then, as an afterthought, he mentioned that there are watches that cost upwards of fifty thousand German marks. My answer to this remarkable man regarding the grandmaster's offer was not without irony, "I recommend you tell him to donate the sum to an orphanage in the Philippines, or to some sort of fund for the development of chess in the U.S." Having understood my position, and acknowledging them himself, he shook my hand and embraced me. "Thanks for everything, Nesh."

"Thanks for everything, Eugene", I replied sincerely. I went out that evening, alone for the first time in a year and a half with a unique mission – how to spend 1,400 dollars in the least amount of time, without buying anything specific. It was easy. And pleasing.

The Greatest Secret of Bobby Fischer

*

I was in the hotel again. I sat in my room with a book in my hand and a certain peace and comfort in my heart until morning came. I listened as the doors of Bobby's apartment opened and closed. The familiar rhythm of steps ebbed and flowed in the hallway. The louder and heavier steps were Bobby's and the light and melodious one's belonged to Torre. I did not want to spoil their fun. Terrified of himself, Robert Fischer was leaving the hotel. That is why I chose to stay put in my own world, aiming to purge myself of any and all emotions.

Morning. I went down to the lobby. At the reception desk I received a letter and a bill for the hotel room, which was paid for a week in advance. I simply had to smile. As early as noon, I received reports regarding the whereabouts of the "elusive" Mr. Fischer. My friends asked me, "So are you going to let it end like this?"

In the game of light and shadow, where the bare silhouettes of people and objects form the only shapes, where there is no beacon for the ships lost in the mist, I danced my dance to the demands of the rhythm and the melody. Those who I aimed to please with my work were found pleased. Even he, who counted as the most peevish and the most eccentric among the geniuses of the sport of chess, would have been lost without me and had followed my rules without question. That morning I felt great pride coming from the fact that for all my twenty seven years, I had for a time, though nonetheless successfully tamed that ungraspable spirit. And so he came to realize his mistake and, in the night, leaving his pride behind, he fled the hotel, out of an unfounded fear for his life. And for all that, he was left with the magnificent piece of knowledge of just how little his 1,400 dollars mattered to me.

And this made me pleased.

At long last I finally opened my eyes to my life, and everywhere around me I saw colors, I breathed the scented air and under my fingers I felt the touch of velvet and silk. It seemed that not everything came down to sixty four squares, black and white. I placed the parchment that contained the reply to my former client's message, and which I had written in my own blood into the beak of Budapest's prettiest dove. I hope he read it before he died:

We reap the straw hiding the secret
That everything that was, still is,
And that nothing is ever lost.

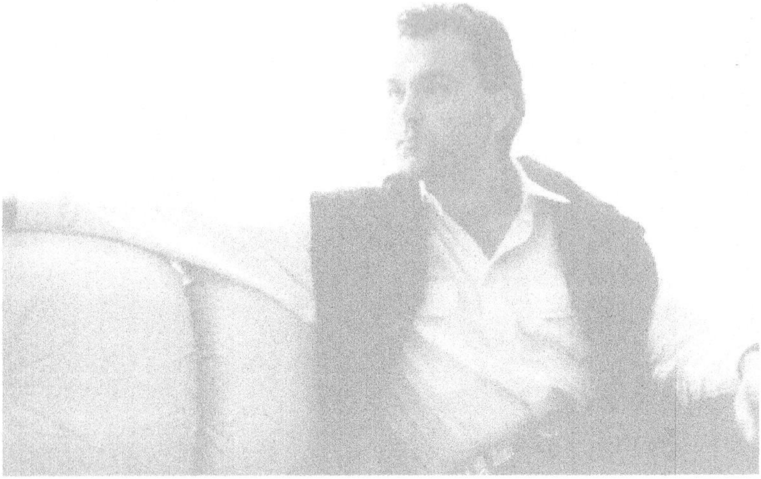

CHAPTER 16.

THE MAN IN THE MIRROR

After our parting, I did not think of Bobby for a long time. The reason is clear. The echo of experience does not overcome the body and mind immediately, but the consequences, which must exist, come later. I suffered from complete mental and physical exhaustion. I stayed in Budapest for several months. I spent the days taking walks, peacefully touring the city, visiting museums, galleries, friends, and concerts. But Belgrade kept calling me. As the days went by, under the weight of what I had done and experienced, and having suddenly lost forty-five pounds for no evident medical reason, I set off into recovery. Life on a razor's edge, daily trials, had brought me all a young man could wish for. The most expensive cars, life in the most exclusive hotels, vintage wines, a limitless supply of my favorite Havana cigars, and of course, the most beautiful girls and women. However, behind all that, there remained a gaping void. The fact I had lived through more than anyone else in my generation, witnessed history being made up close, and received immeasurable experience, did not help me escape the consequences. I drifted through my hometown after my return from Budapest. I continued living in exclusive hotels across southern Europe, up to the point when something had to give. I married and we had our first child, my daughter Natalija, and later, my second daughter, Milena. The next three years I spent in the National Library in Serbia, where I read hundreds of books on the subject of my interest, tons of periodicals available to me in that treasure trove.

Again, theaters, scores of movies, especially from the Belgrade Cinematheque, and then intensive studies of several languages. Maybe one will ask – was it all so hard? It was even harder. But much of it I had to leave out of these writings, partly because it is not yet time for secrets to become known to the public, partly so as not to make this confession too lengthy. Later, on several occasions, Fischer sent me messages indicating safe connections and contacts. However, we knew each other so well that all was to be left exactly as it was.

When I think about it today, Bobby Fischer was in fact the man I knew best and most profoundly. In that regard, there has never been, nor is there now either regret or acrimony. My daily life, however, was interwoven with a past I could neither dispense with nor repress.

One of the saddest moments of my life was when the news that Bobby Fischer had passed away circled the globe. Following the comments of the world media, journalists, and chess players, and especially after Garry Kasparov's pious statement, I could not, and did not want to contain my emotions. My profound grief was inspired foremast by the passing of the genius, but also by the death of the part of my personality that was inexorably bound to him. Thus, I literally lived through what could poetically be described as the loss of a part of my very self.

The will of fate had yet to have its way. In the writing of these memoirs, which I often did in cars, airplanes, hotels, restaurants or gas stations, many turbulent events befell my private life as well. Hellishly difficult and divinely beautiful.

To many of my friends and loved ones, and those who called in from around the world with burning interest for my book and high expectations, I had to explain why I was late in publishing it.

Dreams are God's way of sending us messages – I remember those wise words. Indeed, ninety percent of what is written here, excepting the first, long ago written chapter, was put on paper in the period between April and June of 2010. And then I stopped, brought it all under suspicion: motives and reasons, needs and goals. Over the days gone by, to the people who know me, my colleagues and those interested, I talked about the time and my experiences. But even in moments of peace and introspection I did not want to go back, nor did any particular emotions perturb me, except perhaps pride. However, the web of memories and the

The Greatest Secret of Bobby Fischer

intensity of contemporary events often hindered me in seeking new goals and challenges.

Nights were not peaceful and serene. Since our parting, I have out of habit slept with the light on in the hallway and the television always turned on. Even then, he would come into my shallow dreams.

First he would call out to me and ask for help, and then my nightmare would ensue: for some reason, some powerful force would not allow me to reach him. He needed me, and I could not come to his aid. I remember every such dream. Colors, sounds and scents. Belgrade, Budapest, Tokyo, an unknown city. And when I was nearly ready to give up, into the surprisingly placid, deep reverie came Mr. Gligorić. Young, forty years of age, in an elegant black suit, perfectly groomed moustache and perfectly coiffed hair. An unknown hotel. In the shifted reality it reminded me of a London, the Victorian one in which I stayed several years ago. Only the colors were different. Instead of the ones I remember, yellow, ochre, red, there are green and white walls. Smiling, he says, "Bobby is having dinner in the restaurant downstairs. He doesn't want to disturb you, but he requests you leave out the chapter about him and me. You know the one." Awakening could grow into a layman's belief that dreams are merely a reflection of everyday contemplation, of the experienced, of the repressed, of what is hidden in the far reaches of the mind. Still, I tore up the sheets with the inscription that was fleshed out and finished. I did not intend to continue writing, even though all that was needed was a couple dozen more hours to finish it up and cast the message in the bottle into the sea, lightening the load on my soul, shared feelings with happenstance or intentional seekers of truth and with collectors of the values of the chess spirit and of achievement.

And then I saw him. After so many years. It is a veritable skill to separate the wheat from the chaff, and dreams from dreams. Deep meanings from superficial recycling of reality. This is not a boast: in my mystical understanding of the universe, I always could and knew how to do it.

Bathed in light. An expanse of meadow hemmed with forest. He stands in front of me, all in white. Clean shaven. Long, gray hair, tresses falling to the middle of his back. His eyes closed. I am silent. He opens his eyes. He looks at me with the look I knew and felt better and longer than anyone else in my life. A smile on his face. Then he says to me, "Now I can do what I never could before." Then, like a ballet dancer, or a yogi, he makes several graceful, limbering moves that his unwieldy earthly body could never make. Then, he repeats, "See, now I can do what I never could before". I wake up, and finish this volume.

I sincerely believe there is a promised, other, better world. I also hope that in that world a somewhat different, above all better for himself and happier Bobby Fischer found peace and rest.

I never could play chess, nor is it today among one of my particular interests. But when I arrive there, I will ask him for another go, another walk, just like when once in this world, there was a time we walked shoulder to shoulder.

END

Budapest Aug. 30, '93
2:00 P.M.

Dear Nesha,

Sorry I missed you this morning, and didn't have the chance to say goodbye. Thank you very much for all your help this past year, and I hope to see you again soon. If you need to get in touch with me, please leave a message for me with Aliso. Also say hello to Jojo, Dave, Simon, and the driver whose name I don't recall at the moment. All the best.

Sincerely,
Bobby

ABOUT THE AUTHOR

As a young man, Nenad Stanković (his friends call him "Nesh") was a successful athlete. He played twelve seasons of professional basketball. He is educated in the fields of political science and history of religion. His interests include the mystical elements of Judaism, Islam and Christianity. He has selected and trained hundreds of collaborators in the professions of PR, merchandising and marketing. Today, he is the owner of "Tango & Nesh" a publishing, production and advertising firm located in Podgorica, Montenegro.

For more information, please visit www.fischersecret.com.

CAPTIONS

Pg. 32 Fischer entered his host country without a visa. The request for one was finally made just a few months before he departed. His American passport bore the number 032123930, and the form contains an obvious spelling error in his name.

Pg. 153 The last paragraph of this fax shows that, in some previous correspondence, Fischer had asked about the background of Klaus Ulrich Groth.

Pg. 175 Brilliance after twenty years absence from the chess scene, the first game of "the revenge match of the twentieth century" and Fischer's victory

Pg. 278 One of the letters that frightened the legendary chess master because of its style and handwriting .

The Greatest Secret of Bobby Fischer

"MAY YOU BE DAMNED WHEREVER YOU ARE
(because you crushed my soul with yours);

MAY YOU BE BLESSED WHEREVER YOU ARE
(for you have resurrected me through this book.)"

Made in the USA
Coppell, TX
26 March 2022